CAMPAIGN STRATEGIES AND MESSAGE DESIGN

CAMPAIGN STRATEGIES AND MESSAGE DESIGN

A Practitioner's Guide from Start to Finish

MARY ANNE MOFFITT

Westport, Connecticut
London

Library of Congress Cataloging-in-Publication Data

Moffitt, Mary Anne, 1944–
    Campaign strategies and message design : a practitioner's guide
from start to finish / Mary Anne Moffitt.
        p. cm.
    Includes bibliographical references and index.
    ISBN 0–275–95592–3 (alk. paper).—ISBN 0–275–96470–1 (pbk. :
alk. paper)
    1. Publicity.   2. Mass media—Social aspects.   3. Corporate image.
I. Title.
HM263.M54   1999
659—dc21   98–33613

British Library Cataloguing in Publication Data is available.

Copyright © 1999 by Mary Anne Moffitt

All rights reserved. No portion of this book may be
reproduced, by any process or technique, without the
express written consent of the publisher.

Library of Congress Catalog Card Number: 98–33613
ISBN: 0–275–95592–3
       0–275–96470–1

First published in 1999

Praeger Publishers, 88 Post Road West, Westport, CT 06881
An imprint of Greenwood Publishing Group, Inc.

Printed in the United States of America

The paper used in this book complies with the
Permanent Paper Standard issued by the National
Information Standards Organization (Z39.48–1984).

10 9 8 7 6 5

Copyright Acknowledgments

The author and publisher gratefully acknowledge permission to quote slogans, to quote from previously published material, and to adapt figures from the following sources:

Slogans from the Atlanta Braves, Cellular One, Frito-Lay, MetLife, Miller Brewing Company, Zenith Electronics Corporation, and Nike International were used by permission of each company, respectively.

From M.J. Esman. (1972). The elements of institution building. In J.W. Eaton (Ed.). *Institution building and development.* (pp. 19–40). Beverly Hills: Sage. Copyright © 1972 by J.W. Eaton. Reprinted by permission of Sage Publications, Inc.

For Figure 1.2, adapted from *Managing Public Relations* by James E. Grunig and Todd Hunt, copyright © 1984 by Holt, Rinehart and Winston, reproduced by permission of the publisher.

For Figures 3.11 and 3.12, copyright Nissan (1997). Nissan, Pathfinder, and the Nissan Pathfinder logos are registered trademarks of Nissan. Reprinted with permission.

For Figure 3.13, reprinted with permission, Christian Coalition.

For Figure 3.14, reprinted with permission, Al Salvi.

For Figure 3.15, TM & © 1997 Marvel Characters Inc. All rights reserved. Reprinted with permission.

For Figures 4.1 and 4.2, reprinted with permission, Nissan and Xerox.

For Figure 4.3, reprinted with permission of Avon Products, Inc.

for

Alan
Mary Kathleen
Joseph

Contents

Preface		ix
1.	**The Campaign Professional**	1
	Campaign as Guiding Metaphor	2
	Elements of a Campaign's Structure	3
	Foundations of the Campaign	12
	Issues of Encroachment and Integrated Marketing	23
	A Brief Word About Theory	25
	In Summary	27
	Important Things to Remember	28
2.	**Research Strategies** *Dean Kazoleas*	31
	Research Planning	32
	Sampling	39
	The Research Process	43
	Data Analysis and Statistics	66
	In Summary	81
	Important Things to Remember	81
3.	**Basic Strategies**	83
	Some Definitions	83
	The Bottom Lines	85
	The Goal: How to Create It and How to Write It	93

viii   Contents

	The Objective: How to Create It and How to Write It	109
	In Summary	112
	Important Things to Remember	118
4.	**Message Strategies**	139
	Words as Message Components	140
	Visualization Factors as Message Components	146
	Strategies for Choosing Message Components	157
	In Summary	165
	Important Things to Remember	166
5.	**Communication Selection Strategies**	173
	Definitions Initiate Conceptualization of Strategies	174
	Strategies for Choosing Communication Selections	188
	How Long Is the Campaign?	196
	In Summary	197
	Important Things to Remember	198

References	201
Index	205

Preface

I have been teaching campaign communication for almost ten years. During this time it has been my privilege to see students graduate with majors in communication and public relations and become very successful in their professional work. They tell me that the skills and theory they have learned throughout their college course work prepared them for the "real world." I have gained an immeasurable amount of knowledge from my students, and it has been my pleasure to know them and to teach them.

My research in corporate image—in understanding how persons gain an image of any organization—has led me to understand campaign communication in a distinctive, perhaps even unconventional, way, from the most accepted definitions of campaigns and the most established ways of explaining how to conduct campaigns. This book grounds the conceptualization, the planning, and the execution of a campaign on the Collapse Model of Corporate Image, which directly informs my understanding of campaign communication. I argue that understanding image as contrasting, multiple, and ever-changing opinions, knowledge, and behaviors held by each person has direct implications for the strategy of planning a campaign—in the research, the basic strategies, the messages, and the communication selections.

I also have come to realize that I wanted to write about campaign communication based on my understanding that current books on campaign strategy were somewhat limited in their conceptualization and their explication of the genre of campaign communication. I have examined numerous text books and case study books on campaign communication to use in my classes and even reviewed several for publishers. What strikes me about most current books on campaigns is that they cover research skills, goals and objectives, messages, and channels of communication but not in a definite and systematic "what needs to be done first before you can go on to the next step" kind of way. In other words, a person reading a book such as these could, technically, first decide on the communication channels for a campaign, perhaps then decide on the words and the visuals of the messages, and then even hope that the campaign messages include the information that the organization wants the intended audiences to know. For some campaign strategy books no concerted effort is made to link one step directly and precisely to the next, in order to, in a sense, fashion a system and an order for sequencing the steps.

I envision the conceptualization and the execution of a campaign as a very methodical and organized design. To that end, Chapter 1 argues that the creation and the planning of campaigns constitute a profession. The profession requires knowledge of communication theory and skills and a framework of ethics to guide the campaign professional in her/his work of persuading masses of people to know, believe, and act in certain ways toward an organization or a campaign cause. Chapter 2 explains the basics of quantitative and qualitative research methods so that the campaign professional will understand how to conduct formative research on targeted populations.

Chapter 3 demonstrates that these research findings directly inform what the basic strategies should be. Chapter 4 illustrates that the basic strategies, in effect, "write" the message components and "design" the message formats for the campaign professional to use. Chapter 5 shows that previous decisions on goals and objectives and messages dictate exactly what the proper communication selections should be. My point throughout is that the campaign strategist cannot conceptualize and execute a campaign without this rigorous and thorough systematic organization based on this sequence of steps.

Since I write about "targeted populations" throughout this book, let me explain who are my targeted audiences for this book. It is a fact of public relations and campaign communication that many persons doing professional campaign communication today come to it from another field—journalism, business, management, broadcasting, almost any profession you can name. That is, relatively speaking, most campaign specialists today do not possess college majors in public relations or communication or even business fields.

This creates an interesting dilemma for them. They are the campaign managers and the campaign technicians, but they have no "academic" background in the theory and the scholarly aspects of campaigns as a field of study. They know the practice of campaign communication primarily through their work experiences but not necessarily from an educational or theoretical perspective. This book is for those professionals who want an in-depth understanding of campaign strategy for every step in the planning process.

Of course, not every suggestion I make will be feasible or cost-effective. I admit to being an idealist and to explaining how campaign decisions should be made. But I hope my suggestions present the campaign manager with a look at campaign communication from an organized and accurate perspective; I want to suggest one way that campaign strategy and campaign message design can be conceptualized and can be accomplished. With a framework or a model before him/her for one model for conducting campaigns, the professional can adjust and make the system his/her own.

This effort to write about campaign communication could not have been accomplished without the support of many persons. My students have been my inspiration and my motivation to pursue, explore, and understand the complexity of campaign communication. You cannot appreciate how much I have learned from you. My thanks to Ruby S. Wilsdorf who fashioned the figures and illustrations for the book. Special thanks to my colleague Dean Kazoleas for his good ideas and input on several issues addressed in the book; he wrote the chapter on research with more expertise and more detail than I ever could have done. And to my family, my husband Terry, and our children: I cherish your love and affection.

1

The Campaign Professional

We recognize a professional as one who knows what to do in a crisis or problem situation. If a person needs medical attention and goes to the doctor, the physician knows what questions to ask of the patient and how to examine the body. The physician needs to ask questions like what are your symptoms, where does it hurt, what drugs are you allergic to?

If a person needs legal advice or legal representation and seeks a lawyer, the attorney knows from explanations of the client's problem whether she/he has a case and what research needs to be done to make the case. The attorney knows what paperwork to prepare and how to notify officials of the court of a pending lawsuit.

A campaign manager is a professional in the same sense as a physician or an attorney. If an organization is planning a campaign to enhance its image or to benefit its employees or to react to a crisis such as allegations of product tampering, the public relations manager knows what questions to ask in order to analyze the given situation; knows what research and paperwork need to be done; knows what messages to create and knows what communication selections are appropriate in order to respond to the crisis or to the project. As a professional, the campaign specialist knows how to begin, what questions need to be answered in order to begin, what research needs to be done to plan strategies, and what strategies can lead to the correct messages and the successful execution of a campaign.

The "client" and "patient" whom a campaign manager represents, however, is not an individual or one person. We do not represent individuals. We represent an organization as a singular entity. A campaign professional working for an agency may work with an individual who represents an organization. Another professional doing in-house public relations for an organization may report to a superior within the company. But the bottom line for the campaign specialist is that her/his function is always to represent an organization.

CAMPAIGN AS GUIDING METAPHOR

And whereas a physician heals through medicine and the attorney defends according to the law, the campaign practitioner *serves the organization through the campaign.* The central principle guiding campaign communication and most business communication today is conceptualizing corporate communication principally as a campaign. Whether it be a routine communication by the corporation or a major communication project addressed by the corporation—no matter how large or how minor—it is best to conceptualize any spoken or written communication sponsored by the organization in terms of what kind of campaign will best solve it or address it. The campaign manager working in the corporate world must consider the campaign as the guiding metaphor for doing all kinds of business communication today.

The large and small for-profit and not-for-profit organization of today is obligated to specify carefully planned and appropriate messages to the respective demographics, needs, and attitudes of each audience who relates to and is important to the organization. Rather than throwing out messages to any and all persons in the environment surrounding the organization, today's agency or corporation needs to know not only the traits of the general business environment but the traits of each audience within the business environment—employees, customers, activist groups, retailers, governmental regulators, or the competition. Specifying messages to particular audiences is today's most efficient and most profitable means for business communication by the organization.

This is not to suggest that campaigns are the proper response for only major crises situations or extensive proactive projects of large organizations. I will argue throughout this book that for the small and midsize company or agency, as well, the campaign is the best way to conceptualize its business communication to others. For any business problem—large or small—facing any organization—large, medium, or small-sized—the best way to communicate about a negative or positive situation is to conceptualize a response to it in terms of a campaign. This means identifying all the knowns and unknowns of the crisis (negative) or proactive (positive) situation, identifying the relevant audiences who need to be contacted, and specifying the basic strategies, messages, and communication selections to best inform the various audiences of the situation. In other words, any one negative situation or any proactive proposal—major or minor—is addressed by tailoring messages about it to only those audiences involved or interested in it.

Further, the response to the crisis or proposal lasts for a specified period of time, for just so many months. No matter how minor or damaging the crisis or how small or sweeping the proposal necessitating a response by the organization, the resulting communication is in direct response to one, identified positive or negative situation. The campaign is intended for only those affected audiences and is completed and budgeted to last for a discrete period of time. In terms of focus and memory of the audience and in terms of the number of messages and amount of content needed for any campaign, the optimum length of time to run a campaign is three, four, five, or six months. To get much longer than six months loses efficiency in delivering the content of your messages and works against saturating the intended audiences with your messages. If you think you need seven or more months to get all your messages and information out to your audiences, you should think in terms of two or more shorter campaigns. More detail on determining the appropriate length of the campaign follows in the explanations of basic strategies and in the examination of choosing communication selections.

The real advantages of conceptualizing organizational communication in terms of the metaphor of a campaign are demonstrated in those companies that face no real crisis or project situations or, at best, only face them occasionally. For the organization in a stable environment with no real challenges from, for example, governmental regulations or from its employees or from its sales, protecting the organization simply involves keeping in touch with the audiences who relate to the organization and who have the potential to challenge its image, its sales, its employees' well-being, and its way of doing of business.

Being absolutely clear as to the definition of a campaign is all-important here. A campaign can serve either or both of the following purposes: *to inform or to persuade:*

A campaign is the strategic and carefully thought-out design of a series of messages sent to one or more targeted populations for a discrete period of time in response to an identified negative or positive situation affecting the organization.

ELEMENTS OF A CAMPAIGN'S STRUCTURE

The campaign professional needs to know the basic model of a campaign's structure; this identifies the few but crucial elements that initiate the conceptualization of the campaign. Any campaign is prompted by a situation, represented in this model by *crisis and +project in the upper left-hand corner of Figure 1.1. In some campaign situations, a crisis can stimulate a campaign that also becomes a project. For example, when the Girl Scouts chapter of Chicago faced the crisis of cookie tampering (Center & Jackson, 1989, pp. 293–295), the resulting campaign contained messages addressing the crisis, assuring the affected audiences that no cookies would be sold that year. Additionally, the campaign contained proactive messages requesting donations instead of the cookie sales, which, by the way, pulled in about the same amount of money.

The crisis or project can be any issue from a major problem or large project, or the causative factor can simply be to maintain business sales or image. In the center of the model is the organization itself. It is notably important to view the

4   Campaign Strategies and Message Design

Figure 1.1
Conceptualization Model for a Campaign

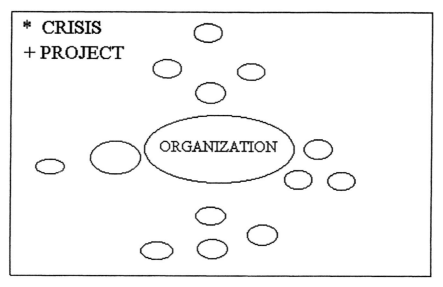

organization at the center, surrounded by any and all the potential populations that may have any relationship to it at all. Within all the possible populations relating to the organization, some have more importance and more consequence than others. Each population itself is an audience of persons who are in the respective population because they share a relationship to the organization; that is, as all employees, as all customers, as suppliers, as the competition, or as community residents where the organization is located.

These basic elements of a campaign represent the starting points for planning a campaign. Just as an attorney or a physician is a professional because he/she knows what questions to ask to solve a legal or medical problem, the campaign specialist is a professional because he/she knows what questions to ask to solve a corporate problem. These elements of the instigating crisis or project, the nature of the organization, and characteristics of the affected populations represent the initial considerations in beginning any campaign. That is, the initial, investigative questions the campaign professional is obliged to ask are what are all the details—factual and rumored—about the crisis or project? What is everything we know about the organization in terms of its mission, its products, its services, its industry, its effects on the persons and environment surrounding it? What are the needs, personality traits, knowledge, attitudes, behaviors, and importantly, the *relationship* of each and every population affected by the named crisis or project?

Answers to these questions are the starting points for understanding and planning a campaign. The corporate campaign specialist is the professional who is obligated to ask these questions and find out the answers to them. Keep in mind that the campaign specialist represents an organization, not an individual. Because of the model's importance, let us look at each of the three elements a little more carefully.

Investigating the Crisis and Project

A negative or crisis event can prompt an organization to conduct a campaign to attempt to correct any damage done to persons and the environment and, secondarily, to rebuild any image damage to the corporation resulting from the incident. A proactive, positive project such as giving additional benefits to the employees or sponsoring a fund-raising campaign to benefit breast cancer research or muscular dystrophy also demands a well-thought-out, strategic campaign to get the information out to the affected populations.

Most persons in corporate communication would agree that these are obvious examples of situations demanding a campaign. But think about this. For small organizations or medium-sized businesses facing no real negative event or any proactive communication needs, the campaign can also serve them as the most efficient and cost-efficient means for communicating their products or services *and* their desired image. Interestingly, most organizations today believe that the only kind of campaign they ever need to wage is an advertising or marketing campaign to sell their products. Their communication needs center around selling the product or the service generated by their business to their customers. Selling their desired image is not often a primary kind of communication, although this attitude is changing as organizations see that managing and promoting a certain image ultimately affects sales.

If messages about sales are typically the most important and common kind of business communication, then why do so many businesses and corporations spend so much money, time, and effort in sending messages to their customer audience by saturating and reaching the entire environment, including all the other audiences relating to them? They want to reach their customers, but they plan messages, choose communication channels, and deliver messages in a kind of widespread dispersal to the general environment and to all the respective audiences surrounding the organization. They reach the community, their employees, the media, and their competition via all the media and personal channels they can afford rather than considering which media best contain the messages that best capture the attention of the *targeted population(s)*.

In order to investigate the crisis or project situation, you need to consider two ways to approach your research. First, the campaign planner needs to consider absolutely every *fact* of the project or crisis. The campaign strategist needs to do an in-depth inventory of every recognized piece of knowledge and accepted truism about the negative or neutral or proactive situation prompting the campaign. You will want to talk to every person who has any knowledge—a lot or a little—about the situation. All this generated information is, first, what everyone involved agrees are the facts—the uncontested, accepted facts—of the situation.

6   Campaign Strategies and Message Design

Next, second, is another kind of information to be collected about the project or crisis. You need to interview probably the same individuals and possibly additional individuals to uncover information that is speculative about the project. This information is opinions and speculations that all your "experts" consider are the possible causes and repercussions of the crisis. That is, this information is not factual in the above sense that it is able to be proven. This kind of information is about what people think might be the reasons for the situation, the fallout from the situation, the effects of the situation on the organization and the related audiences. In short, this kind of information is not directly "provable" but is, instead, opinionated and drawn from the persons most knowledgeable of the situation.

For your factual and your opinionated information, you will need to talk to persons inside your organization, persons outside the organization in the related audiences, and other persons who have direct and related knowledge of the project or crisis. In addition to personal contact, you must exhaust every channel of secondary information. Secondary research sources include the traditional avenues such as library research of relevant books, professional and in-house magazines and annual reports, and "info-track" through the library computer to search periodicals. The more recent technological sources such as the Internet and World Wide Web pages have exploded the information superhighway by providing sources of information such as home pages of corporations, financial sites that provide financial profiles and history and projected growth of a corporation, or newspapers from all over the country.

I want to make these firm distinctions between factual and opinionated or subjective information because the campaign planner must recognize that every proactive and reactive situation contains in it these two kinds of information. I think communication specialists sometimes do not consider that every situation has both facts and opinions imbedded in it. To investigate thoroughly the crisis or the project that demands a campaign response means that the crisis or project must be thought out in terms of both facts and opinions.

I think campaign planners often make a serious mistake as they begin to conceptualize a campaign and ask their preliminary questions about the campaign. They question persons and gather information without regard for what are the facts and what are the opinions. This muddies the waters for later considerations of what the campaign messages should be. If you do not carefully document, or at least have in your own mind, the differences between the facts and the opinions about the crisis or project, you will not be able to plan strategies and messages to confront both kinds of information, later, in the execution of the campaign.

Investigating the Organization

Investigating the organization may seem like a fruitless, or at best, unnecessary part of the conceptualization process of a campaign. For some campaign planners perhaps knowing the details and "ins" and "outs" of their respective organization is a step they consider unnecessary since they feel they already have in-depth knowledge of the organization. Especially for the small-to-midsized organization, knowing such factors as the history, the employees, the management and ownership, the products and services sold, the consumers, or the industry is a manageable task. This is one of the major advantages of business communication for a smaller company or agency.

The larger the organization is, the more difficult it is to know thoroughly factors like the history, the employees, the management and ownership, the product and services sold, the consumers, the industry, the stock and financial picture, activist groups opposed to the organization, all the suppliers and distributors, or the labor unions in the organization. Obviously, the larger the size, the more factors and the more difficult it is to know all facets of the organization.

Knowing either the small or the huge organization is not an impossible task when it comes to conceptualizing a campaign project, however. For the campaign planner, questions to ask here involve seeking out all the information about the company that *relates to the crisis or the project.* Here is how the professionalism of the campaign planner is demonstrated in this second element of the campaign model. The campaign manager should know what questions to ask to get all the pertinent information about the organization and how that information informs the particular campaign at hand.

For example, for a crisis of product tampering, the campaign manager researches the facts and the conjectures of the crisis and puts with this information all the information she/he can gather about the organization as it relates to the product-tampering crisis. Information such as the history of this ever happening before in the company; information on the exact, step-by-step process of how the product is made; information on how each part of the organization is affected in a minor or major way by the crisis; information on image damage or stock price changes; or information on what parts of the organization might be able to discourage tampering in the future, all need to be gathered in order to adequately conceptualize a response to the crisis. Getting answers to these questions will be easy or difficult, depending on how simple or multifaceted the organization and depending on how accessible the information from printed sources and from knowledgeable individuals within the organization. I can envision a company relatively small and simple in structure facing a crisis situation for the first time which, nevertheless, will not have this kind of information at hand.

At the same time, for a project or proactive campaign inspired by the organization, the same kind of information about the organization is absolutely crucial to know before planning strategies for creating messages and for executing the campaign. Information such as the history of the company, knowledge about the product and/or services sold by the company, information about the manufacturing or development process of the product, and information on positive image results or increasing stock process and sales as a result of the charity or fund-raising project, also need to be known at the outset.

It is amazing how *little* can be known about an organization by a person who has worked for the business for ten or twenty or even more years. As a communication and campaign specialist, do not assume that just because you have worked for an organization for ten or twenty years that you know all the important information about your (big or small) company. Common knowledge shared by the employees, along with perhaps sacred stories and other information held by the grapevine is not enough. As the campaign specialist, it is your job to know all information about your organization. Remember, the campaign specialist does not work for an individual as does a lawyer or doctor; because you work for an organization as a singular entity, it is absolutely essential for you to know all you can about all parts of the organization, from ownership style, to corporate structure, to stock and stockholder information, to the intricacies of production and sales.

As the communication specialist for an organization, you are the most important individual or department within the company, if not the only individual or department, to continually educate and update itself about everything inside the organization and everything affecting it from the surrounding environment. With this knowledge in hand, you are ready for any crisis or any project planned by the organization—your "patient" and your "client."

I want to add another facet about knowing your organization. For most campaign strategists, knowing your competition—the other corporations within your industry—should be just as important, or maybe more important, than knowing your own organization. The good advertising and marketing campaign specialist knows about the competitors' products. A political campaign specialist knows about other candidates opposing her/his candidate. The social agency soliciting money to preserve an endangered plant or animal species knows well all the other social agencies competing in the fund-raising marketplace. I caution my students that they, as campaign managers for any kind of organization or any kind of campaign, as specialists in environmental monitoring, will most probably have as thorough a knowledge of their competition as their own organization.

Investigating the Populations

The third and final element of the campaign model is knowledge of and considerations of the targeted audiences. Answering questions about audiences is all-important in the successful design of a campaign's messages. Further, considerations of each audience's characteristics such as its needs, personality traits, and knowledge-attitudes-behaviors ultimately dictate what the appropriate messages should be to successfully complete the informative or persuasive function of the campaign.

The first step in conducting business in a safe environment and in protecting a business from any crisis situation is to know as much as you can about each and every audience that has a relationship to the organization. For example, to ward off any problem or dissatisfaction with your employees—in other words, your employees as audience—you want to consistently ask them for their concerns, questions, and input on the organization itself. For those organizations which deal with employees who belong to labor unions, it is especially important to carefully monitor the feelings and concerns of their respective labor union members.

How do you do this? It is very easy. Chapter 2 on research will demonstrate how to investigate and measure audiences, but this initial step in investigating the populations is to be able to identify all the relevant audiences. The linkage model (Esman, 1972, in Grunig & Hunt, 1984, pp. 140–143) is an excellent reference point for any organization to use to sort out and identify all the audiences that have the potential to affect the organization (see Figure 1.2).

The linkage model serves as a kind of inventory of all the populations "out there" who have the potential to affect any organization. The *enabling* linkage contains all those audiences that allow the organization to exist. Any population in this linkage has the power to control what the organization does and, even, shut down the organization. Perhaps the most obvious population in this linkage is the owners of the organization: the board of directors, including the president, vice-presidents, the chief executive officer and others in direct control of the organization. The stockholders are another "owner" population in this linkage; their ownership of stock makes them a population with a direct reference to the organization. For those organizations that are regulated or monitored to any degree by any governmental agency, the agencies of the government are another enabling population to the organization. For the enabling linkage, the three major populations are the owners, the stockholders, and the government or legal agencies with regulatory power over the organization; these audiences and any other audience that has the power to shut down the organization or permit it to do business are *enabling* populations to the organization.

Another linkage is the *functional* linkage. This linkage establishes every population that has anything to do with the products and/or services that are sold by the organization. It is divided into two functions: the input populations that deal with supplying and producing the product or service sold by the company and the output populations that deal with any step in the process of delivering and selling the product or service.

The major population in the input portion of the functional linkage is the employees. Depending on the structure of the organization, employees can be broken down into populations of upper management, middle management, and line workers or clerical. For some campaigns the three levels of management should be treated as separate populations, and, yet, for other campaigns, it is just as relevant to communicate to all levels of employees together as one population.

Related to this population may be other populations of employees, such as labor unions members or employees organized by the job they perform for the organization. Other populations dealing with producing the product are not direct employees of the organization but nevertheless work for the organization: suppliers of the raw goods into the manufacturing plant or deliverers of any supplies that sustain the organization; truck drivers; loaders and unloaders of the

Figure 1.2
Linkage Model for Identifying Populations

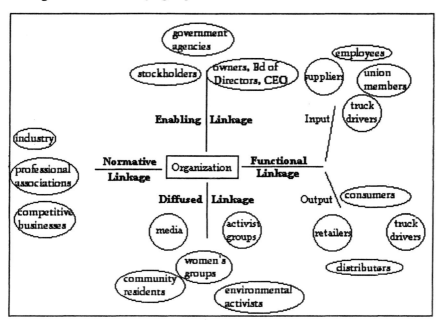

Source: Adapted from Esman, M.J. "The Elements of Institution Building." In Eaton, J.W. Ed. *Institution Building and Development* pp. 19–40, copyright © 1972 by Sage and adapted from *Managing Public Relations* by James E. Grunig and Todd Hunt, copyright © 1984 by Holt, Rinehart and Winston. Reproduced by permission of the publishers.

supply trucks or train cars; satellite industries that supply parts or goods to your corporation. Each of these groups of individuals is a discrete population; all individuals in each population share a similar relationship to the organization. For example, all the members of the labor union(s) may agree or disagree with each other, but they belong to one population—labor union members. Members of the various satellite and supplying industries servicing your corporation are a diverse group of companies and people, but they are members of the one population of satellite industries or, depending on the campaign, members of different populations within the satellite industries population. Your employees, as well, are a diverse, contrasting group of persons who, nevertheless, are members of the one population of employees.

Another set of populations present in the functional linkage are those related to the output portion of the linkage. Populations in the output function directly relate to the delivery and the sale of the organization's products or services. The primary population in this output function is the consumers, or customers, of your products or services. Other populations relating here are the distributors of your products, the retailers and store personnel who sell your products or provide your services, more truck drivers who deliver the goods to the retailers, and other businesses that might depend on your services in order to produce their services.

Another linkage that inventories possible populations relating to your organization is the *normative* linkage. This linkage is best described as the industry to which your business belongs. In other words, this linkage contains the major population of all the businesses that compete against you in the marketplace. These are all the businesses that sell similar products or similar services as you do.

Competing businesses (your organization's industry), by the way, is a frequently forgotten or disregarded population in the conceptualization of a campaign. Again, campaign specialists not only must know all there is to know about the organization they work for and are paid by; they are also absolutely obligated to know all they can about the competition. Monitoring competing businesses within your industry and within all those industries related to your industry reveals a crucial population that you must recognize. For some campaigns you will be obligated to communicate to them as an audience. Other populations present in the normative linkage are the professional organizations or associations to which your organization belongs or to which your employees may belong.

And, finally, the *diffused* linkage is discussed last because, simply put, this linkage contains any other population that cannot be considered the owners, the product or service handlers, or the competition. Populations in this linkage relate to your organization but from a definite "outside" stance. Typical populations are the media, the communities your organization(s) are located in, activist or environmental groups that picket your company or your industry, or women's groups or minority groups that might protest your company or your industry. This linkage is, in truth, "diffused," since it may contain any group of persons who organize to support or protest your organization. It may contain any population drawn from any of the media; for some organizations and some campaigns awareness of the media as a related and important population is crucial in executing the messages of a successful campaign. Cultivating a positive image in your residential communities and, perhaps, in other relevant geographical areas identifies other populations that may or may not be important targets in a given campaign.

One final consideration—a somewhat confusing situation related to identifying all the possible populations—needs to be mentioned at this point. Sorting individuals according to a population is not as neat and clean as it may appear from the linkage model. Let us say that a person named Joseph Ring lives in Bloomington-Normal, Illinois, and works for State Farm Insurance as a computer programmer. Ring is a member of the employee population. Ring is also a member of the community residents population. Consider that Ring might also be a member of an environmental group concerned about saving and preserving the rich farmland of central Illinois. Ring also belongs to a professional association of computer programmers where he regularly meets with other programmers who work for other companies.

Suppose that you are planning a campaign for State Farm Insurance to persuade the community that additional buildings need to be built on rich farmland surrounding the Bloomington-Normal community. And here is Ring who belongs to at least four populations relating to State Farm Insurance and this campaign, some populations possibly in disagreement with each other. If you are planning a campaign on behalf of State Farm Insurance, you will be creating multiple messages respective to each of the various populations that Joseph Ring belongs to. Yet he is one individual.

My suggestion here is to be careful not to assume that each population you identify has a different, discrete group of persons in it who are separate from the members of the other identified populations. This fact does not have to complicate your strategies, however. You simply assume the responsibility of creating messages appropriate for each population; if members of one population share membership in other populations, they—in theory at least—will necessarily receive multiple messages, messages consistent and respective to each population they belong to. This can be a good situation for you as campaign manager. Joseph Ring will receive multiple messages about your campaign, consistent with his various memberships in multiple, albeit disagreeing, populations.

The campaign professional gets started by asking questions—by knowing which questions to ask first. Knowing the importance and the definition of a campaign is your first consideration in representing your organization. Next, knowing the three elements of the conceptual model of a campaign identifies for you which questions to ask of the project or crisis, the organization, and the possible audiences to target. And, finally, knowing how to identify every population that might have a relevance to the campaign under consideration is your final preliminary consideration in conceptualizing the campaign.

FOUNDATIONS OF THE CAMPAIGN

With this conceptual framework of project/crisis, organization, and audiences as investigative starting points of the campaign in mind, we are now ready to explore more particularly the components of the campaign structure and those major assumptions that guide the planning and execution of a campaign. To begin, the campaign specialist must have in mind the differences between a population and a public.

A Population Is Not a Public

A population has already been defined as a group of individuals who share a relationship to the organization such as all employees, all consumers, all stockholders. A public has commonly been defined as a segment of persons within a population who share—not a relationship to the organization—but characteristics such as commonly held or shared knowledge, similar attitudes, behaviors, needs, psychographics, or demographics.

For example, within your population of stockholders are some persons who know a lot about your organization and some who know little. Within your population of employees are those who like the company and like working for the company and perhaps those who are indifferent toward the company and perhaps those who genuinely dislike the company and their jobs. These "groupings" of persons *within any given population* who share a knowledge (a lot of information or a little) or an attitude (like a lot, are neutral, dislike intensely) can be viewed as publics, or individuals who share a certain knowledge, attitude, or image position.

I want to make this distinction between typical, established definitions of a population and a public very clear since I think the term "public" is so often misused. A campaign specialist will hear and read about "public" every day. Most often, the term "public" is used, incorrectly, as reference to a population. It is important to be very clear as to the differences between population, a group of individuals relating to the organization, and public, often thought of as a segment of a population relating to the organization on different terms. These are two entirely different concepts, and recognizing the distinction is a must for the campaign specialist. Understanding and employing these two concepts has important repercussions for conducting research into populations and publics and, similarly, is crucial to the later creation of messages and choices of communication selections for the campaign.

The terms "audience" and "population" are synonymous terms. Remember that the audience or the population is defined only on one measurement—the sharing of a *relationship* to the organization, such as employees, community residents where the organization is located, members of the media corresponding or accepting correspondence from the organization, customers, etc. *The only factor that assigns persons to the same population is that they all share the same relationship to the organization; they do not share any other factors such as information or attitudes or needs to be categorized as a population.* Members are placed in a population or audience because they share a relationship to the organization, and that is the only trait they have to share to be considered a population or an audience.

The treatment, definition, and selection of public positions is always from within a population. This necessarily gets a little more complicated since a singular characteristic or multiple traits (knowledge, attitude, behavior, needs, psychographics, demographics such as sex or level of education or annual income, positive or negative image, lifestyle behaviors, leisure activities, etc.) can identify the various public within a population.

A Public Is Always "Public Positions"

I want to offer a radical, new definition for the commonly assumed definition of public as a segment of a population. I present, instead, the term "public position(s)" rather than the term "public." It is important for the campaign professional to understand the difference between a population/audience and a public

14   Campaign Strategies and Message Design

(see Figure 1.3). But it is even more important for the campaign specialist to understand the definition and explanation of a public. *Your understanding of how a public (and image) is conceptualized has a direct impact on how you, as campaign manager, plan messages and choose communication selections to deliver your messages.* Traditionally, publics have been segmented from a population based on a shared opinion such as all the individuals who hold a positive image or all those who share a psychographic factor such as similar lifestyle behaviors or those groups who share a demographic factor such as gender, income, or marital status.

Another, more accurate way to determine publics is not to look for a shared factor and then group individuals who share this factor, thus creating a segment, or public from a larger population. Rather, the process is to look for all the "public positions" within each member of a given population. The campaign manager does this by researching in the targeted populations all the shared factors that each population member possesses, individually. In other words, the determining of public positions does not work by grouping persons into segments or publics from a population based on their shared factors but, instead, to find out all the multiple images or "public positions" that each person has within himself/herself toward the organization. In essence, then, the concepts of public and image are the same construct. If one factor or attitude toward an organization defines a public position in the traditional sense, then conceptualizing a person as having multiple factors or attitudes toward an organization dictates that image (each singular factor or attitude) and public position (based also on shared factors) are the same entity. Let me explain.

My research into corporate image processes has been in the area of understanding how images are developed in persons relating to an organization (Moffitt, 1992, 1994a, 1994b; Williams & Moffitt, 1997). The focus is on how image is received in the audience rather than on how the organization creates and delivers its image to targeted audiences. This research examines what factors go into the process of how a person gains a positive, negative, or indifferent image(s) of a corporation. This focus on the members of a population and/or public positions is a bit different from most public relations research, which focuses on how the organization creates and delivers its image to its audiences.

This focus on image in the audience has led me to define a public as *any one, singular factor (opinion, image, psychographic, demographic, behavior, etc.) held of an organization.* That is, if an individual has some positive opinions of a company and some negative opinions of the same company, and consequently, some positive and negative behaviors toward the organization, each positive opinion plus each negative opinion plus each positive and negative behavior are all images toward the same company. According to this model, one person has multiple images of a corporation, perhaps many more images of a corporation the person knows well and perhaps fewer toward a corporation known less well.

Research into the image of State Farm Insurance in the home office community of Bloomington-Normal, Illinois, yielded findings to confirm this model of

Figure 1.3
Collapse Model's Conceptualization of Image and Public

Each person possesses multiple images of each organizational issue which can change moment to moment.

Employees
I think the organization
- is good to employees by providing good benefits
- is negative to employees by requiring strict attention to time
- has good policies for promoting employees from within
- has been accused of gender discrimination

Products
I think the organization
- has a good product for quality
- but the product is too expensive

Community
I think the organization
- is good to community by providing jobs
- is bad for community by driving up real estate prices
- is good to community by providing tax revenue

Groups of persons share primarily one image toward each organizational image which remains constant and never changes.

We all believe all the time that the organization is good to its employees.

We all believe all the time that the organization has quality products.

We all believe all the time that the organization is always good for its community.

image (Moffitt, 1994a, 1994b; Williams & Moffitt, 1997). When residents of Bloomington and Normal were interviewed about their images (that is, their opinions and knowledge) of State Farm, findings were that each resident had multiple images of this major corporation dominating the community. Each resident held some positive, some negative, and some different opinions, or images, of State Farm. Not surprisingly, some respondents in the study—typically, the employees or family members of employees—had many more positive images while other, nonaffiliated residents tended to have more negative or indifferent images, usually because of State Farm's effect on the community's real estate inflation, higher taxes, and zoning.

The major finding here is that any individual has many, changing opinions or images of the same organization. This makes sense. Consider for a moment an organization you know well, such as the place where you work or the university you graduated from or the company a parent worked for. Each of these organizations has its good points and its bad points and, additionally, points of information that are not particularly bad or good but just pieces of information. If you think about one of these organizations and consider all the positive, neutral, and negative opinions, knowledge, and images you have of it, you can see that image is not one generalized concept but a collection of multiple images, multiple images that are easily changeable and flexible. This is an all-important realization for the campaign professional; any organization you work for will have multiple images in the eyes of the persons who respond to it or relate to it. Other image studies' findings are consistent with this model of multiple images within each person (Alvesson, 1990; Baskin & Aronoff, 1988; Boulding, 1977; Fombrun & Shanley, 1990; Dowling, 1986; Grunig, Ramsey, & Schneider, 1985).

A public has most often been defined as a group of individuals within a population or a segment of a population who shares an opinion or a behavior or an image of a company. That is, within a population of employees are those who like the company and can be grouped as a public and those who do not like the company are classified as another public, also within the population of employees. Traditionally, efforts to identify publics has been a process of grouping individuals according to shared traits (Grunig & Hunt, 1984).

However, given my model above that any one person can have some positive, some negative, and/or indifferent images toward the same corporation, it becomes impossible to group persons according to shared images. How can a person be assigned to a positive public when she/he also belongs in the indifferent or negative publics? The possibility of shifting public positions, and multiple public positions, within a person cannot allow for a person to be neatly plugged into a group of other persons who share the same factor.

What if the person you talked to yesterday about the benefits of the corporation likes the corporation because of the good benefits, but when you talk to the same person today about the corporation's policy of not allowing unions, this same person expresses a negative opinion or image of the corporation. For the issue of benefits, the person has a positive attitude or image; for the issue of allowing unions, the same person holds a negative image or attitude. What is demonstrated here is that one person can have several images or opinions of the same organization and that these multiple images can be flexible and changeable. The dilemma for the campaign professional becomes, then, how to create campaign messages for population members who hold all kinds of images—for example, based on attitudes, opinions, knowledge, behavior, needs, psychographics, demographics—and who can change these images from day to day and even moment to moment.

Research into the image formation process supports this new model of multiple, varying images/publics with each individual (Moffitt, 1994a, 1994b; Williams & Moffitt, 1997). Other studies into image would agree that it would be impossible to, for example, take a population of 1,000 persons and from this 1,000-member population, assign persons to publics based on a singular, shared piece of knowledge, attitude, behavior, or image of the organization. To demonstrate, suppose I am seeking the image of an organization in the residents of the community where the organization is located. Suppose I ask these persons in the 1,000-person population if they feel that the corporation is good for the community, is bad for the community, or has no effect on the community. And suppose that from the answer to this question I have 300 who feel the corporation strongly benefits the community, 200 who feel the corporation has a negative impact, 400 who feel no effect exists, and 100 who have no opinion at all. Technically, we have determined four public positions from this population based on the factor of what effect the corporation has on the community.

Now, what happens when we ask these same 1,000 persons different questions related to their image of the corporation, perhaps questions about how good or neutral or bad they feel the corporation treats their employees and treats their customers. For each of these two questions we will end up, again, with a possible three or four *or more* groupings of persons with differing answers to the "treats their employees" question and "treats their customers" question. It is evident here that each question provokes a different assortment and alignment of "public position" configurations.

This seeming confusion over multiple and changing images presents a dilemma for the campaign professional—how to target and appeal to all these images possessed by a population. The solution is not difficult, however. While I will explore in much detail exactly how to plan strategies, messages, and communication selections to cover the wide range of images held by the population, let me state here that the project for the campaign manager simply shifts away from grouping individuals and delivering messages to groups to identifying all the possible images held throughout the entire population membership and delivering messages to all these images or public positions shared by the population's members.

This shift away from segmenting a population into publics and consequently targeting publics instead of populations might, at first glance, seem like a return to the earlier, traditional practice of targeting populations, rather than the more scientific model of targeting publics. However, it is not. The new model does not advocate simply communicating messages to entire populations based on the relationship that the population has toward the organization; this would dictate that the messages would appeal to only one primary factor—that of the relationship defining the population. The new model advocates using the tools of research to explore and reveal all the various public positions or images shared by all the members across the population so that messages can be created to appeal to all (or most) of the public positions, not to appeal to a singular relationship defining the population.

This new model's recognition of multiple images/multiple public positions has direct repercussions and more advantages for the campaign strategist today. The increased number of messages that this model dictates must be sent suggests that the more and varied messages targeting the more and varied images possessed by an audience will insure a more efficient, more thorough, and more successful campaign.

Labeling Kinds of Campaigns

Another, fundamental component of the campaign based on this concept of population and public position informs how to recognize and to label the kind of campaign you are conducting. Most campaigns target more than one audience, but, nevertheless, *it is the kind of population targeted in the campaign that labels the kind of campaign being waged.* The campaign professional, as campaign strategist, must always have within his/her conceptual framework an understanding of what kind of campaign is being planned. Knowing the kind of campaign means knowing the targeted populations inherent to it. The kind of campaign is determined by the crisis or project stimulating a campaign response, and, more importantly, by the populations that will need to be communicated to, given the crisis or project. Further, each kind of campaign carries with it its respective approaches and procedures for eventual completion.

In addition to these ways for defining campaigns are two other, larger frameworks for defining and labeling campaigns. You will often come across the terms "crisis management" and "issues management." To explain, in a local sense, campaigns are defined by the crisis or the project that stimulates or gives cause for the campaign and, also, defined by the targeted populations inherent to the campaign. In a more general sense, any campaign can also be explained as crisis management or, as in the sense of a more positive goal, as issues management.

Pfau and Parrott (1993) have presented a more concrete framework for defining campaigns. They classify campaigns as commercial, political, and social issue. The commercial campaign is typically planned on behalf of an organization and falls into either marketing, advertising, or public relations. The political campaign persuades voters in order to get a candidate elected or, perhaps, targets Congress in order to affect legislation. The social issue campaign is waged at potential charity donors in order to support an issue of social, usually charitable, interest to society such as a fund-raiser for a worthy, non-for-profit cause. These are the strict "textbook" definitions for the most commonly waged campaigns found in society today, but a closer look at why and how these campaigns are executed today suggests that often the boundaries between them are often blurred.

The three kinds of *commercial campaigns* are marketing, advertising, and public relations. While marketing and advertising are very close in purpose and in populations they intend to persuade, the field of business communication makes some distinctions between them. Marketing as a field of business was created first; its purpose is to place a company's product or service in the marketplace and, hopefully, carve a unique space and create a singular demand for the product within all the competitive and related products or services. It involves for the organization the process of placing the product or service out in the public sphere to potential consumers for purchase. Obviously, the process of marketing is, for any organization, absolutely crucial for the existence of the company; no business can continue without sales of the product and/or service to sustain it.

This singular need to sell products led to the more specified and narrow field within marketing of advertising. The singular purpose of advertising is to sell the product and/or service of the organization. For both marketing and advertising—differing but related fields of business—the purpose of the campaign, the project, is to sell the product of the organization. For both marketing and advertising, the primary targeted populations are consumers and retailers. The advertising campaign and marketing campaign share the approach of sales and the procedure of targeting potential customers and store owners to accomplish sales.

For the third kind of commercial campaign of public relations, the project/crisis situation and the targeted populations are radically different from advertising and marketing. Within the field of public relations the potential for numerous kinds of public relations campaigns exists, given the numerous project and numerous crisis situations that can prompt a public relations campaign response and given all the other populations (besides consumer and retailers) to whom the practice of public relations is obligated to communicate. In terms of populations, the function and approach of public relations is to respond to any one or more of all of the other potential populations, in addition to the consumer population.

Let me give an example of why the kind of population is the major determining factor, especially given the complexity of reasons giving rise to a public relations campaign and given the multiple populations that can come into play. Consider that your organization suffers accusations of damaging the environment, such as the tuna fish industry faced with findings of killing dolphins as well as killing tuna or the *Valdez* oil spill in Alaska by Exxon. When the organization faces a crisis situation such as these—Starkist tuna or Exxon oil—it sends a press release to the newspapers or the broadcast media, which is media relations public relations. If the press release gets into print or on the air, that kind of public relations becomes community relations. If a letter goes to the stockholders to explain the organization's response to a crisis, that kind of public relations becomes investor relations or financial public relations. If an employee newsletter contains the organization's response to the crisis, it is classified as internal or employee relations.

As a campaign professional you must have a thorough appreciation of the shift in the kind of public relations, given the different population to which the press release is sent. In just one campaign reacting and managing just one crisis, multiple kinds of public relations are played out because each target population defines the kind of public relations. The bottom line here is that the campaign manager must appreciate that each population demands its respective response and demands messages respective and unique to it.

A final consideration of public relations campaigns involves the concept of populations and offers another distinction between public relations and marketing/advertising. For a typical public relations campaign multiple populations are often targeted, rather than the one or two populations of consumers or retailers, typical of advertising and marketing. For example, in a crisis situation such as an environmental group attacking the organization for water pollution, the campaign manager is often obliged to communicate to the activist group members, the media, the employees, the stockholders, any governmental regulatory agencies, the affected geographical region's residents, and perhaps the industry as primary targeted populations. Even for a project campaign, or issues management campaign, to benefit the employees, the campaign is obligated to inform not only the employees but their families, the corporation's owners and top management, the stockholders, the organization's financial analysts and benefit consultants, and perhaps the media and regulatory agencies. Very rarely can a singular public relations campaign (either crisis management or issues management) necessitate communication to only one, two, or three populations.

Whether a crisis or proactive project as campaign situation, public relations' function and approach is to deal with all crisis situations affecting the product or any part of the organization and to deal with all project situations outside of direct sales of the product. It is clear that public relations is distinguished as a field of business communication by its greater responsibilities in communicating about more issues and in communicating to many more populations on behalf of the organization. Public relations is responsible for managing all crisis situations and for other proactive or project situations outside of sales.

Responding to such a variety of crisis and project situations and communicating to such a wide range and diverse set of populations—not only consumers—opens up multiple, numerous campaign responsibilities for the public relations campaign specialist. For public relations, crises as diverse as accusations of product tampering, of insider securities fraud, of truck driver strikes, of environmental pollution and activists' outcries, of union labor strikes, of dissatisfied employees, of media misrepresentation, and even of problems of a competitive business that call into question your business and the entire industry as well, all demand a public relations solution—not a marketing or advertising solution.

For public relations, also, in terms of proactive projects that might involve giving benefits to your employees, making fund-raising efforts to support a worthy cause, working to enhance relations with the media, making cooperative efforts with a competitive organization, improving the image of the organization, and promoting positive ways to improve the oceans, forests, or residential communities surrounding an organization, all demand a public relations response—not a marketing or advertising one. The bottom line for any kind of public relations campaign is that its function is to manage the image of the organization, not sales of the organization's product. By addressing and correcting a crisis problem or by executing a proactive campaign on behalf of the organization, the public relations specialist is, in essence, managing the image of the organization in the eyes of all the affected populations. A public relations approach and function for the organization is not to sell the product but to sell the organization itself, the image and reputation of the organization as a whole, to all its relevant populations. In order to accomplish this, public relations is obligated to deal with all minor and major attacks on the image of the organization.

For *political campaigns* the campaign's purpose and respective targeted populations are much more singular and focused than public relations commercial campaigns (Pfau & Parrott, 1993). A political campaign's purpose is to get a candidate elected or a piece of legislation passed. In terms of populations affected, a political campaign obviously targets voters or constituencies and necessarily the media as primary audiences. Within a large mass of voters needed to get an individual elected or legislation passed might be smaller populations according to political districts or other geographical distinctions; the size and needs of the campaign determine if voters and geographical regions need to be treated as singular or as multiple audiences.

The final broad classification of campaign in our society today is the *social issue campaign* (Pfau & Parrott, 1993). Described as a campaign to benefit society or to benefit a social/charitable cause, it needs to be recognized as taking two forms. The social issue campaign is usually recognized as a campaign waged to attract believers or followers to a cause such as: the stop-smoking movement campaign embodied in the National Smoke Out Day; the various environmental campaigns to save the forests, the tropical rainforests, the oceans, the whales; the medical-issue/social-issue campaigns advocating breast cancer research and early detection, AIDS research, and birth control methods; and the greatest social issue debated today, the prolife and prochoice campaigns clashing over the issue of abortion. Altruistic causes have been supported by not-for-profit organizations and agencies, for example, fire departments' Toys for Tots, American Legion's summer junior baseball, or police departments' nationwide support of the DARE campaign against drugs.

However, the second most recent movement in social issue campaigns is for-profit-oriented organizations to execute or to support a social-issue campaign. In this situation, a for-profit organization elects to support financially and support additionally, often through their employees' efforts and employees' time, a social cause. This necessarily affects the altruistic nature of traditional social-issue campaigns as executed by not-for-profit agencies and blurs the lines between a strict definition of a public relations campaign managing the image of a corporation and a social issue campaign supporting a worthy cause. For the profit-driven organization or business, press coverage and public recognition drawn from supporting a social cause enhances its image and also accomplishes a public relations function for the organization. As such, a profit-oriented organization that conducts a social issue campaign can help a charitable cause and also help its image in the eyes of those persons exposed to the social issue campaign messages.

This move to manage image through support of a social-issue campaign is one of the hottest moves in campaign communication and in business communication today. An interesting twist to this is when a corporation supports a cause related to its product or service, such as State Farm Insurance's support of Mothers Against Drunk Driving and Students Against Drunk Driving and Budweiser's campaign, Appoint a Designated Driver. Out of all kinds of campaigns—the three commercial, the political, and the two social issue campaigns—the profit-driven organization's execution of a social issue campaign is the most recent innovation in campaign communication. Other examples are Ryka athletic shoes' campaign against violence to women, USA television network's campaign against all kinds of prejudices, and Ben and Jerry's ice cream campaign to save the tropical rainforests.

The commercial campaigns of advertising, marketing, and public relations, together with political campaigns and social-issue campaigns of not-for-profit and profit organizations, typify the major kinds of campaigns. However, other kinds of campaigns are found in society. Celebrity figures, entertainment personalities, and sports heroes often conduct campaigns through their publicists to manipulate their images and keep their names in the public eye; they might lend their support to a social issue or conduct a straightforward image (or public relations) campaign to foster and to maintain their image. Michael Jackson actively conducted an image campaign granting Oprah Winfrey an interview and later carefully orchestrating public appearances, which included covered activities with wife Lisa Marie Presley, in an effort to counteract accusations against him of child abuse. Michael Jordan fosters his "good guy" image and athletic prowess through his advertising campaigns for Nike, McDonald's, and Hanes. Many sports figures lend their support to United Way. And whenever an author, actor, or celebrity has a book or movie to publicize, she/he makes the rounds of the talk shows.

I want to suggest that even though these campaigns are consistent with image and public relations campaigns—and even advertising campaign definitions—when the source of the campaign is a famous athlete or entertainment figure, the publicity, sales, and image management efforts conducted within the framework of a social issue or advertising campaign really qualifies as a separate kind of campaign. When any famous person conducts a campaign to enhance her/his image and if the messages are not in support of an advertising campaign, the campaign is a *publicity campaign*. When a famous person lends his/her image to an advertising campaign, the campaign is an advertising campaign, with the celebrity serving as a visualization factor in the advertising campaign.

Another kind of campaign found throughout the world today is, unfortunately, the *terrorist campaign* waged by political factions throughout the world. A unique kind of campaign, nevertheless, it contains for the perpetrators planned messages and hurtful, violent acts as messages to support their goals to selected audiences. The Irish Republican Army, Middle Eastern religious factions, uprising African nations, and, in the United States, the Oklahoma City bombers exemplify sources of immoral and inhumane campaigns to hurt those groups of people opposed to their "ideals." These can only be labeled as terrorist campaigns.

ISSUES OF ENCROACHMENT AND INTEGRATED MARKETING

Having discussed the various kinds of campaigns offers a framework for discussing an extremely controversial issue in business communication today, especially in the area of commercial campaigns. The campaign professional today must be aware of the hotly discussed issue of encroachment, or integrated marketing, since it affects most persons who work in any of the campaign areas.

The rise in importance of the role and function of public relations for organizations today gives rise to encroachment. It is a practical or financial issue, actually, for mostly profit-driven (although also for some not-for-profit) organizations. Research findings gathered by those in advertising and marketing have suggested for several years and even recent decades that the American consumer has become very skeptical of advertising claims of some marketing and advertising for products and services.

This is easy to see and to appreciate in light of the recent trends in advertising products. Without actually contrasting the early advertising messages of the 1940s and 1950s through to today, let me just briefly demonstrate some of the general trends in advertising messages. Whereas early messages of this century spoke only of the product and its superior qualities, messages in advertising have now become so creative and so subtle that they often only suggest the product or the organization, sometimes without even naming the product or the company. Creativity and attention-getting devices that often only hint at the product serve as persuasive devices to the targeted consumer, rather than claims of superior qualities of the named product.

The claymation raisins singing "I heard it through the grapevine" sell raisins without mentioning the ingredients or benefits of this product. The M&M candy figures ("melts in your mouth, not in your hands") are now actors in little dramas, giving no direct mention to M&Ms as candy or as candy that melts in your mouth. For several athletic shoe advertising messages, young adults are pictured sweating and panting, playing basketball or jogging, with no mention of how the shoes are made or of how they are better than the competition; in fact, for several of these products no dialogue is present at all, only a picture of the shoe at the end of the message.

Consistent with this trend for advertising messages that are implicit rather than explicit, the trend toward clever entertainment in order to sell products recognizes that the image of a company can also sell products as well as good will. As discussed above, one of the most exciting and innovative trends in business communication today is for the organization to send out messages about itself as a company—messages about its image, messages that the corporation is environmentally friendly or socially responsible. The organization conducts a public relations campaign(s) to foster a particular image to its audiences—an image about the corporation as a whole and not a campaign mentioning sales of the product. The corporation communicates about itself in a two-step fashion—first, communicating a strong image of the corporation as a whole which, secondly, leads consumers to buy products and leads to general good will in the community.

Given the sophistication of today's consumer, corporations are beginning to see the merits and the importance of fostering image first; then hopefully sales will follow. Sales are fostered not through direct mention of the merits of the product but, instead, by attracting the customer because of a certain corporate image.

The "encroachment" and "integrated marketing" terms are generally the same principles and refer to the dilemma the organization faces in its turn to public relations campaigns as well as marketing and advertising campaigns. Given that most organizations have their advertising and marketing departments in place, the tendency is for the corporation to use the advertising and marketing departments to conduct public relations image-enhancing functions. Therefore, the terms encroachment or integrated marketing signify that the advertising/marketing departments doing conduct relations functions for the business.

This combination of marketing and public relations operations and functions is not a new phenomenon. The controversy, however, is largely for those in public relations. Many public relations professionals contend that the combining of functions is a boon for public relations, because this calls attention to public relations' importance for an organization. And then there are public relations professionals who decry the integration of advertising and public relations, noting instead that the two kinds of business communication are different enough from each other that they should be considered different entities, conducted only by campaign professionals in each area who understand the intricacies of advertising versus public relations.

As a campaign professional you will need to know that the controversy surrounding encroachment and integrated marketing exists, and you need to grasp the significance of the controversy for your work as a campaign manager in any of these areas. Of course, ever since marketing, advertising, and public relations have been instituted as areas of business communication, companies have had departments named marketing that do, by definition, public relations work in image management and departments named public relations, which are in fact responsible for advertising and marketing products. This has always caused confusion for companies, for their campaign specialists, and for applicants who want to apply for positions in advertising, marketing, or public relations. The recent controversy of integrated marketing emerges as a more significant issue than the traditional confusion over department names. The recent emergence and emphasis on public relations image management to indirectly affect sales and community good will calls into question the roles of advertising, marketing, and public relations in this new turn in business communication.

A BRIEF WORD ABOUT THEORY

My students hear the word "theory," and most of them think of boring, complicated models and in-depth explanations of phenomena that have no direct relation to practical skills or working for an organization. Not true. *All good theories explain and predict behaviors and knowledge.* What wonderful tools to have at hand as a campaign manager: the ability to explain and predict organizational behavior and to comprehend campaign skills and knowledge. Understanding those theories that have a direct relevance to the organization and the campaign provides the campaign professional with a guide for understanding the "health" of the organization and the "legal" intricacies of the organization.

To be sure, this entire book is primarily theory-based. In order to explain campaign strategies, to understand campaign decision-making processes, and to comprehend the skills necessary to execute these strategies and decisions means a dependence on theories and, especially, *the explanation and predictive qualities of theories.* So, while the remaining chapters will call up theories to frame research and to explain all the steps necessary for conducting a campaign, this introductory chapter explains what theoretical understanding the campaign professional needs to begin to conceptualize a campaign.

The fundamental theoretical understanding is provided through systems theory. I want to stress that no campaign professional can operate effectively as a campaign strategist without an appreciation of how systems theory explains organizations. It is very easy to understand, requiring just common sense knowledge about organizations that you probably already have experienced and already know. In a nutshell, systems theory contends that anything that happens to one part of an organization—from within or from without—can have repercussions for all the other parts of the organization.

When business and communication researchers first became interested in studying the organization as a unique communication entity, with its own set of rules and behaviors and expectations, systems theory made the most sense and was easily adapted. The earliest studies, labeled closed system theory, examined issues such as the communication and behaviors within the organization, the flow of information within the organization, who had the power, grapevine, or informal communication patterns, and managerial roles versus technical roles.

While these findings are interesting and explain an organization, the major breakthrough in systems theory was the move to understand an organization not only internally, as an autonomous unit supposedly functioning by and within itself, but also externally, in its relations with the environment and outside forces that shape and affect it. This new move to open systems theory recognized that to understand any organization means to acknowledge the effect of outside forces as well as the internal operation of the organization.

This fundamental appreciation that any organization functions internally, in unique ways and externally, from forces it might have little or no control over, is crucial for the campaign manager to appreciate. A good campaign professional is always aware that at any time a crisis can erupt and impact the organization, or a project can emerge as absolutely necessarily for the well-being of the organization. This constant attention to internal and external factors that might affect any part of the organization, and hence the entire organization, is the job description of the campaign professional. Monitoring the environment in order to protect the organization and manage its sales or image, to get a political candidate elected, to raise funds for a social cause, or to publicize a celebrity rests on assumptions of systems theory; that is, any organization acts as a system in that any factor impacting one part of the organization can have repercussions throughout the organization.

The campaign professional is always ready for any factor to enter the organizational system. Another look at the linkage model's inventory of populations identifies potential trouble spots (Esman, 1972, in Grunig & Hunt, 1984, pp. 140–143). A proxy fight by stockholders or a scandal with the owners exemplify factors emerging in the enabling linkage; for example, note how Phar Mor's embezzlement of money by the owner led to numerous Phar Mor's closings and almost company bankruptcy. A labor strike, truck driver strike, product- tampering allegation, or a customer's dissatisfaction are potential issues surrounding the populations in the functional linkage. If a competitive business suffers a crisis, your organization does too, simply because it is in the same industry. For example, the murders of women students on the University of Florida campus called into question the security on all university campuses across the United States. And finally, poor relations with the media or environmental or activist group protests can emerge from the diffused linkage. Witness the image damage brought to Denny's restaurants from allegations of racism and damage to the entire furrier industry from activists against using animal fur for clothing.

As a campaign professional you need to be aware of and have a sense of whether your organization is in a dynamic or static environment. For some organizations and industries, they are always in a dynamic environment, perhaps because of careful governmental scrutiny of their product or because the nature of their product engenders activist, environmental, or women's groups watchful eyes, or because the competition within their industry engenders fierce competition for the marketplace. Advertising messages of the phone wars, the cola wars, and the tennis shoe wars exemplify combative messages naming and attacking the competition emerging from a dynamic environment. For other organizations, they enjoy a relatively static, trouble-free, and financially stable existence. However, even an organization or an industry in a static environment can suddenly face a crisis. For example, financial losses have resulted from weather phenomena such as hurricanes and forest fires, which have led to billions of dollars in losses paid on claims for insurance companies, leading several to go out of business.

IN SUMMARY

The campaign professional is a "fixer of people problems." If a story comes out in the media alleging that the organization has spilled oil and damaged the environment, the tuna fish catches have been found to kill dolphins, the organization's financial analysts are guilty of insider trading, or that the company has turned a blind eye to sexual harassment allegations, the story is dumped on the campaign professional's desk. "Here. Fix this." Business communication specialists do social science, not hard science. We work with people. We are not chemists or mathematicians or computer programmers. The organization and its audiences are the clients and the patients. The problems or project challenges faced in the ongoing work of a campaign manager demonstrate *the boundary role of campaign manager between the organization and the environment.* What you are about is always persuading and informing persons without and within the organization about the organization. Dealing with human beings is an inexact science. We can survey or interview the populations, but we can only hope for accurate responses. We can create messages and deliver them to our targeted populations, but we can only trust that the messages will be noticed and received as we intended them.

This recognition of the limitations of a career framed by communication to humans is not mentioned so as to consider it a negative or impossible situation. Rather, it is the challenge of informing and persuading "people" that makes the job so much fun and so rewarding when it works.

As much as the campaign specialist must accept the challenge of communicating to masses of people in support of her/his organization, the campaign manager has one more, very important responsibility. The campaign specialist is obligated, as well, to protect the environment from the organization. Organizations are run by people, *and* they make mistakes—intentional and unintentional—that can hurt others and our planet in the process. The ethics of the profession absolutely dictate that if the campaign manager discovers the corporation's abuse to people, to animals, or to the environment, this manager reports it to the upper management and attempts to correct it.

I am sure some professionals reading this are smiling at the prospect of the campaign manager reporting organizational abuse to those in charge who might very well have condoned it. I am not claiming it is always easy to do. For some companies whistle blowing might mean your job. But it is the right, the ethical, thing to do. Only when the campaign specialist is respected as the ethical voice and an accepted expert on damage control for the organization, will the managerial role of campaign specialist be respected within and without the organization.

Anyone in public relations is aware of the bad press the term "public relations" suffers every day. I tell my students in my public relations management classes that two things will legitimate completely the field of public relations and will remove the bad press surrounding its practice: first, when public relations professionals become the accepted ethical voice of the corporation and are accepted as protectors of the environment and, finally, when public relations professionals accept research as the very foundation of planning and evaluating of successful campaigns.

Ethical decisions are struggled over every day by employees aware of their organization's deceptions. How many employees working for Exxon knew that the company spokesman was wrong in his claims that the Alaskan shoreline was clean of oil and animals were restored to Prince Williams' Sound? How many employees working for tobacco companies had insider information for decades about the link of smoking to cancer? How many Dow Corning employees and personal physicians suspected the danger of breast implants and said nothing? How many Union Carbide employees knew of the real atrocities of the gassing in Bhopal, India, outside the official announcement put out by the company?

The good news here is that even out of all these disasters, the truth emerged through some individuals' willingness to expose the coverups and through the efforts of the media to get to the truth. Even more exciting for fields within business communication is that as a result of this turn to telling the truth and protecting the environment, companies are beginning to realize that being ethical and responsible means goodwill toward the organization, which, in turn encourages a positive image(s) and, ultimately, more sales.

IMPORTANT THINGS TO REMEMBER

- The *campaign* is the most important principle in business communication today.

- Initial conceptualizations of a campaign include considerations of the instigating crisis or project, features of the organization, and traits of the targeted audiences.

- The linkage model is a means for identifying any population that has importance to the organization.

- Population and public are two different concepts. There is no concept of "general public" out there; consider, instead, all the relevant populations that are important to the organization.

- A population is a group of individuals who share a relationship to the organization, such as, all the employees, all the customers, all the stockholders.

- A public is, rather, a "public position." A public position is one position that is shared by a group of individuals within a population; the position can be a piece of knowledge, an attitude, a behavior, a demographic, a need, a schema, a psychographic.

- The Collapse Model of Corporate Image views image as the same concept as a public position. An image is viewed as any one position toward an organization, such as, positive knowledge, negative opinion, need, behavior. Multiple and everchanging images toward any one organization are possible within every individual, multiple images of which some can be negative, some can be neutral, some can be positive toward the organization.

- Three major kinds of campaigns are commercial, political, and social-issue.

- Three kinds of commercial campaigns are marketing, advertising, and public relations.

- Encroachment, or integrated marketing, is when the organization has the advertising or marketing departments do public relations functions

- Systems theory explains the need for campaign communication; that is, if anything good or bad happens to any part of the organization, the entire organization can be ultimately affected.

2

Research Strategies

Dean Kazoleas

The purpose of this chapter is twofold. First, it is designed to provide the public relations practitioner with the basic tools needed to design and conduct original campaign-related research, as well as to analyze results. Second, it is written to provide public relations professionals with the knowledge, tricks, tips, and techniques to critically evaluate information and research generated by others. To that extent, this chapter does not offer a comprehensive in-depth review of all research design and statistical analysis techniques, but rather it offers a quick, down-to-basics approach that focuses more on what is ordinarily used as opposed to special cases or circumstances.

This chapter will examine three methods or types of research. The main focus will be on conducting interview, survey, and focus group research. Additionally, some emphasis will be placed on two other types of research that public relations professionals often need to pursue. These are first content analysis, for examining media or examining participant responses for patterns and/or trends; and second, simple experimental research for testing sample strategies and messages. Examples of the applications of these research techniques will be drawn from a wide array of public relations campaign areas, including community relations, corporate image, corporate culture, health/risk prevention campaigns, and investor relations.

RESEARCH PLANNING

The research techniques discussed in this chapter are broad in nature and applicable to many public relations projects. To that extent, the techniques are not broken down and categorized by the specific roles they may play in the collection and analysis of information. However, typical campaign-related applications and suggestions will be forwarded throughout the chapter as research and analysis strategies are presented.

Campaign-Related Research

It is important to know the terminology that many professionals use to differentiate between research that is used to develop campaign strategies as opposed to research that is used to evaluate campaign effectiveness. The term *formative* research applies to research that is conducted before and during the campaign development stages (Atkin & Freimuth, 1989). Examples of formative research, which is also sometimes called "formulative" research, are background research, segmentation research that identifies audience profiles and tests possible message strategies. The term *interim* research is also used to describe research that is conducted during the implementation of the campaign. On the other hand, *summative* or *evaluative* research refers to research that is used to determine if the goals and/or objectives of a campaign were met (Flay & Cook, 1989). Examples of summative research might be original research such as public opinion surveys, focus groups, or research that is obtained from other sources such as sales information, enrollments in social action programs, or behavioral observations.

The distinction between original research and secondary research is an important one. Original research examines the targeted populations of a given campaign, and secondary research is gathered from outside sources about the organization, the intended audiences, and/or the campaign itself. The focus of this chapter is placed on the design, implementation, and evaluation of original research, regardless of whether the practitioner conducts it or whether it is provided by hired consultants. The area of secondary research is not given in-depth coverage; however, secondary research can still be a valuable source of information. The results of previous research, government statistics, marketing data, census data, library research, and sales figures are examples of secondary research that professionals can use as baselines in the development of goals and objectives in a campaign.

Nonetheless, secondary research can be a valuable tool to the campaign professional, especially given the ability to amass large amounts of research information via the Internet. Comparatively, this takes little time and is relatively inexpensive. An example for planners of social action and health campaigns are the sites and information available at the "Fedworld" site (http://www.fedworld.gov), which is a directory of most federal government agencies and institutes. These government agencies routinely post the results of research, and many have extensive archives that can be searched at no cost. Examples include statistics on the economy, the impacts of regulation, results of studies on the spread of disease or the use of hazardous products (like cigarettes), and many more. In summary with this information so readily available, the lack of resources is hardly an excuse for a lack of secondary research.

Why Do We Need Research?

Research can serve several functions, the first of which is meeting critical information needs. Good campaign strategy is based on precise knowledge of the targeted populations' profiles and what motivates the individuals who comprise that population. Research allows the practitioner to better understand the targeted population and what can change their attitudes, beliefs, and behaviors.

Research can also help us predict specific responses to campaign messages. Some messages can have unintended effects, while others may be confusing. The goal of any well-planned campaign is to meet a set of stated goals and objectives. It is always better to know ahead of time whether or not there is at least a probability of attaining success with a certain set of campaign strategies.

Research can also be used to drive a campaign. A quick look at a popular newspaper like *USA Today* or the nightly news will tell you that the media like to report the results of research, such as surveys. Releasing the results of your research can get you news coverage, and much more. The example below will highlight how research results can be used to gain media coverage.

Example: A community activist group with a goal of building an ice arena in a medium-sized Midwestern city had been working to influence local government officials' attitudes regarding the need for an ice arena. The group commissioned a random telephone survey of 350 individuals spread across the community. The results were released to the press. The net result was a 1/3-page article in the local newspaper and interviews on a number of local radio stations, with corresponding news coverage. The report was also presented to the city government. In this case, the research actually became a campaign message strategy and was effective in generating awareness and attention.

Research is necessary and, as noted above, can be used as part of a campaign message strategy. However, public relations professionals have to plan for research when they are developing budgets and time lines for their campaign proposals. An excuse that is often heard for the lack of research is "that budget considerations won't allow it" or that "there is no time." Even a small campaign is expensive to implement. When the costs of staffing, printing, postage, message development, overhead costs, and media use are combined, the monetary totals can be overwhelming. The question that campaign planners have to ask themselves is, "Do I want to put my reputation on the line, without a sound informational base?" or "Am I willing to spend large of amounts of my employer's or client's money on a campaign without information which predicts at least some chance of success?" Hopefully, the answer to this question will be no. In the end, every public relations and campaign professional knows that they cannot guarantee results. However, if things do not work out, it is much easier to explain failure when working from an informed and well-researched information base, than from a position based on conjecture. Finally, if research were used to evaluate success, often these results can explain what went wrong. Data may be worth their weight in gold when a client has to be told why a multimillion-dollar campaign failed to attain its objectives.

Research Ethics

Before discussing the "what's out there" of research and the "how to's," a few words need to be said about research ethics. The ethical researcher always has the participants' best interests in mind. This means treating participants with dignity and respect. This means telling the truth and keeping your promises.

The ethical issue most likely to come up is in the area of participant *anonymity* and/or *confidentiality*. *Anonymity* means that you can in no way track a certain response or answer back to a specific individual. *Confidentiality* means that although you can track "who said what" or who responded in a certain way, you will not divulge that information. Often individuals who engage in socially questionable or illegal behaviors are afraid to speak freely because they fear negative consequences. A promise of anonymity will often get them to complete a survey or participate in a focus group.

TIP: When reporting results, if you have a very small sample of respondents from one particular part of an organization, or a few individuals with unique titles, you may choose not to report the number of respondents for certain findings. If you have promised anonymity, reporting the results with corresponding sample sizes in these areas may leave others the ability to attach responses to individuals, resulting in a loss of anonymity.

Research Validity and Reliability

Although some would argue that the issue of research validity is best left to those "social scientists" in the academic world, nothing could be farther from the truth. The results of research are often used to make decisions regarding strategy, planning, and the use of resources such as money. More to the point, when conducting research, approving research, or paying for research, it is the public relations professional who is putting his/her reputation on the line. Basing decisions on invalid research findings, or "bad" results does not guarantee negative outcomes, but it increases the probability of such outcomes. Similarly, decisions based on valid research results do not guarantee positive results. Again, the additional information only increases the probability that goals will be attained and that results will be positive.

Experimenter Effects

In common everyday language, the question that research *validity* asks is "Am I assessing what I think I am assessing?" or "Am I measuring what I think I am measuring?" In the case of campaign-related research, one of the questions that has to be asked is "What else could be impacting my findings?" Unfortunately, the answer to that question is "many things," one of which could be the researcher.

The term *experimenter effects* refers to changes in participant responses that may be caused by the research professional. Perhaps the researcher, through some action, gives an indication of a preferred answer, or on a controversial topic, asks a question in such a way that it leads the subject to what they might consider "the socially/politically correct" response. The lesson for the research professional is to be as neutral as possible because the end result of experimenter or researcher effects is bad information. In this case, the responses of participants have been affected by factors that you did not control for or are of which you are unaware. The goal of a research professional is to understand what caused participants to respond the way they did. Every influence, no matter how small, detracts from your ability to do so.

Threats to Validity

Social scientists often go through lists of factors that threaten the validity of research results, many of which are rare. However, there are several steps that researchers can take to minimize the risk of conducting "bad" research and getting "bad" results. Six basic threats exist to the validity of campaign-based research that will be examined in this section. These are selection effects, history effects, maturation effects, mortality effects, instrumentation/measurement effects, and testing effects. Although these terms sound technical, some are quite common and can have devastating effects on the results of campaign-related research.

Selection effects imply that the sample of individuals that you conduct your research on are not representative of your target population. In other words, the people that you chose for your research are not like the people that you want to apply your results to, which could lead to campaign failure. For example, let us say that you are conducting community relations research examining the attitudes of homeowners who live in close proximity to a proposed dump site for your company's waste products. If you want to gauge the homeowner's opinions, whom should you ask? Simply put, it should be a sample of homeowners, or those people that are likely to be impacted and involved by your company's decision. Given that, would you conduct your survey at the local high school? Probably not, because high school students may not necessarily have the same level of involvement, knowledge, attitude, or ability to mobilize as do those homeowners. The bottom line on preventing selection effects comes in two easy steps.

First, whenever possible randomize your sample (this technique will be discussed later in the chapter). Randomization does not guarantee that your research results will not be affected by an uncharacteristic sample, but it will go a long way. Second, when planning sampling techniques, always segment your publics as carefully as possible, profiling important characteristics. When drawing samples for research, they should be drawn from those individuals who meet your segmentation profiles. If you are paying for research or using previous research findings, look for the use of randomization and ask yourself, are the participants representative of my target population? If the answer is no, it is best not to put confidence in the results of that research.

Another threat to the validity of research is known as a *history* effect. This means the participants may have been affected by an "event" that impacts the way they respond to your messages, or survey questions. This event could be a major news story, an announcement of new government regulations, or a company's announcement of downsizing in the near future. Examples of research that can be affected by a history effect are longitudinal research (e.g., examining the effects of message strategies over the course of a campaign), or shorter term pretest, posttest research where there is at least some time between the measurement of responses to strategies. The problem that history effects present is that the campaign professional will not be able to accurately assess the impact of the campaign messages on the targeted publics. If the effects are strong enough, the failure or even the success of the campaign may be impossible to attribute to either the campaign strategies or the unintended "history" event.

What the researcher has to remember is that participants do not live in an isolated environment. What they see and hear impacts their knowledge, attitudes, beliefs, and behaviors. When conducting research, a smart professional always asks the question "What else could be contributing to or affecting my findings?"

Example, investor relations: If a company uses quarterly surveys of investor confidence as a benchmark of their effectiveness, researchers must pay attention to what comes from the media just before those surveys are distributed. An announcement of a government investigation or FTC rules violation may cause investor confidence to dip sharply right after that announcement. However, those attitudes may change quickly based on the findings of the investigation or the news that no violation has occurred.

More importantly, do not assume that a history effect occurs because of an unplanned event. In today's competitive marketplace companies will fight for market share, and sometimes that means attacking the competition. An excellent example is the attacks by the makers of ibuprofen-based pain medicines on Tylenol, when there were reported cases of liver damage when Tylenol was taken with alcohol. If participants in a survey saw these ads, that may have changed the way they processed and responded to Tylenol's advertising campaign. The end result is that a population's view of Tylenol may not have reflected the success or failure of Tylenol's advertising strategies, but rather may have been driven by the negative advertisements and subsequent news coverage that accompanied it.

A good way to find out about possible history effects is to talk to participants when conducting research. An example of this was a research professional who was testing the effectiveness of certain types of messages on participants' cognitive processing. One set of messages being tested was promoting alcohol moderation, with a sports star as the main spokesperson. At the end of the first test session, the researcher asked the participants what they thought of the messages and what they thought about the surveys and measures they had completed.

It came to light that the sports star in the messages had been arrested the night before, for several illegalities, including public intoxication. Furthermore, about five percent of the participants knew about it, and the researcher did not. This is an excellent example of a history effect and demonstrates that the best way to monitor for this effect is to keep an eye on what is going on in the world while you are conducting and/or testing campaign messages, as well as to talk to your participants. If you suspect that an issue or event has affected the perceptions of the target groups or populations, you can always use interviews, focus groups, and surveys to ask them.

A related threat is called *maturation*. Again, this sounds technical, but this is a real threat to public relations research. Maturation means that the participants in a study have changed in a certain manner. Usually, these are internal factors, and some examples are increases in physical variables such as age or, more likely, changes in variables such as a population's level of issue awareness, involvement, constraint recognition, attitudes, and beliefs.

James Grunig's noted situational theory of publics (See Grunig & Hunt, 1984; Grunig, 1989) suggests that certain portions of publics will mature. He states that publics can move from unaware latent states to more active, aware, and involved states, as they gain information. For the research professional who is involved in testing campaign messages, this may mean that the campaign messages planned for the later stages of a campaign may have to be retested after the campaign has started to develop. This is especially true on topics where there are truly latent publics who, once made aware, may mobilize quickly. An example of this is the NIMBY (Not In My Back Yard; Rabe, 1994; Simmons & Stark, 1993) effect. Test messages assessing an organization's image as a positive contributor to the community may evoke a different response once participants learn that the company wants to open a large manufacturing facility in the middle of the community.

What can help detect these effects? The use of a control group (a group usually unexposed to the campaign messages) will help protect against history and maturation effects. If you use control groups, the assumption is that whatever changes occur in the research group due to events and or audience changes, will also occur in the control groups, thus allowing for comparisons to be made. For example, you could measure attitudes in a community that does not receive exposure to the campaign message. (For an example of this, see the Stanford Three

Community studies; Flora, Maccoby, & Farquhar, 1989.) Even if you use randomization and control groups, do not assume that you can control for these threats to validity. In research nothing is ever certain, but the use of a control group and randomization will greatly decrease the probability of basing a decision on bad information.

A fourth threat is called *mortality*. Mortality is the loss of subjects from the research pool for reasons such as leaving an organization, losing interest, and/or leaving the geographic area. Although this threat sounds sensationalistic, it actually can happen and happen easily as can be seen in the following example.

Example: A public relations specialist is conducting research on a population's attitudes toward an upcoming referendum on a city's marijuana laws. The size of the city is approximately 50,000 and includes two large corporations and a major university. The current survey is an interim evaluation of a population's reaction to a series of advertising messages. A previous study showed moderate support for the passing of less stringent penalties for possession. The results of this second survey conducted in July indicate a strong shift in attitudes, with many favoring strong sentences for possession. Did the campaign fail? Not necessarily, since in summer months many college students may return home, and generally they tend to be more liberal. It is possible that the opinions did not shift but rather the sample. In this case a good part of the sample may have dropped out of the research.

A quick way to look for mortality effects is to note sample response rates and to compare sample demographic profiles. If there are changes, you may want to investigate further.

Another threat to the validity of the research techniques discussed in this chapter is referred to as *instrumentation* or *measurement* effects. In this case it is the instruments or measures (surveys and/or interview guides) that cause problems. The use of extreme, poorly worded, and socially insensitive items can lead to problems with validity. Individuals may react to these items in different manners, and to that extent the items may not be assessing what you think they are supposed to measure. Similarly, the use of different instruction sets can also lead to different responses. Later in the chapter some tips will be presented on increasing survey validity and reliability. Instrumentation effects can be avoided if a researcher uses care and forethought.

Related to instrumentation effects is a threat called the *testing effect*. This effect will most likely occur during formative message testing. In the most common scenario researchers tend to have participants complete a survey assessing their attitudes, positions, or behaviors, and then expose them to one or more sample campaign messages. After they are shown the sample message(s), they are then given either the same or a similar survey so that any change can be measured. Can you see what is wrong with this picture? With shorter messages some subjects may be answering similar questions within minutes of completing the first questionnaire. The end result is that the participants may remember how they answered the questions on the first "test" and will respond in the same way. Thus, this effect is called the testing effect. A keyword to watch for when evaluating research completed by vendors or professional research firms is the use of a "pretest posttest" design. This technique is highly susceptible to testing effects. Similarly, so are opinion polls that sample the same individuals during a short time period. Without adequate time between surveys, participants are likely to remember their previous responses.

You can take a few steps to avoid testing effects. First, if possible, use different items or place the items in a different order. Second, if this is a major concern because short messages are being tested, select a different type of design (see the section on experimental research below), namely one that uses a control group for comparisons as opposed to pretesting participants. If longitudinal (over time) opinion polling is being conducted, try drawing a new random sample during each research cycle. In the end testing effects can occur, and campaign professional have to be aware of them, know how to spot them, and know how to avoid them.

On a similar note, the reliability of measures, scales, and surveys refer to their consistency. Does a similar set of items, supposedly measuring the same concept, issue, or attitude get a similar response. If the answer is no, then what are they measuring? If you are thinking, "we cannot be sure," you are correct. Measures need to be reliable in order to be valid. Following some of the simple rules outlined in the section on survey research below will also help to increase the reliability of your measures and surveys.

SAMPLING

In the previous section, it was suggested that random sampling techniques could be used to control for certain threats to the validity of research that is conducted. However, when discussing research, clients often ask why is there a need to draw samples of respondents or participants when conducting research? They also often ask, "Why use samples; can't we just ask everyone?" The simple answer is that samples save time and save money (clients tend to like this answer!). Conducting research is time-consuming, and it is expensive. Can you imagine the cost of doing research without the use of sampling? What would the cost of doing a nationwide opinion poll be if you had to send a survey to everyone—roughly $80 million in stamps alone, and it would take weeks to complete. The irony is that once you completed the project, the information would be of little use, because by then public opinion would have changed. The bottom line is that sampling allows the researcher flexibility, speed, convenience, and in the end it does save money.

How big a sample? A wise old statistics professor once said that "God rewards those with large sample sizes." The bigger the sample, the more confident you can be in your results. For example, imagine that your boss asks you to predict how 100 employees who are in the room next door will vote on an upcoming union contract. If you pulled one person out of the room and got her/his opinion, would you be confident that it represents the way they would all vote? What about if you asked ten? You would definitely be more confident than asking just one, and twenty would make you even more confident. The bottom line is that the larger the sample, the more confident you can be in your results.

This concept is due to a factor known as *sampling error*. Simply put, as sample sizes increase, sampling error decreases. So a sample of 200 individuals will have less sampling error associated with it than a sample of 50. However, the good news is that once sample size reaches 100-200 randomly drawn individuals, it takes large increases in sample size to get even small decreases in sampling error. That is why national political polls can survey 1,500 people and generalize to the opinions of all 260 million Americans. Once you hit 200 people, you could go to 1,000 people and get only a very small decrease in error, which means it would not be worth the time or money to draw the bigger sample.

Sampling Strategies

Random sampling is the most basic form of sampling. The term random refers to the fact that every member of the population (or public) has an equal chance of being selected. An example might come out of a community where names of registered voters are drawn at random from a list of registered voters. To perform this type of sampling, each name on such a list is usually assigned a number, so the researcher could draw numbers at random or use a computer to generate a list of random numbers. The individual with the corresponding number is added to the list of participants.

Although random sampling seems simple enough, how do you draw a random sample out of a pool of 20 million New Yorkers? With that many names it would be fairly time consuming and expensive to randomly draw a sample of 10,000 names. A simpler approach, especially when the names of potential members of a sample are found in lists, is to use *systematic random sampling*. In this case randomness is still maintained in that every member will still have an equal chance of being chosen. To perform this type of sampling procedure a researcher would first randomly choose a starting point in the list of potential names. Next, a *sampling interval* is chosen. The sampling interval is the number of names that will be consistently skipped when choosing names from the list of the selected population. For example, a sampling interval of fifty would mean that every fiftieth person in the list would be chosen. *The key to systematic sampling is that the sampling interval must guarantee that the researcher will move through the entire pool or list at least once.* If the interval is not big enough, then the problem is that those individuals at the bottom of the list do not have an equal chance of being chosen. The result is the loss of randomness and perhaps generalizability.

A second critical component to any randomized sampling technique is the sample pool. If you draw a random sample, you now have (or are assumed to have) a representative sample of the pool from which you drew. Can you see the problem with this statement? What if the pool or list is not representative of your target population? This means that you have to make sure that your sample pool is representative of your target population. If you are working on a political campaign and your goal is to find out how women will vote on a certain issue, sampling the opinions of males and females would lead to inaccurate predictions, because the sampling pool was different from the population you are targeting.

The aforementioned sampling techniques drew individuals from the general population. But individuals in the population can be very different. People can be categorized by a large variety of demographic, sociographic, and psychographic factors. A sampling technique that focuses on these differences or "strata" in the general population is known as *stratified sampling*. Stratified sampling involves the identification of groups or "strata" in the intended audiences. After the different groups are identified, random sampling techniques can be used to draw samples from each of the groups within the general population. For example, in political campaigns individuals can be segmented on the basis of political party affiliation. Thus, a researcher might sample the opinions of Democrats, Republicans, and Libertarians.

There are two forms of stratified sampling. Most often, the researcher will choose random samples within each strata that represent the proportion of that group in the actual population. This is referred to as *proportional sampling*. For, example, if current surveys have found that 50 percent of Americans claim to be registered Democrats and 49 percent Republican, a researcher doing opinion polling might draw a sample that is 50 percent democratic and 49 percent republican. However, sometimes researchers will choose to use *disproportional samples* and select an equal number of participants from each group within the population. An example of disproportional stratified sampling could be found in a campaign that targets the current customers of a company and their beliefs regarding the quality of customer service that is currently provided. Although there may not be an equal number of registered customers who use the product in every state, the public relations professional may elect to draw a sample of 100 customers from each state.

There are times, however, that due to resource limitations, random sampling is not possible. For example, a limited budget may not allow for the cost of a telephone survey, or a topic that deals with a socially sensitive issue may make it difficult to draw a random sample. Nonrandom sampling techniques can then be used. But, caution must be used when interpreting their findings, because your results are always limited by the sample that is drawn. In this case, it may be harder to draw inferences and make generalizations from your sample data, because you will not be sure if the information you obtain is truly representative of your targeted audiences.

The first type of nonrandom sampling to be discussed is called convenience (a.k.a. accidental) sampling. *Convenience/accidental* samples are gathered much like their name implies. In this case the researcher collects data at a certain location and surveys those who are at that location or are passing through. If someone has ever tried to poll your opinions on the street or in a shopping mall, you have been a participant in a research project that utilized convenience/accidental sampling techniques. The key to using this type of sampling is to understand that your location is the key to identifying the profile of your participants. In most cases people at or passing through certain areas will share many demographic, geographic, and perhaps sociographic qualities. For example, in Los Angeles if you surveyed passersby on Rodeo drive in Beverly Hills, you might be getting individuals with different demographic backgrounds as opposed to those you might sample at a more mainstream shopping location, or a small "strip mall." The bottom line to using this technique is to know that your location dictates your sample. Beyond that, this technique is an effective and low cost sampling mechanism if it meets your research needs.

Purposive samples are usually made up of populations of individuals that may have very specific characteristics or have characteristics that do not exist in large numbers in the general population. In these cases, a researcher may decide to purposely pursue and "hand-pick" subjects when they can be found. Professionals who develop campaigns that target health-risk behaviors often have to use this type of sampling. If campaign planners wanted to test messages about using clean needles when "shooting" up to avoid AIDS targeted at intravenous drug users, they might have to seek out such users. They could not conduct a random telephone poll nor could they do a mailed survey. Could you imagine your reaction if someone called your home one evening and asked if "you were a user of illegal intravenous drugs!!!?" Do you think if someone did use intravenous drugs that they would be quick to publicly admit it? Probably not. In this scenario researchers might seek out drug users (perhaps at methadone clinics or rehabilitation centers) and ask them to participate.

Snowball or *network* sampling techniques are also used by researchers to get at difficult populations. The term "snowball" is used because the researcher asks current subjects to bring other participants with a similar profile. In turn, those new participants are also asked to bring acquaintances and/or friends who share the desired characteristics. Since you are drawing a sample based on an initial participants social network, you can also see why this technique is sometimes referred to as network sampling.

An example of a network sampling strategy could be the case of the researcher who is developing message strategies to get HIV positive individuals to practice safe sex. It may be difficult to get subjects because of the social stigmas that are sometimes associated with the HIV virus. When the researcher recruits some participants who are HIV positive, they make ask those participants to bring in a "friend or two" who are also HIV positive. In the end the researcher gets a sample with desired characteristics but hopefully without having to expend large amounts of time or financial resources to do so.

In summary, research professionals use sampling to save time, manpower, and money. It is important to remember that your research findings are only as good as your sample. If you can have confidence that your sample is representative of your campaign's targeted populations, then you will have enough confidence to apply the findings of your research to the development of your campaigns.

THE RESEARCH PROCESS

Research professionals and academic social scientists will often note that all research designs have their advantages and their disadvantages. Many will argue that one technique is inherently better than another, and many individuals specialize in a certain type of research. However, the smart researcher lets the research question dictate the best method to use.

Collecting data and always using a certain technique is analogous to a mechanic who always uses the same tool, no matter which tool best fits the job. Furthermore, a variety of methods can be used. For example, when developing messages for an image campaign, a researcher might start out with interviews of an organization's management and employees to find out what is the image that they want to portray. A second step could be the use of focus groups and surveys to identify the images that external audiences may have. Finally, experimental methods could be used to test competing message strategies. In some situations, multimethod approaches may provide a greater quantity and quality of information. However, often campaign planners are limited in terms of time, manpower, and money so choices will have to be made. The key is to remain flexible and to choose a method that provides valid answers to your questions, while meeting your constraints.

Interviewing

Interviews may not be the most efficient way to collect information on a certain topic, issue, or situation. In comparison to the use of survey techniques, interviewing takes more time and perhaps more manpower, depending on the sample size that is chosen. In contrast, interviews can be used to gather in-depth information on a topic or issue, especially when they are used as "pilot" or preliminary research. There are a few basic rules that can be used to increase the probability of getting good response rates to interviews and to increasing the quantity and quality of information that is obtained.

Preparation is a key component to successful interviewing. An interview guide with prioritized questions/need items should be prepared in advance. The interview guide is really no more than a survey that contains the items that are to be asked of the participants. The guide should also include probing questions in areas where more detail may be needed.

In addition to probing items, the items should also be prioritized in some manner. Prioritizing items is important if schedules change, or if some new and unexpected information is brought up by the participants, or if things do not go as planned. If any of these events occur, a prioritized interview guide increases the probability of obtaining important information as opposed to less crucial data. This is especially true when conducting the first set of interviews in a series. At the beginning of most research projects, it is often difficult to predict the speed at which individuals will move through a survey or where probing questions maybe needed. This tends to be especially true if the issue or questions deal with controversial topics.

Similarly, to increase the flow of information, try to keep questions in "conceptual categories" so that the participants' ideas can more easily flow on a topic. Finally, a good interviewer usually has practiced the interview several times before the actual interview is taken. The credibility and professionalism of a public relations practitioner may come into question if she/he starts fumbling over the words of the interview guide or gets confused while reading a survey he/she has supposedly developed. If assistants are used to conduct interviews or if the research is contracted, make sure that those who conduct the interviews are similarly trained and practiced. Fumbling over items not only leads to mistakes but also may impact the credibility of your company.

Preparation can also include *preparing the participant.* If the questions are complex, or require some in-depth analysis, a prepared participant will give more complete and perhaps more valuable responses. In the age of e-mail and facsimile (fax) machines, a preliminary list of topics can easily be sent to participants. If the interview treads on a sensitive topic, advance warning may also serve to better prepare the participant and to decrease defensiveness.

When conducting the interview, try to choose a setting that makes the participant comfortable but is also convenient. Low response rates and a high number of "no-shows" should not surprise a researcher who requires that participants fight rush-hour traffic to come to the researcher's office location. Additionally, a comfortable setting increases the probability that the participant will relax, be focused, and be willing to engage in thoughtful dialogue. Contrast this to a situation where a participant is uncomfortable or is distracted by loud noises or people walking by. In the end, the loss of focus, as well as the loss of participant desire, may lead to the collection of less information.

Last, *allow the participant the ability to skip questions if she/he so desires.* Forcing individuals to discuss issues that are uncomfortable may lead to nervousness, defensiveness, hostility, and in a worst-case scenario, the use of lies. If a respondent does not want to answer a question, she/he should not be obligated to do so. Noting the ability to skip questions and promises of anonymity and/or confidentiality will often help the researcher to get the participant to relax and begin the disclosure process.

Flow is also an important component of a good interview. The experienced researcher learns to manage the interview and let probing questions add to the flow of information. Similarly, if time does not appear to be a factor in a particular interview, the researcher can skip items as the interviewee begins discussing a topic and later return to the unanswered items. In the end, a good interview sounds like a simple conversation, with the same verbal components, and similar nonverbal components such as good eye contact, the use of gestures, and positive body orientations.

Focus Group Interviewing

Focus group research is very similar to interviewing; however, in this case a group of participants will be surveyed. There are two advantages that focus groups have over interviews. First, participants can synthesize or "work off" the answers provided by others, often providing greater depth and insight into attitudes and positions on issues. Second, the interviewer can ask in-depth probing questions of an individual or the entire group, which can lead to even more synthesis.

Focus groups are a useful formative research tool for exploring a population's pre-existing levels of awareness, involvement, and constraint recognition, as well as knowledge, attitudes, and beliefs. Similarly, they can also be used to pretest message strategies before launching a campaign or, in the middle of the campaign, to assist in making strategy modifications. Finally, focus groups can also be used as part of the summative research process to help explain campaign success or reasons for failure.

The term focus group research is one that is often heard in discussions regarding public relations research. The concept is a simple one. Groups of individuals who are similar to the target group profile are brought together and are asked to answer/discuss questions. On the surface this type of research appears rather simplistic and easy to conduct. However, without careful planning and experienced moderators, focus group research can be an expensive waste of time and resources.

Planning

When it comes to conducting effective focus group research, three areas of concern have to be put at the top of the list: planning, conducting, and analyzing results. There are several keys to conducting effective focus group research. The first step to getting good results is wise planning and organizing. Planning for focus group research is not difficult but takes a lot of attention to detail. In terms of planning there are four major issues: the setting, the participants, materials, and recording. All are important, and problems with any of these factors will in all likelihood impact the quantity and/or the quality of your data.

There are several things to note about the setting. First is that it must be comfortable and neutral in nature. As a researcher you want the participants to be comfortable with and focused on the task at hand. Anything that distracts participants may affect their level of involvement and the quantity and/or quality of their responses.

The *setting must also accommodate interaction.* Tables and chairs must be placed in such as way to facilitate discussion among all participants. To demonstrate the use of seating arrangements Figure 2.1 presents examples of preferred and unpreferred seating arrangements. The first two examples (square and round) allow for equal participation and interaction by all participants. In the last two examples participants at one end may have difficulty communicating with participants at the opposite end of the configuration. If oval or rectangular

46   Campaign Strategies and Message Design

Figure 2.1
Suggested Seating Arrangements for Focus Groups

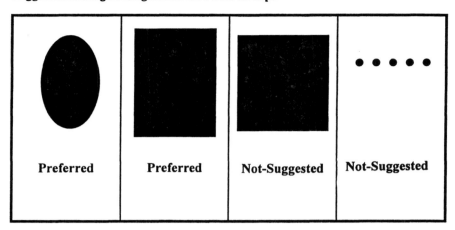

shapes must be used, try at all costs to minimize their length and the distance between participants.

The setting should also be conducive to recording if a record of the session is to be kept. Firms that specialize in research services will often have facilities with hidden or recessed audio and/or video devices. If such a facility cannot be used, choose a setting that will allow for the inconspicuous use of cameras and/or microphones. Be careful to test equipment beforehand to ensure that all participants are captured on tape, if video is being used. Similarly, test microphones and tape recorders to make sure that all participants can be heard on audio recordings. Last, if recordings of any type are made, make sure you get the written consent of the participants to use those recordings. If legal or ethical issues arise in the future, obtaining prior consent could save your reputation and/or large legal fees.

When discussing the issue of *participants,* one word should come to mind. The term "representative" should be at the heart of every decision made regarding who will participate in the research. The objective of focus group research is to uncover feelings, knowledge, attitudes, and beliefs of individuals in the target population. That means that the participants in your focus groups should represent a cross-section of that targeted population. The further the psychographic, sociographic, and demographic profiles of your participants move from the profiles of your targeted populations, the less likely the data you collect will be helpful when making decisions.

Size is also an issue. If the group is too small, then interaction is limited, and domination may occur by one or two individuals. If the group is too large, you may also have limited interaction. In larger groups some individuals may be nervous to speak up and may acquiesce to the opinions of others. Similarly, a fair degree of "social loafing" can also occur when using large groups. Social loafing refers to a situation where people in a group do less, because they assume others will do the work. This will tend to happen in large groups, especially if the group contains several dominant individuals.

Materials are also an important concern. Decisions should be made in advance regarding the use of interview guides (as always, prepared well in advance) by both the interviewer and the group. If issues are complex, it may save time and effort if each member of the group is provided with an interview guide. Similarly, consider if the group needs something to keep track of their discussions or needs a white board to diagram issues or attributes of some process. Things like paper, markers, white boards, and tape are handy to have if participants decide they would like to have something to write on or draw diagrams on for the group. Last, do not forget that you can also have focus group participants respond to surveys after the session is over. If additional information is not desired, feedback on the focus group process might be useful, especially if you have unexpected results. Similarly, demographic and psychographic information on participants can sometimes help match issues with audiences.

The *recording* of information can be a troublesome issue. First, the presence of recording equipment can raise participant doubts of the sincerity of promised confidentiality. Furthermore, in some situations (for example, organizing a cultural change campaign in an organization) the presence of recording equipment may cause individuals to withhold or present untrue information because they fear retaliation. In these extreme situations, it may be best to either simply take notes or hire a transcriptionist to develop a transcript of the session.

If recording equipment is used, there are some tips and techniques that can minimize their impact. First and foremost is the notification of the participants. In certain situations where the loss of anonymity may lead to negative consequences or if the discussions will focus on a socially "taboo" topic, participants may suspect that sessions are being recorded. You do not want to be second-guessed by your participants. The worst-case scenario is the one where you do not inform or receive consent, and the participants notice a hidden microphone or notice movement behind a one-way mirror. A good number of people have probably had Psychology 101 and may recall participating in an experiment. How did you feel when you noticed the hidden microphone, or heard voices behind a "mirrored wall?" In this situation, the end result is mistrust, and any information obtained will be unusable, or at least suspect.

Second, when using recording equipment, make sure it is unobtrusive. Humans in general are fairly vain creatures (you may not like cameras in your face) and are often nervous about being recorded. Placing the equipment in a position that is usable but where it is "out of the way" is of the utmost importance. If the site you have chosen cannot accommodate your recording needs, simply choose another site.

Conducting

The ability to moderate and conduct focus groups is one that is learned and takes time to develop. However, there are some suggestions that can help the public relations practitioner conduct effective focus group research. Acclamation, participation, and conversational management are all factors that will impact the way that the groups interact, as well as contribute to the usefulness of the data that you collect.

When it comes to conducting focus groups, there are a few simple techniques and a trick or two that can improve the quantity and quality of the information you get. The first step is to get everyone *acclimated* to the focus group environment. This also means getting the participants used to the recording equipment if it is used. It is a good idea to "break the ice" with some introductions and some simple instructions. If you can manage, try to start off with issues that are relatively neutral in nature and will allow for participation. Once the participants get used to the setting, the process, and one another, they will be ready to explore deeper issues.

Participation is the key word when conducting focus groups. You want everybody to participate. There are a few problems that you will face if participation is your goal. First is that fact that some individuals are just much more extroverted and dominant than others. Second, some individuals tend to be more introverted and are likely to say little. The end result is a situation where one or two individuals will dominate the discussion, and their opinions will drive the results that you collect. The question you have to ask is "Why run a focus group with six to eight individuals if you are only going to get the opinions of two or three people?" It is a good question, and the answer is that you should not. There are some tricks to getting people to participate and some techniques that can be used to shift the focus away from dominant individuals without seeming rude or without injuring egos.

To get everyone to participate, you must first keep a mental tab of how much individuals are speaking. Time does not have to be equal, but you should try to include everyone at least once when discussing major issues, unless they state that the topic makes them uncomfortable. If you want individuals to contribute, do it by asking them. During a pause, simply turn to that individual, use their name and say "what do you think." It is hard to resist and say nothing when the speaking turn has been given directly to you. Use this technique to keep everyone involved and to maximize the amount of information that is contributed to the discussion.

How do you get the speaking turns away from those that dominate the discussion? One trick is to use both nonverbal and verbal cues to give the speaking turn to another participant. This technique is outlined in the tip below.

TIP: As soon as the dominant individual pauses after a statement, thank him/her directly for his/her comment (this causes him/her to stop speaking) and then without stopping turn your body away from the person and gently motion with your hands toward another participant, as you ask that participant (using his/her name) what he/she thinks on the issue. The end result is that you have just complimented the dominating individual and have diplomatically taken the speaking turn away from him/her.

This technique takes a little practice, but it can be very useful.

As in interviews, *flow* is also important during focus group discussions. Whenever possible try to keep the conversation flowing smoothly. If time permits, allow the group to maneuver through a set of issues that may not be consecutive on your list but are considered high priority in nature. Probing questions should come only after the group has reached a natural stopping point. However, if the group gets too far off track, bring them back by asking them to focus on a more relevant issue associated with the current question. If possible tie your probe to one of the participant's responses (use her/his name), and you will find that the group will quickly get back on track.

While flow is important, so is *silence*. The temptation will be great to fill the silence when a question or issue is presented to the group and no one quickly answers. The practiced focus group moderator learns to be patient and lets an individual in the group formulate or synthesize an answer. This is much easier said than done because silence in conversations even for ten seconds seems like an eternity. However, it is the participants who you want answering the questions, and if they notice that you will start for them, groups will often work off your cues.

Although counterintuitive, flexibility and the opportunity to discuss unplanned issues may sometimes be crucial to attaining quality results. Some practitioners may find this approach unsettling, because it implies abandoning the focus group interview guide or script, to let groups explore unexpected issues. However, the loss of control and the loss of time may well be worth the cost, especially if the information that comes to light provides answers to your questions. Similarly, it is also wise to let them complete an in-depth exploration of issues that gain importance once the session has begun. This is not a contradiction with the tenets of scripting and control mentioned previously in this chapter but rather speaks to the issue of flexibility.

Verbal summaries can also help manage the discussion, as well as help simplify analysis. *Summarizing* refers to the process of providing the group with a quick verbal summary of their overall feelings on a certain question or issue. You might phrase it as, "If I were to summarize what the group is saying on this issue, I would say that two themes have. . . . ." Summarizing adds value to the focus group process in several ways. First, it provides a natural ending point for a topic and a transition to a new area. Second, it allows the group to get an idea of where they are on certain issues, especially if the conversation changes the positions that individuals hold. Third, it keeps the researcher on track with the "meaning" of the group's responses, which will greatly aid the researcher when performing subsequent analyses (see Figure 2.2).

Analyzing Results

The analysis of focus group results can be time consuming depending on the length of the interview guide, the length of the focus group sessions, how sessions were recorded, and the diversity of opinions. The goal in analyzing results

Figure 2.2
Techniques for Effective Focus Groups

1.	Choose a site and setting that is neutral, comfortable, and allows for both interaction and recording.
2.	Participants should represent a cross-section of a targeted population.
3.	Limit the group to a manageable size, usually 6 to 8 individuals
4.	Recording equipment should be as unobtrusive as possible.
5.	Allow the group to "synthesize" responses by giving them time to discuss issues among themselves.
6.	Do not be afraid of silence. Let the group ponder issues and make them begin the conversations.
7.	Try to include everyone; this means using interpersonal and conversation management techniques to get quiet individuals to contribute.
8.	Do not let one or two individuals dominate the group. Use turn-taking techniques such as eye contact, body movement, and the use of names to distribute the participation.
9.	Be careful not to give off "cues" or "tips" as to how you feel on certain issues, and try not to respond to what you feel are good or poor answers. You may inadvertently "contaminate" your data with your opinions.
10.	After some discussions of major issues stop the group and offer them a summary of what you see them saying. This is especially important if a lot of information has been presented and/or positions have shifted. You might even use the phrase "Could I sum up what you are all saying now as....".

is to identify relevant themes, issues, or responses to each of the questions posed to the group. Often this is completed using a technique called content analysis. In common terms, *content analysis* has the researcher categorize the responses into major content areas or themes. This is usually done on a question-by-question, or an issue-by-issue basis. For example, if the focus group was being conducted to identify why participants voted for political candidates, major areas could be party affiliation, past record, credibility, physical attractiveness, or any other reasons that may have been mentioned.

Some researchers may choose to limit this analysis to a simple listing of themes or issues, while others may prioritize themes based on their prevalence or the frequency with which they were discussed and also on the importance or strength of an issue as identified by participants. In either case, information on conducting content analysis will be found later in this chapter.

Survey Research

One of the most well known and most popular types of research is survey research. Survey research is popular because it is often simple, reliable, and an inexpensive method of meeting informational needs. As noted, survey research can be a powerful tool to help the campaign practitioner develop, monitor, and evaluate campaigns. Surveys can be used to assess attitudes, beliefs, knowledge, perceptions of image, and behaviors before campaigns begin, as well as identify changes during the course of a campaign. Finally, surveys are also a powerful tool to determine if change has occurred after the completion of a campaign. However, if care is not taken, survey-based research can be a waste of time, money, and other resources. Worse, the result may be bad decisions based on bad data, which can cost "PR" professionals their contract, their client, and perhaps their reputation.

Open-Ended versus Closed-Ended Questions

One of the first choices that has to be made when constructing a survey is the type of questions that will be asked. Will the survey consist of open-ended items or will it consist of close-ended items (such as short answers with scales or check boxes). Both can be useful in obtaining information, and both have major advantages and disadvantages. The key to deciding is to identify the type and depth of information you need and how prepared you are to get that information.

Open-ended questions have several advantages. They allow individuals to supply the categories of responses to questions. Furthermore, they also allow the individuals to provide a longer and more in-depth answer, which means more information. Open-ended questions are often useful as pilot surveys, which can be used to identify responses, issues, attitudes, and concerns for inclusion on subsequent closed-ended survey items. This technique is especially useful if the public relations or campaign professional has little experience with the issue or with a particular public. In this case, the use of a pilot survey with open-ended items can lead to a much stronger and more valid survey tool by identifying the main ideas or concepts associated with an issue that the research professional may have missed.

Open-ended items do have several disadvantages. First, they take time to complete, which can mean lower response rates or higher costs to conduct the research if interviewers or telephone survey specialists are used. Furthermore, the results are relatively unstandardized, take time, and are subjective to analyze. An example of how subjectivity enters into the process is a project where individuals may be using different terms to describe the same phenomena. The end result is that the researcher has to make subjective choices when interpreting results, deciding which terms fit into which categories.

Closed-ended items have a good number of advantages. First, they are easy to complete and easy to analyze. Ease of completion usually means higher response rates. Furthermore, the numerical rating given by a respondent is often used in the data analysis, which means there is very little subjective interpretation on the part of the researcher. Closed-ended items are also simpler to complete and less mentally taxing, which can mean more items and less fatigue. If interviewers or phone surveyors are used, closed-ended surveys can reduce the cost of salaries and toll charges. The last advantage is speed. Because closed-ended response formats are faster to complete, require little coding, and can be analyzed quickly, large samples can be drawn quickly. Speed and timeliness are often necessary in the middle of a campaign, especially if messages and strategies have to be responsive to a competitor's campaign messages.

In contrast to open-ended items, closed-ended items are limiting. If the questions are vague or poorly worded, they leave little room for the respondent to clarify their responses. If this occurs, the research professional has almost no way of knowing what the respondent based an answer on, because there is no supporting information. Similarly, closed-ended items are also limiting in that the respondent is forced to limit her/his response on a fairly small scale. Social scientists often call this "restriction in range." This means that an individual who felt moderately strong on an issue, might choose a rating of "5" an a scale of 1 to 5, while a person with extremely strong feelings would also be forced to choose a "5" on the same scale. In sum, closed-ended items may not capture all of the intensity of attitudes or feelings because they often use a small range of responses.

After the discussion of the pros and cons of both open-ended and close-ended items, it is evident that both can be useful and that both have their drawbacks. The availability of resources such as information, time, and money will also to some extent dictate what choices are made. Finally, they are not mutually exclusive. A research professional could include a few open-ended items at the end of a survey to capture missed responses or extreme feelings that the survey did not allow to be expressed. Finally, the following section will detail a few tips on how to write effective survey items that may help to minimize some of the disadvantages associated with either format.

Rules for Writing Effective Surveys

The key word to writing good surveys is to think *participant.* Never lose sight of what you are trying to learn about your participants with the survey. Furthermore, try to think like your participant when writing items. Ask yourself "Could person X understand this?" or "Will the participants become confused, tired, or bored?" Similarly, "Is this survey easy to complete and/or will the participants want to complete it?" Figure 2.3 offers a few suggestions of response formats that research professionals currently use.

Although these rules sound simple, the author has often been amazed at how researchers can quickly lose sight of such simple considerations as writing for a specific audience. Overall, there are some simple steps that a campaign professional can follow to minimize the risk of constructing a "bad" survey.

Figure 2.3
Suggestions for Survey Rating Systems

Likert Scale	Str. Disagree Disagree Neutral Agree Str. Agree 1 2 3 4 5
Semantic Differential	Unfavorable _ _ _ _ _ _ _ Favorable
Yes/No	Yes ____ No ____ Undecided/Don't Know ____
"Scale of 10"	On a scale of 1 to 10, with a 1 representing a "bad image" and a 10 representing a "good" image, how would you rate Acme Corp. ____
Grunig's System	On a scale from 1 to 500, how would a ban on the sale of cigarettes affect you, personally? ____
Demographic Data	What is your age? under 20___ 21-25___ 26-30___ 31-35___

The first rule is that *each item should measure one concept or idea.* For example, avoid "and" questions such as, "The message was easy to comprehend and very persuasive." The participant is forced to decide if he/she should focus on the part of the item measuring comprehension or if he/she should evaluate persuasiveness. The research professional will have no way of knowing which parts, or if both of the questions were focused on by each participant. Therefore, to increase item reliability, each item should represent just one idea, issue, and/or concept. If two are represented, the researcher does not know if the participant is answering part or all of the question.

Another writing tip is to *avoid the use of extreme language.* Refrain from calling ideas "stupid" or referring to positions as being "ignorant." Individuals will tend to stay away from extreme terminology. Similarly, be careful when using terms that make reference to an individual's ethnicity, gender, or habits. Use *currently acceptable* and *politically correct* labels to assess ethnicity. *Refrain from using slang terms* for describing behavior, for example, "Would you consider yourself a boozer?" as opposed to "Would you consider yourself a heavy drinker?"

Although expertise is a touchy area, the professional public relations practitioner knows her/his limitations. One limitation that faces all professionals is that no matter what we think, we do not know it all. Therefore, when writing surveys, it may be wise to base the survey on the results of interviews or focus groups. However, if resources such as time and/or money do not allow for this inductive approach, a simple technique is to include a few open-ended questions at the end of the survey. These can be content analyzed (see the section on content analysis) to identify key issues that may have not been picked up by the survey. However, as was previously discussed, open-ended items take much longer to analyze and interpret; therefore, the use of "catch-all" open-ended items should be kept to a minimum.

Getting accurate answers and high response rates is another reason to follow some simple rules. A good research professional always *takes the survey himself/herself.* By doing this, you quickly identify typographical and/or mechanical errors, confusing questions, and perhaps biased questions. Taking it yourself also allows you to get an estimate of how long the survey takes to complete. This can help you to either cut the survey to reduce fatigue or to try to simplify the response scales to make the survey less mentally taxing.

As noted in Figure 2.4, likewise, to get better responses, make the survey simple to complete. This means always providing a cover letter or statement as well as instructions. Furthermore, this also suggests that response formats need to be kept as simple as possible. The more difficult the survey is to complete, the less likely individuals will be to complete it. Similarly, the more difficult it is to complete, the more likely that mistakes will be made, which can lead to questions regarding the validity of your research and the reliability of your survey.

Collecting Survey Data

There are many ways to collect survey data. Three main survey collection techniques will be discussed in this section. These are surveys collected by mail, telephone, and electronically. Mailed surveys are a quick and efficient method of collecting data. A list of names and addresses is obtained, and your sample is drawn from the list. However, the down side to mailed surveys is that they can be expensive, for two reasons: first, because the cost of postage is high and you have to pay it in both directions; and second, because response rates are extremely low. Social scientists often report that (Frey et al., 1991) mailed surveys tend to get a response rate somewhere between five to fifteen percent. A fifteen percent response rate tends to be good for mailed surveys. The more specific the target population, the better the response rate. However, the more specific the profile of the target population, the more it will cost to obtain a mailing list. In the end, mailed surveys can be very expensive to produce, distribute, and collect.

There are several tips that a researcher can follow to maximize response rates. The first is to always include a self-addressed stamped envelope for returning surveys. Do not assume that individuals will want to participate and that they will be motivated enough to supply a stamp, address an envelope, or go to extreme lengths to return questionnaires. Second, always include a letter explaining the nature of the survey and that it is not part of some sales process. Many

Figure 2.4
Tips and Techniques for Effective Surveys

1.	Always include instructions for participants; do not assume that everybody knows how to fill out a questionnaire.
2.	Each item should measure only one issue, feeling, attitude, knowledge, etc.
3.	Higher numbers/ratings should indicate more positive outcomes/higher quantities of characteristics. Adjust your rating scales accordingly.
4.	When possible avoid switching rating systems in the middle of the survey.
5.	Always give respondents the option of a "don't know" rating or the ability to skip the question.
6.	Rating systems should always have an odd number of categories to allow for feelings of neutrality or uncertainty.
7.	When assessing concepts, factors, or characteristics that can be quantified and when there are a large number of possible responses (e.g. number of miles driven in a year), consider creating categories or a series of intervals that participants can choose from.
8.	When constructing items that will have participants choose a range of values (e.g. annual income), make sure the intervals or categories are evenly spaced.
9.	If you do provide categories for continuous variables (i.e. age and income), try to keep the number of categories between 5 and 8. Too few or too many categories could make it difficult to accurately segment populations.
10.	Take the survey yourself. Make an effort to think hard about answering each question. Doing this can catch typos, identify the threat of fatigue, and spot confusing questions.

individuals are justifiably distrustful of anything in the mail. Third, use official looking envelopes and letterhead. While having introduction letters printed on blank paper and using inexpensive envelopes may save money, they may also look enough like "junk mail" to get discarded in an early sort of the mail. Using business-quality letterhead and envelopes may at least get you past the "sorting stage" where less important junk mail is discarded.

Incentives can also be used. The inclusion of a small amount of money, such as a dollar has been shown to increase response rates (Paolillo & Lorenzi, 1984), over no incentive or the promise of rewards such as a lottery entry. Feelings of indebtedness can be used to drive response rates; however, those feelings may not be held equally across all demographic groups, so be sure to compare the demographics of your respondents against those of your intended audiences.

Finally, target your surveys as closely as possible to reach your intended populations. It will be hard enough to get a high level of response if your audiences are not aware of a problem that potentially faces them. Do not make it harder by doing a general mailing. Given the cost of postage and materials, it may be worth a few extra cents per listing to pay for a more focused validated mailing list. In the end, there seems to be one constant across all survey research techniques: the better the profiling, targeting, and the sample, the better the response.

Although response rates from telephone surveys tend to be higher, they cost more in the form of tolls and manpower. They are also becoming increasing more unreliable as there are increasing proportions of unlisted phone numbers and individuals who refuse to take part in surveys. These numbers are growing in part because surveys are sometimes used as a ruse to make a sales pitch. Furthermore, as the number of telephone fraud/scam incidents increase and gain media attention, public cynicism will also continue to grow. If telephone survey techniques are to be used, there are several tips that can increase response rates and improve the quality of the information that is received.

First, always begin the telephone scripts with your affiliation, the purpose of the call, and if you so choose, how you acquired their number. It is important to quickly note that you are not selling anything and that the call will be fairly short. This leads to the second tip: keep phone polls short. Would you take thirty minutes in the evening to spend time on the phone with a pollster? Probably not! Telling the participant that the call will be short will increase response rates.

Another tip is to train your interviewers. An interviewer who stumbles over the questions may lose credibility and may try the patience of the participant. The scripts should be almost memorized and the interviewers carefully trained in how to record certain responses. Why bother to spend time and money on a survey, if the data will be unusable because the interviewers have made too many mistakes? Following is a tip on how to select effective telemarketing services to conduct research.

Tip: Many better survey research and telemarketing organizations will allow you access to listen in on calls to check on the quality of the telephone interviews. Look for a firm that offers this option. Also, ask if the company has an internal quality control mechanism.

Although data have not been presented on this issue, the generalizability of telephone surveys may also come into question as the number of Internet users increase. Since those who use the Internet tend to be from upper socioeconomic demographic groups, researchers in the future may be more likely to receive a busy signal from a number whose listing includes an Internet user than one where there are no Internet users. The end result is that the participants of telephone surveys may be less likely to represent the general demographic patterns that are found at random.

Surveys can also be collected electronically, via fax, or by the Internet. The key factor here is to understand who has access to this technology and who uses it. If the individuals who have the access and use these media fit your target profile, these methods are simple and inexpensive mechanisms for collecting data.

Suggestions for targeting surveys might include the use of list servers and solicitations on chat lines. Furthermore, surveys can be included as options on websites. If these tactics are used, ease is the key. The simpler to complete and return (for example, check boxes or a simple button to return the responses) the better the response rate. Caution must be used, however. The Internet does little to accurately identify the sender of a message. Moreover, it is also often impossible to differentiate single versus multiple respondents. This means that one individual could respond 100 times or more by simply repeating the survey or worse by simply reclicking the send button. The same is true for other electronic media such as fax machines. The person you send a fax to may not be the person who receives or returns it.

Overall, the growth of the telecommunications and telecomputing industry is to the benefit of campaign research professionals. These channels can be used with great forethought and care. However, relying on these mechanisms for getting information to a demographically broad population may lead to problems with validity and unreliability.

Content Analysis

This section discusses an analytic technique known as content analysis. Content analysis does simply what its name implies; it categorizes participants' responses to questions, statements, or messages. Additionally, content analysis can be used to categorize media content for use in formative and/or evaluative processes. Content analysis can be used to categorize statements and responses obtained from research participants via open-ended survey questions, interview results, and statements made during focus groups, or from the media. These data could be obtained during the formative research process to identify public positions, identify issues, identify images, and assess a group's reactions to general message strategies or actual campaign messages. It can also be used in the summative or evaluation phases of campaign research to examine if campaign messages were effective and to assess the key factors behind success or failure.

As with most research techniques, content analysis, taken at face value, appears to present the public relations professional conducting research with a daunting task. However, content analyses are relatively simple to perform, but they demand a much greater amount of time, especially when compared to other types of quantitative analyses. This section will forward some "how to's" about content analysis. Furthermore, some techniques and tips will also be forwarded to allow the researcher to be better informed and to save time, which usually equates to saving money. The areas of planning, preparation, and analysis will be covered in this section.

Planning for Content Analysis

When discussing the issue of planning, it is best to start with the mechanics of actually collecting the information. Ease is the golden rule in this case. Make the content analysis process as simple as possible. There are several things that you can do in terms of ease. For example, if you are content analyzing surveys, it is best to keep open-ended questions on a separate page from close-ended items. This is especially true if you are analyzing large numbers of surveys. This technique allows the researchers to simply tear off the page(s) with open-ended items and start processing the close-ended items. If you follow these suggestions, make sure the page(s) with the open-ended items is/are numbered with the identification number of the survey to allow the matching of responses. This suggestion also speeds the analysis process because the researcher can begin analysis on closed-ended items, while performing the content analysis. Again, this is mainly true when there are large numbers of participants or there is a large amount of data due to longer surveys.

Preparing to Begin the Content Analysis

If the content analyses are being performed on participants' reactions to message strategies or the results of focus group sessions, the issue of what constitutes a separate response comes to the forefront. Again this sounds complex, but the issue is a simple one: what counts as a response; is it the use of a word, a sentence, or do you count three minutes of discussion on an issue as a single response. These are issues that the researcher will have to determine in advance to allow for more accurate and more efficient data analysis. Here is a tip on simplifying analyses when you are analyzing participants' responses to message strategies or specific messages.

Tip: When asking participants to write their comments to message strategies or actual test messages, give them response sheets with lines that are numbered. Then give them specific oral and written instructions to start each new response on a separate line. This allows the researcher to easily see where one response ends and a new one begins.

When analyzing recordings of focus groups, it is best to sometimes have these transcribed. Once you have received the transcripts, you can go through and identify and number each separate response. Therefore, there are no disagreements over what constituted a response, and more important, it is easy to reference a response when there are disagreements or when more focus is needed on a certain response category. If videotaped information is obtained, the researchers may need to identify issues by the tape counter or run time, to make absolutely sure that there is no disagreement over what is being categorized. When dealing with audio and/or video recordings, it is very easy for independent researchers coding the same material to be focusing on different segments of tape or statements. If this happens, the data you obtain are now worthless because you cannot link the analysis with specific content, and the whole process becomes a waste of time and money.

In sum, based on the suggestions contained above regarding the collection of responses, it is clear that when it comes to content analysis, a little planning goes a long way.

Conducting Content Analyses

The term *content analysis implies that you are analyzing the content of actual, written, or recorded events*. This means that you examine the statements, actions, or responses and place them into content categories. A simple example would be to draw a sample of news stories that mention a campaign that you may be conducting. You could then categorize them as being positive or negative in nature. Alternatively, you could identify themes that the articles discuss; these could be questions of causality, praise, criticism, or any other specific content area that you choose. Finally, remember that content analyses can also be conducted on open-ended survey items and on recorded records of focus group sessions.

The first rule is to be as *specific as possible*. Vague category definitions make responses much more difficult to categorize and lead to increased unreliability and questions regarding the validity of your findings. As mentioned before, you may think that these are problems that only academics should deal with, but you are wrong. Unreliability and invalidity mean bad data, poor accuracy, and will lead to bad decisions. Remember that campaigns are expensive in terms of time, manpower, and money, and as a professional you are staking your reputation on the decisions that you make. Taking a few extra hours to more carefully define categories and train coders (those who actually categorize responses) will give you the piece of mind about the decisions you make based on the information you receive from these analyses. Second, to increase reliability, category definitions should be as mutually exclusive as possible. That means if a response fits in category A, it should not fit into category B, C, or D.

Category systems and definitions do not have to be complex. Simple examples are to code the responses simply as positive, neutral, or negative in nature. Other methods could include examining mention of a certain aspect of a message or mention of an issue. These examples can also be used to code media coverage, or statements by the media. More complex category systems could code responses as positive or negative but rate them on degrees of positiveness or negativeness. Similarly, category systems could also break the concepts of positive and negative into subcategories that mention what the participant was responding to. For example, if the respondent's response was negative, was it to the medium or quality of the message, or was it targeted at the actual copy of the message, or the sponsor. The examples of responses such as "I think the message was boring" and "I think that the message was full of lies" are both negative in nature but are indicative of some very different thought processes.

The Use of Theory in Content Analysis

Theory can also play a role in the use of coding categories. For example, those working on health-based campaigns could use a category system based on similar theories from the domains of public health and persuasion. The Health Belief Model (Janz & Becker, 1984) and the protection motivation model (Prentice-Dunn & Rogers, 1986; Rippetoe & Rogers, 1987) specify components of health-based messages that have to be included to facilitate message effectiveness. These are factors such as severity of harm, certainty (susceptibility), an explicit recommendation, and a mention about the efficacy of the response. A campaign planner could code responses to test messages and see if respondents mention any of these components. A more sophisticated analysis could examine the types of negative statements or counterarguments that individuals make targeted toward these areas. Message strategies could then be developed to counter the negative responses.

Quantifying Responses

In the academic arena, some researchers would say that looking at numbers is not necessary and that the presence of a response or category of responses is enough. Take caution with such statements. Because resources such as time and money are limited a researcher has to be able to judge the pervasiveness, or magnitude, of a certain mindset that exists in the minds of the profiled populations. Often the campaign planner will be forced to choose between message strategies due to limitations of time, manpower, and money. Having an idea of widespread perceptions, as opposed to those that are held by only a few individuals will facilitate prioritization and speed the campaign development process. Second, the quantification of responses also allows the researcher to identify response patterns with individuals (if the information is matched with questionnaires containing other items, or demographic information) and allows a much higher degree of audience segmentation.

Finally, the use of numbers allows for the use of a two-way symmetrical model of communication. Having information that shows evidence of large-scale attitudes or beliefs, needs, or desires, allows the researcher to better make suggestions on policy and actions. If no quantification of responses is undertaken, arguments regarding the strength, and depth of knowledge, opinions, attitudes, behaviors, images, or needs cannot be made. These numbers are a great tool to generate change in a client or sponsoring organization. To get a better idea of how quantifying results can leverage influence, note the example about recycling below.

Example: A recent recycling campaign was conducted on a university campus to increase the recycling of paper and cans among target populations. One major barrier listed by focus group participants and 88 percent of those completing surveys was inconvenience due to a lack of bins. The sponsoring organization had been hesitant to order more bins because of the lower levels of use. When the client saw the results of the research, they quickly ordered a large number of new bins.

The recycling campaign example also provides an excellent demonstration of the way research can be used as part of a two-way communication and change process. In this case, the original goal was to increase recycling behavior, and the client's actions (lack of bins) were resulting in lower recycling. By conducting the research and quantifying the sentiments of the targeted populations the public relations professional was able to change the organization's behavior to better meet goals.

The last aspect of content analysis is compiling results. As previously mentioned, these analyses usually involve categorizing statements or actions into set category themes. To report these data, one can simply mention the percentage of times particular themes, issues, or actions were mentioned. Alternatively, a researcher could also focus a report on predominant themes and omit lesser occurring themes. The choice to do this is guided by concerns over resources and client needs. However, it is often better to include all themes, so that if future projects are undertaken, comparisons can be made regarding the presence of certain issues and the relative volume or magnitude of those issues.

Statistical significance tests for content analyses can be conducted by associating other variables with response sets. A simple example is the breakdown of themes by participant gender (male or female). This analysis could be conducted by using a chi-square analysis, which would indicate if the differences in the listing of themes by males and females were due to chance. The issue of conducting statistical tests will be discussed later in this chapter.

In summary, content analysis can be performed on a wide variety of written works, recorded works, and participant responses. Similarly, it has also been noted that interviews, surveys, and focus groups can all be used as pilot research to facilitate more in-depth examinations of issues.

Experimental Research

Experimental research can be one of the most powerful tools in the campaign developer's arsenal. Experimental techniques can be used in the formative stages of campaign research to test message strategies, actual campaign messages, and variables highly related to effectiveness such as recall, or comprehension. The term experimental research refers to the use of a research technique where the investigator examines the effects of a variable, or stimulus (like a sample message), while controlling for other factors such as the individual characteristics of the participants, the environment in which the messages or stimuli are viewed, or the process by which the messages are delivered. Experimental research also allows the campaign professional the option of testing a variety of message components by comparing their effectiveness against each other.

This section will discuss some of the definitions and concepts involved in the use of experimental techniques. This will be done to give the researcher a solid foundation for assessing research that has been performed by others, as well as to prepare the campaign developer to conduct simple experimental research.

Experimental Research Techniques

Technically, experimental research is defined as research where the investigator examines the effectiveness of one or more variables or factors on some subsequent outcome (like attitude change) while controlling for outside factors. The criteria in this case are that the researcher must control or vary some aspect of the predictor variable, so as to determine its effectiveness on another variable or factor. A simple example would be the case where a campaign research professional experimentally tests the effectiveness of public service announcements (PSAs) that were identical in content but had the lines delivered by different celebrities. In this case the researcher could examine the effectiveness of different sources on subsequent attitude change.

The key to good experimental research is the notion of control—control of all other factors, except those that you want to vary. If you want to assess the effectiveness of message one against message two, then the only thing that should be different between the two groups you show the messages to are the messages themselves. The setting, procedure, and participants should be identical in nature. The goal of experimental research is to be able to make valid comparisons and to be confident that the only differences between groups or messages are those that you control.

Before discussing the "how to's" of experimental techniques, there are a few terms that need to be defined. The first term to be presented is the phrase *experimental group* or "condition." This refers to a group of participants who will be exposed to some message or stimulus that has been constructed by the researcher, and it usually contains one or more variations of the factors that the researcher is testing. In contrast, a control group is a group of participants who are exposed to either nothing, or are given an irrelevant message in place of the experimental message.

The second term, *random assignment,* applies to the random placing of participants in groups. Supposedly, this will eliminate selection effects by spreading out individuals who have similar traits or mindsets equally across groups. The good research professional will ask questions about such factors and make sure that the respondents are fairly evenly distributed. The third set of terms refers to the time at which measurements are taken or surveys are administered. Pretests are surveys or measurements that occur before exposure to a test message or stimulus. A posttest is a survey or measure that is administered after the participant has seen or been exposed to the test message.

When conducting experimental research, the investigator will have to make several choices about the way that the research will be conducted. Generally, the main choices in experimental research fall into the categories of choices regarding the use of participants, choices regarding how and when factors will be measured, how comparisons will be made, and the time frame of the research project.

How participants are assigned to groups and how many messages or stimuli they are exposed to is the first set of choices the research professional has to make. Usually, participants are *randomly assigned* to groups, which means that each participant, no matter what sample pool they were drawn from, has an equal chance of being assigned to any of the experimental conditions. An example would be if participants for a project were provided by a marketing research firm. Upon arrival they might be randomly given a number between one and three, and depending upon which number they drew, they would be exposed to a different stimulus or message.

Conversely, researchers can also *match* (a.k.a., matched groups design) so that individuals with certain characteristics are assigned to certain groups so that comparisons can be made. Matches can be based on demographic, sociographic, or psychographic factors.

Similar to the placement of participants into groups is the issue of "how many messages or stimuli will they be exposed to." *Independent groups design* expose participants to one stimulus while *repeated measures design* usually involve participants by exposing them to two or more message stimuli.

Example: A campaign researcher wants to develop a message to persuade individuals to oppose an upcoming state regulation. The researcher develops three prototype messages, which are similar, but have a different source presenting the message in each of the three commercials. If the researcher uses an independent groups design with a pool of 100 participants, she/he might have twenty-five participants see each message and use the other twenty-five as a control or comparison group. The repeated measure design might have seventy-five participants see all three messages, but in a varied order, and use twenty-five participants for a control group.

The advantage of independent groups designs is that the participants are exposed to just one message or stimulus, and if care has been taken to limit other factors, the researcher can have some confidence about the validity of responses toward those messages. A second advantage to independent groups designs is that they are usually easier to conduct and require less time and preparation. Third, data analysis also tends to be less complex when dealing with independent groups designs. However, if a campaign developer needs to test five sample campaign messages, the issue of differences among groups can be a question. Although randomization through the use of random assignment will usually equalize differences between individuals by distributing persons with similar characteristics across groups, there is no guarantee that all the groups will contain similar psychographic or sociographic profiles. In this case the researcher might want to consider the use of a repeated measure design and have each participant view all messages.

In the *repeated measure design*, subjects are often exposed to more than one message or stimulus. This means that factors such as the order in which participants are exposed to messages may influence their perceptions regarding them. Research professionals use a technique called counterbalancing to make sure that the order that participants view messages in does not impact their findings. Counterbalancing simply means that the researcher changes the order in which messages are presented. All possible combinations of order are used. If more than three messages are used, this can be complex, time consuming, and very expensive if you are paying for participants. However, this design gives you more confidence that differences in ratings are not due to the differences among the groups that participants were assigned to but are attributable to the changes in the message factors that you controlled. The main disadvantage is that the viewing of multiple messages may influence the way that the information in later messages is processed or received. Technically, if you have counterbalanced the messages (varied their order), this threat should be minimized and will be spread out across all groups; however, you will never be completely sure of that if it does happen.

The issue of measurement—almost every individual has heard of this aspect of experimental research, when he/she has heard or used the term pretest or posttest. The choice the campaign research specialist has to make is whether or not a pretest is needed to get an assessment of how an audience feels or reacts before they are exposed to the campaign message. Simply put, the choice is often between the use of a pretest and the use of a control group that is not exposed to a message. What it will often come down to is the researcher's certainty that random assignment has equally broken individuals with traits, or mindsets, that might impact the findings evenly across groups. That is a big assumption, and researchers have to be careful to look for differences among groups by tracking demographic and sometimes psychographic characteristics. So the threat of validity if you are using a control group is the threat of a *selection effect* which simply means that the differences between participants can impact your results.

The use of a pretests can give the researcher more confidence in any change that a test message(s) produce(s), but it will raise other concerns. Namely, pretests can lead to *testing effects*, by sensitizing participants to certain issues, and/or impacting the way they answer questions on a subsequent survey. To make a comparison of message effectiveness the researcher will administer a posttest survey after message exposure. When the analyses are undertaken, pretest scores will usually be compared to posttest scores.

However, to avoid the sensitizing effects of a pretest, many researchers will use a posttest only control group design. This means that participants in the test or experimental groups are NOT given a pretest. They are simply assigned to a group, given some instructions, and asked to complete a posttest survey after viewing the test message. A control group, or group that is not exposed to a message, will be used as a baseline or comparison group. In the data analysis phase the participants' posttest ratings will be compared against the ratings of the control group. If there are differences, they are usually attributable to the factors that the researcher varied. The following details a basic experimental technique.

Example: To perform a simple experimental comparison, choose a source or message factor that you want to vary. Next, construct two test messages that are identical except for the factor that you want to test, which should be different for each group (for example, use of different celebrity presenters). A control group that sees no message can be used to assess baseline attitudes. Randomly assign subjects to one of the three conditions; then show each group their respective message. After seeing the messages, the participants should be given a survey to assess their attitudes or ideas. You now have a completed project and can compare the effectiveness of both messages against each other, as well as the control group's baseline attitudes.

Quasi-experimental Designs

This is one of those phrases that you might try to impress friends with, if you want them to believe you are truly a research professional. However, this is the type of experimental research that many campaign practitioners undertake. The term quasi-experimental design is used because the research does not incorporate some of the controls that are found in normal (laboratory/research facility) experimental techniques. Quasi-experimental designs usually apply to tests of messages or strategies in the "real world," where the investigator cannot randomly assign individuals to groups and cannot guarantee that the experimental and control groups are equal in all respects.

These designs are often easily identified by the use of the term *cohorts* to describe participants. In this case the research may use different departments or facilities of an organization, different communities, or different regions of the country as participants. Even though the facilities or communities are different, they are usually chosen because they have a certain set of similarities, referred to as cohorts. The groups must be similar enough to allow for comparisons, but differences will exist and should be carefully considered. The key to the successful use of quasi-experimental designs is the match between cohort groups. If the groups are different on a set of variables that influences the way the participants respond to the stimuli, then the results will be invalid.

One of the best set of examples was the Stanford Three Community Study and the Five City Project. In these research projects campaign developers were attempting to test factors that impacted health message effectiveness, with a goal of reducing heart disease. Researchers varied media types and the use of interpersonal communication channels in the different communities. The end result was a quasi-experimental design, which used individual communities as participants.

In the Stanford studies researchers had to match the communities in the research project as best they could and live with the differences that existed between communities. If possible, differences can be assessed and factored out at a later time, but this can sometimes be difficult.

Cohorts can also be similar groups of individuals that were surveyed or assessed at a different point in time. Much of the research you hear about in education regarding SAT and ACT score decreases is considered to be quasi-experimental research because the researchers use cohort groups of college juniors from previous years. Although a high school junior in 1960, may be somewhat different from a high school junior in 1997, they are considered to be similar in terms of development, knowledge, and abilities.

The advantage of a quasi-experimental design is that the results are typically more generalizable to the "real world," especially if you used "cohort" groups that were representative or your target populations. Remember that if you test messages in a research facility, you are artificially controlling a key factor in the attitude behavior change process; you are forcing the viewer's attention. In the use of quasi-experimental techniques the participants may or may not see your message based on their media habits, a process that is much more reflective of actual human behavior. Here is a tip that explains an effective use of quasi-experimental research design.

Tip: Rural areas are often prime candidates for testing campaign messages and strategies. Usually, there is enough distance between cities and towns that they often have different newspapers, different radio stations, and different television cable systems. This means that you can control who sees what and make comparisons regarding the relative effectiveness of message strategies.

The disadvantage is that you have less control over factors that may impact the participants' responses to test messages. Furthermore, the threat of confounding factors like history effects are also a problem. You do not have control over factors such as breaking news, competing campaigns, or other factors that may influence responses to your messages.

DATA ANALYSIS AND STATISTICS

Well you have your data! The next step of the research chain is the one that often drives fear into the hearts of many who at one time or another were forced to take statistics 101. So grab that calculator and those old notes and prepare to analyze data the way professionals do. Start by putting those old notes, old textbooks, and calculators on a shelf somewhere else, because today most research specialists use the computer, and many use the same programs that you might use every day.

Preparation

There are several methods and programs that can be used to analyze your collected data. The first suggested method is to use that spreadsheet that resides on the hard drive on your personal computer. Programs such as Excel™, Quattro Pro™, and Lotus™, offer a wide variety of statistical functions, usually many more than are needed for even sophisticated research.[1] These programs are often easier to use because you simply enter your data into columns, and then select variables or factors you want to analyze with the click of a mouse. Even better, all three "Windows" versions of these programs offer "tip" and "answer wizards" that will walk you through the process.

A second method is the use of specific statistical analysis programs such as SPSS for Windows™, SAS™, and Statistica™.[2] All these programs offer both lower level statistical routines, such as the ability to summarize data, or run basic analyses, as well as highly advanced routines such as factor analysis, and multivariate regression routines. For the number and computer weary, do not fear! Data entry and analysis in these programs is similar to entering the data in spreadsheets, and statistical routines are run with the click of a mouse. They all also offer the ability to create high-quality charts and tables from the raw data, although some may not have the complex editing and layout controls available in the spreadsheet programs. However, programs, such as SPSS for Windows, offer tables add-ons that give the user much more flexibility in the creation of presentation and camera-ready charts and graphs.

Last but not least, there are professional survey research packages out there that combine survey generation with data and report generation. These programs are usually fairly expensive but offer the user the ability to manipulate questionnaire items, select report statistics, construct charts and graphs, as well as generate high quality finished reports. Programs such as Survey Pro™ [3] allow the user to "do it all." However, a price is paid in the form of limited analyses, statistics, and report formatting options.

Data Entry

Using the computer to analyze data is simple and very efficient. But some may ask where to start. The first place to start is by creating a codebook for your data. Computers can only interpret numbers, and this means that you have to turn all of your responses into a meaningful number. Often this is easy enough. When you have your completed surveys, you start by first numbering the questionnaires from one to whatever. You might also wish to code the survey identification numbers by geographic locations (e.g., numbers 1,000-2,000 are from New York) or by facility or some other demographic variable. Some of the more knowledgeable readers may be asking, why use this extra step? The answer is that if you discover a mistake in the data, it easy to go back and find the original survey to validate the correct response. If they are not numbered, this can be a time-consuming, tedious, and/or an impossible task.

---

[1] Excel is a product of Microsoft Corporation; Quattro Pro is a product of Corel Corporation; Lotus is a product of IBM.
[2] SPSS for Windows is a product of SPSS Inc.; SAS is a product of the SAS Institute; Statistica is a product of Statistica Inc.
[3] Survey Pro is a product of Apian Software.

Similarly, the use of numbered surveys allows the research professional to perform quality control checks on data and analysis that were completed by independent vendors. A random sample of five to ten surveys could be drawn, then checked against the data. A quality control check may take time, but then again, it is your client, your employer, and your credibility on the line!

The next step is to assign each item or variable a number or column in the spreadsheet. For each item you also develop a code for the response. The most pragmatic approach is to use the response scale included on the survey, which makes interpretation fairly painless. For example, if an item assesses attitudes on a five-point Likert scale (Strongly Agree to Strongly Disagree) assign each type of response a number from one to five. If you assessed geographic location, you could assign number codes to cities or states. Gender simply becomes males are "1," females "2." Once that is decided, you simply enter the data on each questionnaire into the computer. The most important part of the process is to make sure that you put each response in its correct column in the computer. If you make a mistake, the computer will not catch it! They are truly "dumb" machines and are limited by their programming and the data they are given.

Some tips on developing codebooks and coding data are important to note. First, when assigning codes to scale items, higher numbers should consistently reflect larger amounts of something, or more positive outcomes. If you have negatively worded items, these responses should be "reversed" or recoded so that the responses are consistent with other items. Note these items carefully, for many a researcher has tried to track strange results and found the root of the problem: forgetting to reverse negative items. Making larger numbers indicate higher quantities of some characteristic, attitude, or behavior also makes sense if you would like to create charts or graphs at a later point. An audience of clients can quickly become frustrated when on "charts 1, 3, and 6 larger numbers indicate better outcomes, and on charts 2, 4, 5 larger numbers indicate negative outcomes."

Organizing and Aggregating Information

Although the computer will often analyze the data for the practitioner, it will not interpret the results or show the practitioner where to begin. The first place to start is with the topic of organizing or aggregating data. Many assume that once a questionnaire is written, the results will be magically compiled. Unfortunately this is not the case. Usually a researcher asks more than one question about awareness or inquires about several attitudes toward a company's products or reputation. However, many do not know what to do with those items when they are done. Do they look at one or all of the items? The simple answer is that they should create a scale out of those items. If there were five items measuring different aspects of awareness, these could be summed (added together) to form an awareness scale. So, instead of having to look at five items, the researcher can now look at one number for that variable or concept. The technique tip in Figure 2.5 goes into greater detail on how to create scales from survey items.

You have now simplified your data into scales measuring factors such as trust, awareness, attitudes, and/or behavior, with accompanying data on other factors such as demographic, geographic, or sociographic variables. What is next?

The smart researcher can validate her/his data and look at general patterns among responses by running a "Frequency Analysis." A frequency analysis reports the relative percentages of each chosen alternative or rating; for example, how many people gave a rating of 5, how many people gave a rating of 4, and so on (see also Figure 2.9). Moreover, the frequency analysis can also detect "dirty data" or typos made during data entry. If, for example, the researcher would have made a mistake or "typo" when entering data and entered a "3" instead of a "2" for a female, this analysis would have alerted us to this mistake by indicating that there was a third category for gender.

Choosing Analyses

The preceding section made data analysis appear to be completely automated. To some extent that is true. However, it is the research professional who will choose what analyses to conduct and what statistics to interpret. For example, if a researcher asks a few questions about a population's beliefs regarding passage of a new law, the investigator could report a mean rating. However, can a researcher report a mean value for a factor such as gender. "The average participant in this study scored 1.5 on the gender scale, which puts them somewhere between a male and a female." This does not make much sense and seems to go right along with the average American's 2.2 children. The difference in this case is the difference in the type of variable or factor that is being analyzed. Factors such as gender or political affiliation are considered to be categorical variables or more technically "nominal" variables. This means that we can assign numbers to them to look at how often they occur, but the numbers are meaningless. If Republicans were coded as a "1" and Democrats by a "2," does that mean that a Democrat is worth 2 Republicans (perhaps if you were President Bill Clinton, but otherwise not).

Ratings of attitudes, beliefs, and physical factors such as age are usually referred to as "interval" level or "ratio" level data. This means that the interval between numbers is fairly even, and in the case of "ratio" data there is a true zero point. More importantly, for these variables higher numbers do mean more of something, and we can look at average or *Mean* ratings. The lesson here is that although a computer will analyze whatever you tell it to, the researcher still has to know what to ask for and how to interpret what is produced.

Statistics

Descriptive statistics do exactly what their name implies: They describe distributions (patterns of responses) of data. Descriptive statistics can tell us such

Figure 2.5
Technique: Forming Scales

If you measure a variable such as awareness of an issue or image of a company with more than one item, you get an increased range of scores and higher reliability. But how do you take those 3, 5, or 6 items and combine them into one score or scale. You simply tell the computer to sum each participant's responses to form a scale (Hint: Most computer programs have a SUM function).

ITEM	RATINGS
	SD D N A SA
1. I think ACME Inc. is an honest company.	1 2 3 <u>4</u> 5
2. I believe that ACME can be trusted to do the right thing.	1 2 3 4 <u>5</u>
3. I believe that ACME would not release false information.	1 2 3 <u>4</u> 5

RESULT
This participant's score would be 13 (4 +5 + 4) on a 15 point trust scale, which has a possible low of 3 (3 x 1) and a possible high of 15 (3 x 5).

things as what the "average" person responded, what was the most frequent response on a questionnaire item, or who was in the middle of a range of scores. But they can also tell us much more; for example, they can tell us if individuals have high levels of awareness of an issue or have strong or weak feelings. Furthermore, they can also tell us if the individuals in our populations are thinking alike or if there a wide range of feelings. Many statistics courses and books often spend little time on these "low level and "basic" statistics. They would rather spend their time focusing on the "high" level and "power" statistical techniques like factor analysis and canonical correlations. However, it is these low level statistics that often are the most meaningful and allow the deepest of interpretations.

In this section we will discuss four types of descriptive statistics. The first look at "what's average" or "what's the most popular response" and are called central tendency. The second group we will examine is how spread out are the scores or how are they "dispersed." We will also look at how evenly spread out the responses are spaced (a.k.a. skewness), and the similarity of response patterns across the range of response choices.

Who's average? Often clients will deliver a report for analysis that contains "average." The question you have to ask is what's average? Is it the arithmatic average? The most popular response on the survey item? or is it the middle score? These are all considered averages, and the public relations practitioner who puts his/her reputation on the line and values his/her position needs to know the difference among these numbers and that certain factors can greatly influence them.

Example: As part of a community survey, a researcher draws a subsample of ten homes that lie within 2 blocks of a proposed shopping center. To get a better idea of the homeowners' attitudes, values, and background they decide to look at the average value for those homes, which comes out at $ 200,000. Who lives in a $200,000 house? When the researcher sees that number, they profile the homeowners as individuals that have a higher than average education, tend to more conservative, and are professionals like doctors and lawyers. So when they invite the owners in for a focus group and find out that many of them have lower paying jobs, are lower income brackets, they are totally surprised. When they inquire about the value of the homes, the researcher finds out that nine of the ten homes are worth $20,000, and one is worth approximately $1.8 million dollars. What happened? Where did the researcher go wrong?

In the example above the practitioner decided to look at the *mean*, better known as the arithmatic average. The problem is that statistics like means are sensitive to extreme (high or low) scores or responses. A better indicator in this case might have been a different kind of "average" called the *mode*, or the most frequent response. In the example above, it would have given us the most accurate picture of the population that we wanted to characterize (see Figure 2.6).

A second type of descriptive statistic looks at how spread out the responses were, or to use a more technical term *"dispersion."* It is important to know if the individuals that responded to your survey questions tended to agree and gave similar ratings or if they disagreed and gave different ratings. The mean only tells you how the "average person" or how the most people (mode) responded. Statistics like the *standard deviation* (denoted as s^2) tell you on average how far people are away from the mean. The standard deviation sounds complex to understand but it really is not. The standard deviation gives you an idea of how spread out the responses to a given item were in relation to the mean in standardized form. Standardized means that the arithmatic mean of the distribution is the zero point, and each one unit above it represents the average distance from the mean. In the normal bell shaped distribution 68 percent of the sample will fall within one standard deviation of the mean.

Some reports will report the *standard deviation* and a statistic called the *variance* of a distribution of responses. These numbers report the same thing. The only difference is that the variance is a statistic that tells you how spread out responses are in "squared" (for example, x^2) units from the mean. So the variance of a distribution is simply the standard deviation squared (for example, if the standard deviation is 2, then the variance is 4). Although it might appear odd that one would use a measure of dispersion in squared scale units, statisticians do this because the variance is easier to use in conducting higher level statistical tests.

Skewness refers to the shape or symmetry of the distribution of responses. The optimal shape for the pattern of responses is called a "normal curve," where the responses are fairly evenly spaced with higher numbers occurring in the

Figure 2.6
Types of "Averages" or Central Tendency Statistics

Statistic	What does it tell you?	What does it look like numerically?
Mean	The "average" score or response	2+3+5+5+5= 20 ÷5 = 4 = Mean
Mode	The most frequent response	2, 3, <u>5, 5, 5</u> Note, that there are three 5's therefore 5 = Modal value
Median	The "Middle" score or response	2, 3, <u>5</u>, 5, 5 since there are 5 numbers, the Median is the middle or third number, with a value of 5

middle. Recall that in a normal distribution of scores the mean divides the data in half, and that roughly 68 percent of the responses fall within one standard deviation (see Figure 2.7) of the mean.

The normal distribution is symmetrical and looks like the classic bell curve. However, sometimes response patterns are skewed. Examples might be if you ask a question that a certain group or audience has strong feelings about or if you were giving a test on awareness of an issue, and everybody had a high level of awareness. The result would be a large number of high scores or a large number of low scores or selections. Either of those distributions would be considered "skewed" because the responses were not evenly distributed around the middle of the range. Skewness is important because first it can tell the researcher if participants gave strong or highly charged responses, but it can also

Figure 2.7
Percentage of Population: The Normal Curve

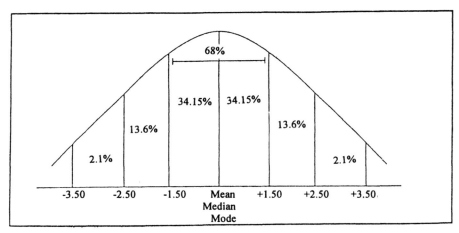

tell us if our surveys are weak. If 90 percent of the participants in a survey rate their response as a 5 on a 1-to-5 scale, that item may not be strongly worded enough. This is called *restriction in range* and limits our findings because our measurement system was not sensitive enough to discriminate between those individuals who have truly extreme feelings, as opposed to those who might have only moderately extreme feelings.

The secret to interpreting skewness is to look at the "tail" of the distribution of scores (see Figure 2.8 on interpreting skewness). If individuals gave a lot of high responses (tail going off to the left), the distribution is said to be negatively skewed. Although this sounds counterintuitive, this is the way skewness is determined. Similarly, if there were a lot of low scores (tail going to the right or in a "positive" direction) the distribution is said to be positively skewed.

Figure 2.8
Interpreting Skewness

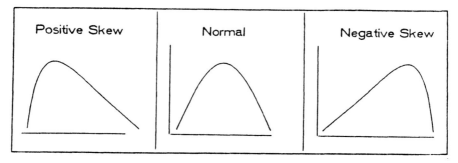

Kurtosis, although sounding rather technical, refers to the peakedness of the distribution (or curve) of your responses. If individuals to a large extent agreed or had similar feelings when responding to a given survey item, the distribution of scores would be leptokuritc or very peaked. Looking for a peaked distribution of responses can often be used when identifying demographic or psychographic profiles during the segmentation of target groups or publics. For, example, if you are looking at individuals' attitudes during a campaign to increase awareness about the need for a municipal bond referendum, you might break out individual attitudes on the basis of family status. If you examined those participants' responses which had children in public school, you would get a quick picture as to where they stand as a group. If the distribution was peaked (a large number of respondents giving the same response/rating), you could say that they had similar attitudes on that issue. On the other hand, the individuals in the sample may have had very different ideas, attitudes, or feelings, and so their ratings would be spread out across the rating scale. This situation is referred to as a platykurtic distribution (Hint: notice that platy-kurtic rhymes with the word flat), with a wide level of dispersion. Figure 2.9 below demonstrates what these distributions might look like if you were examining some spreadsheet or statistical output.

Figure 2.9
Computer Results Indicating High or Low Levels of Kurtosis (Peakedness)

Rating	Frequency	%	Rating	Frequency	%
1	23	23	1	5	05
2	68	68	2	32	33
3	5	05	3	37	34
4	2	02	4	21	21
5	2	02	5	7	07
Note: 91% of these respondents gave an answer of 1 or 2; this is a peaked distribution. Conclusion: These individuals have similar attitudes on this item.			Note: Response patterns are spread out, showing a fairly flat distribution of responses. Conclusion: These individuals have a wide diversity of opinions on this item.		

Significance Testing

In data analysis and statistics the $100,000,000 question when looking at differences between groups or at relationships between variables is *"Are there statistically significant differences?"* Although this sounds like a sophisticated concept, statistical significance simply tells if differences between groups, patterns of responses, or relationships between variables are due to chance. Think of it this way. If someone put 200 pennies in a box and also puts in two dimes and if you were given one sample of two coins to guess what is in the box, is there a chance that you might draw the two dimes? Yes, because you are sampling at random, there is a chance! The question is how certain will you be about your results. Statistical significance answers the question: how certain can you be that your findings are not

This is accomplished by choosing a confidence level or probability level (p). Most social sciences use the $p = .05$ level. This number simply means that if a result and its related statistic achieve statistical significance, you can be 95 percent confident that the results are not due to chance. If this number is set to .01, then you would be 99 percent confident, and so on.

Several factors impact statistical significance. The first is sample size. As discussed earlier in this chapter, as sample size increases, we are more certain and confident of our results. Hence, as we add participants, it gets easier to achieve statistical significance. The second factor is the amount of error associated with our estimates. Simply put, many significance tests look at the amount of error or "slop" that is contained in the data we obtain. The more error, or dispersion (if you were thinking the bigger the standard deviation you are correct), the less sure we are that groups are truly different or that true relational patterns exist.

An excellent example of how these factors work together can be seen in the second way that the term *confidence interval* is used. This term is also used to denote the degree of confidence in which researchers, usually pollsters, have in their findings. Polls results often reported in the media are usually linked to a confidence interval that is reported with the results (for example, "these results were accurate to with +/- 2 percent"). While not tests of statistical significance, these numbers tell us how confident the researchers are in the generalizability of their findings to the actual perceptions of the target population. For example, if the results of a public opinion poll stated that 60 percent of those polled agreed with a policy statement, +/- 2 percent, that means that there is a 95 percent (if 95 percent confidence interval was chosen) probability that the actual population's agreement level would be in the range of 58-62 percent.

Without going into great statistical detail, it is best to say that these "confidence intervals" are also a function of the confidence level chosen by the research professional (for example, 95%, 99%), the sample size (the more people, the smaller the interval), and the amount of variation in ratings (the more agreement, the more confidence).

T-Tests, F-Tests, and Chi-Square

You have collected your data and want to find out if there are significant differences based on differences between certain groups such as gender, geography, or political affiliation. What test do you use? If you are comparing the differences between the mean ratings of two groups, you would use a t-test. t will vary from about zero and will increase (or decrease if negative) as the differences increase. *A t of less than one (e.g., a fraction or percentage such as .76) is always not significant.* Remember that the p level or significance level of t must be .05 or below for t to be statistically significant. If it is not, then any differences are considered to be due to chance. Last, when interpreting t, use caution. A significant t value does not automatically mean that the results support your predicted conclusions. All it tells you is that the means of your groups are different and not which one is smaller or larger. Figure 2.10 demonstates how you come into the process and where you have to decide what the numbers really indicate.

The *analysis of variance test or f-test* assesses differences between the means of three or more groups. As with *t, f* will also range from zero to whatever. *Again, an f below one will indicate a non-statistically significant relationship.* As always *f* must be statistically significant at the .05 level. If not, then any differences are said to be due to chance.

What happens, however, if you are working with categorical data and do not have means to work with? The differences between categorical data are usually tested with a statistic referred to a Chi-square, which is denoted as X^2. Chi-square reports whether or not the reported proportion or percentage of responses

76   Campaign Strategies and Message Design

Figure 2.10
Interpreting t Test Results

Scenario: You are a campaign planner and want to construct a campaign message to help keep teens from dropping out of school. You predict that using The President of the U.S. as the presenter in your video PSA, will be more effective than using Michael Jordan. You conduct a preliminary test study, run the statistics and receive the results below.

Test Message One: President of the USA Mean 2.99 (scale of 1 to 5)	Test Message Two: Michael Jordan Mean 3.59 (scale of 1 to 5)

Sample Statistical output:
Group one: **Mean 2.99** | Group two: **Mean 3.59** |
t value: 2.45   df = 124 | p= .023

Results and Interpretation: Were there differences between the groups? Yes for two reasons. First, the means were fairly far apart. Second, the differences were statistically significant, which means they were not due to chance. Since they were significant do they support your predictions? No! You predicted the president would be more persuasive, but the data show that Michael Jordan did a better job at persuading teens, which is reflected by the higher ratings.

---

across given categories varies from what would be expected by chance. Consider the example of asking a group of participants which candidate they are going to vote for in an upcoming election. If there were three candidates, we would expect an equal number of participants to select each of the candidates. However, as the percentage of responses moves away from what would be expected by chance, the more confident we are that the differences in the choice of candidate was not due to chance. *Thus, as Chi-square increases, the probability that the results are due to chance decreases.* Again the *p* value for statistical significance must be below .05 or any differences are said to be due to chance, or random fluctuations. A quick summary chart describing t, f, and X^2 can be found in Figure 2.12, which is presented later in this chapter.

Critically Evaluating Significance Tests

Be careful! As previously stated, statistical significance only tells us that our data are not due to chance. Differences between groups, or relationships between variables can be significant but not in the direction that we expected. For example, an employee relations specialist might note that there are significant differences between the opinions of union and nonunion employees on the issue of the value of the union (see Figure 2.11). This researcher may also note that the results are significant. Does this mean that the union members rate the union higher? No! It may be the case that union employees have to pay union dues and

Figure 2.11
Statistical Significance Can Be Misleading

Question: I value the services the union provides.
SD D N A SA
1 2 3 4 5

Group	Mean Rating	Statistical Significance
Union	2.8	Yes, $p < .05$
Non-Union	3.2	

TIP: Even though the results are statistically significant, non-union members rated the value of the union higher than union members. These results are the exact opposite of what was predicted. All statistical significance says is that the results are not likely due to chance. Use caution when reading reports because statistical significance says very little about the actual "meaning" of data, such as the meaning of employee ratings.

not get many benefits while nonunion members get the same benefits negotiated for, without having to pay dues. The end result is that the results are the opposite of what would be generally predicted, but the differences are statistically significant (see Figure 2.12).

Significance also does not indicate meaningful. If a large sample is drawn, almost any minuscule difference is significant. To that extent in the "Big Picture" real differences might not exist between groups on such issues as attitudes, awareness, or behavior (for example, means of 2.6 vs. 2.7 on a five-point scale), but these differences may attain statistical significance. The knowledgeable practitioner looks at the data, the results, the significance tests, and from there develops conclusions. The example below helps put things in perspective.

Example: A "PR" practitioner is doing some formative message testing to select which commercial will be used to improve an organization's image. Two messages are tested and the differences in audience favorability and image ratings are statistically significant. On a five-point scale audiences gave message 1 a rating of 2.4, and message 2 a rating of 2.6, and again these differences were statistically significant. Does the use of message 2 over message 1 really improve the company's chances for success? No, unfortunately both ads received low ratings and probably would not improve the company's image. Even though the differences in ratings achieved significance, on a five-point scale they were not large enough to warrant confidence in the effectiveness of message 2.

Continuous Variables and Correlations

The above descriptions of significance tests dealt with the issue of comparing distinct groups or segments against each other. However, what happens when the information we are looking at is not broken down into categories, but rather

Campaign Strategies and Message Design

Figure 2.12
Summary of Basic Statistical Tests

Statistic	What does it tell me?	How do I interpret it?	What should I look out for?
t T-test	Are there differences between two groups?	Bigger is better; look at the p value for significance.	Look at the means of the groups! Differences can be significant, but the means may not be in the direction that you predicted.
F ANOVA	Are there differences between three or more groups?	Bigger is better; look at the p value for significance. Also note that an "F" of less than one always means the effect is due to chance.	Look at the size of the differences between the Means! With a large sample almost any difference will be significant, but the differences may not be meaningful.
R Correlation	Is there linear relationship? r varies between -1 and +1.	As r gets closer to +1 or -1, it indicates a stronger relationship.	Ask is the relationship linear? If the relationship between the factors is not linear, this statistic is practically useless and can be misleading.
R Multiple Regression	How big an effect does a variable have relative to others?	As R gets closer to +1, it indicates a stronger relationship.	Larger numbers mean larger effects. Look at the significance level. If it is over .05, that means that the effect is due to chance.
X^2 Chi-Square	Are the patterns of responses due to chance?	Look at the level of significance. As X^2 gets larger, results less likely due to chance.	Chi-square is used to assess differences in response patterns on categorical data. Look for patterns.
λ Lambda	Are the patterns of responses due to chance?	As Lambda gets bigger, results are less likely due to chance.	Used with categorical or nominal data. This is a more conservative estimate of the difference between groups than chi-square.

is continuous, such as age or income. To examine associations between continuous variables, researchers tend to use *correlational analyses*. Again, this only sounds complex, because what they are doing is looking at the relationship that one variable (e.g., age) has on another variable (e.g., importance ratings given to a good pension plan). A better nonpublic relations example might be the associations that we see in the media between cigarette smoking and getting lung cancer, or even more basic, the relationship between eating larger amounts of fatty foods and gaining weight.

Correlational analyses look for patterns between variables, and the main statistic researchers use is Pearson's r. The statistic r is easy to interpret; it ranges from -1 to +1, with 0 in the middle. As r gets closer to +1 or -1, the relationship is stronger; as it gets closer to zero, it indicates a weaker relationship.

There is one basic rule that cannot be violated by any researcher when using correlational analyses. The rule is that r is an indicator of a *linear* relationship. For those of you who may not remember the information you learned in that geometry class, linear means straight line. The relationship may be far from perfect, but the pattern the relationship falls into must be in a general linear pattern and not form a curve or have an area at one end which flattens out into a shape like an "L."

If the relationship is nonlinear, let us say in the shape of a curve, "r" will indicate that no relationship will exist, and many will interpret that to mean no relationship at all. The problem for the researcher testing campaigns is that some variables can have curvilinear effects on others when conducting campaigns. The best example is the effect of repeated exposure to a message on changing attitudes (see Petty & Cacioppo, 1979). The more an individual is exposed to a campaign message, the more they will begin to remember, and the greater the probability of having an impact on that individual.

But what happens after that individual has seen the message fifty or 100 times? Heavy television viewers could see a message on numerous channels at different times. Is the message still as effective the fiftieth time or the one hundredth time it is viewed? The answer is no! Don't you get sick of certain ads that you see a large number of times? In the end the message will be less effective and may cause a negative reaction. The result is a curvilinear relationship between seeing the message and attitudes. As the message is new and novel, attitudes increase but will start to flatten out with exposure. After a moderate-to-large number of exposures the message will have no effects and may generate a negative response forming the second half of the curve.

Knowing this, we can say that there tends to be a curvilinear effect for repetition on attitude change. However, if the correlation coefficient r is used to assess the strength and statistical significance of this relationship, it will tell us that there is little if any relationship between repetition and attitude change. Many individuals misinterpret that this means there is no *linear* relationship between these variables. The bottom line when using correlations is to choose the scatterplot/plot command in your computer program to examine the relationship; as the shape of the plot looks like a U or an inverted U, the relationship begins to be curvilinear.

Multiple Reg... What?

If r examines the effects of one variable on another, what happens when you have more than one variable that can cause effects in knowledge, attitudes, beliefs, or behaviors? Researchers use a technique called multiple regression, and it simply examines the effects of more than one predictor or independent variable on a related variable.

Consider the example of an antismoking campaign. What predicts who will smoke? A researcher could speculate that beliefs about the relationship between smoking and cancer might predict smoking behavior. The goal would be to convince those individuals with little knowledge or low levels of beliefs that smoking causes cancer. The researcher could then survey individuals, ask them if they smoke, why and where they smoke, and if they know/believe that smoking causes cancer. This investigator could then determine the relative impact that variables such as did parents smoke, do their friends smoke, do they engage in social activities where smoking is the norm, and the impact of knowledge about cancer have on smoking behavior. In this case a multiple regression would be conducted, and the investigator would report several statistics.

First r, which is the *multiple correlation coefficient* would be reported, which indicates how good all of those factors are at predicting who will smoke. *r ranges from 0 to +1, and bigger numbers indicate stronger relationships.* Again, however, r must be statistically significant to be deemed as a valid predictor. Second, the researcher will also report a statistic known as the standardized regression coefficient for each of the predictor factors. These statistics are often referred to as Bs or bs better known as beta weights. These are not really that complex. The B for each predictor will range between -1 and +1, with higher numbers (moving away from zero) indicating stronger effects. This statistic indicates the relative effect for each of the predictor variables, while controlling for all the other variables that are included in the analysis. This means that the researcher can see the relative effect of knowledge regarding cancer versus the effect that parental smoking might have had. As always, the Bs have to be statistically significant or else the effect could be due to chance.

In summary, multiple regression analysis allows the researcher to examine the relative effects of multiple variables or factors on attitudes, beliefs, or behaviors. This can be a powerful tool for the public relations practitioner, because messages and strategies don't exist in a vacuum. Understanding the relative strengths of any approach leads to more successful campaigns. Furthermore, regression is also a powerful tool in identifying what factors influence targeted behaviors. As in the example noted above, there is more than one factor that influences smoking behavior, some more powerful than others. Regression is used to identify the strength of these factors, so that strategies can be developed to deal with many or all of them.

While regression is a powerful statistical tool, there are many different types of quantitative and qualitative techniques that are available to today's professional. The key to success is to have some knowledge of the research process, and to be able to choose the appropriate test for the task at hand. Figure 2.12 offers a final summary of some of the statistical tests and techniques mentioned in the chapter.

IN SUMMARY

This chapter has presented a wide array of information and suggestions regarding the use of research in the development of campaign strategies. In most cases the techniques that were presented are not difficult to use but do take some planning and forethought. With any of these techniques, it is planning and forethought that will often determine the quality and usability of your results. Some practitioners like to take the "just do it" approach. This mindset will not work well if research is to be an integral part of the campaign process. Without careful planning and a strict attention to detail, the results of research can quickly become useless, reflecting a large waste of time and money. However, the real danger is that the distinction between useless data and "bad" data is usually difficult to make. The end result is that tainted results will not be seen as useless but will be used to make decisions regarding strategy, media use, resource allocation, and subsequent evaluation. Nonetheless, research needs to be part of every campaign and can be a powerful tool in developing more effective campaign strategies and generating change in the minds of many populations, including the media, and the clients of public relations professionals.

IMPORTANT THINGS TO REMEMBER

- Formative research is done before a campaign, interim research during a campaign, and evaluative or summative research after the campaign to measure its success.

- Formative research is crucial in developing target audience profiles so that messages can be designed to maximize effectiveness and achieve desired results.

- The campaign strategist must recognize threats to the validity of research so that research findings are sound and accurate and can be relied upon when making decisions on factors such as targeting, message design, and channel selection.

- The campaign strategist must know how to use various sampling techniques in order to gather an accurate sample of respondents who truly represent the entire target population.

- Analyzing data involves assuring that the data are "clean" or error free, choosing the appropriate computer program, running statistical analyses, and interpreting the results.

- Descriptive statistics can tell us what the "average" target individual perceives, how spread out target opinions are on certain issues. And whether or not the population as a whole is largely undecided or holds an extreme position.

- Significance testing (t-tests, ANOVA, correlation, chi-square, etc.) assesses if the differences between responses and groups are due to chance.

- Significance tests only tell us if differences can be attributable to chance; they do not tell us what those differences mean, or their implications.

3

Basic Strategies

Formulating the basic strategies is the first step in the execution of the campaign. True, the campaign professional possesses an understanding of the theoretical framework needed for conceptualizing any campaign, that is, the knowledge of all the models, theories, and definitions that inform the process of setting up any campaign. The campaign specialist also possesses the general knowledge and skills needed for setting up a research design and collecting and analyzing data informing any campaign situation and possesses the general skills needed for researching the organization, the crisis or project situation, and the targeted populations for the particular campaign at hand. These are routine, but crucial, preparatory steps needed in the conceptualization of a campaign.

But a campaign does not actually begin to be executed until the basic strategies are decided. The basic strategies lay the groundwork for creating the campaign messages and, later, for choosing the communication selections that will deliver these messages to the appropriate audiences. It is absolutely imperative that the campaign professional know exactly how to determine the correct and appropriate basic strategies for any campaign situation at hand. Further, if basic strategies are incorrectly or impartially drawn, or, which can also happen, not laid out at all, the campaign's success is jeopardized even as it begins.

SOME DEFINITIONS

Given the crucial role that basic strategies play in formulating the messages and ultimately deciding the communication channels and selections for a campaign, it is somewhat surprising how generally and incompletely most campaign strategy textbooks have typically explained and defined them. What is evident in many business communication and marketing strategy books is a failure to

84   Campaign Strategies and Message Design

link the basic strategies directly to the message design and to the communication selection choices. That is, most business communication management books offer a definition of basic strategies as goals and objectives and then, almost as a separate operation, explain how to create campaign messages. The role of basic strategies—the goals and objectives—to directly inform the content and design of campaign messages and to determine the personal communication selections and media channels is often not thoroughly explained or not explained at all. In other words, the direct links between basic goals and objectives to messages and between messages to communication selections is not stressed or only implied.

The Goal

Let us first examine the most typical definitions of goals. Most traditional definitions of goals are some kind of "generalized ends" (Grunig & Hunt, 1984; Hunt & Grunig, 1994) or "general directions" of the campaign (Rayfield et al., 1991). Kendall (1992) theorizes goals as answers to problem statements, and McElreath (1993) states a goal is "abstract and difficult to quantify." Simmons (1990) defines basic strategies as global objectives. Advertising and marketing books on campaign strategy often assume, not surprisingly, that the primary goal of their kind of commercial campaigns is sales. In fact, the concepts of goals and objectives are often not fully explored nor even mentioned since the implicit goal of product sales is so fundamental to campaigns in these fields (Bogart, 1990; Ind, 1993; Schultz & Barnes, 1995). For advertising and marketing, concepts of goals and objectives are collapsed into the unified, guiding strategy of sales. The singular strategy becomes, in essence, the linking of the product to consumer to facilitate sales (Schultz & Barnes, 1995). In the case of political campaigns, the issue of strategy takes a completely different turn with no reference to objectives; strategy is understood as primarily style, such as campaigning as an incumbent, as a competent candidate, or on charisma (Trent & Friendenberg, 1991).

My understanding and definition of a goal is radically different from these typical definitions. Instead, I offer a rather focused and precise definition of a goal as any desired effect or desired change in the targeted audience by the organization. This definition eliminates the "generalities" from most conceptualizations of campaign goals and focuses, instead, on just one concept and one principle specifying a goal—a singular change in the intended audience, a change in either knowledge, attitude, behavior, or other image.

The Objective

The concept of objectives has been most typically defined as measurable actions in support of the goal (Baskin & Aronoff, 1988; Grunig & Hunt, 1984; Hunt & Grunig, 1994; Kendall, 1992; McElreath, 1993; Nager & Allen, 1984; Pfau & Parrott, 1993; Rayfield et al, 1991; Simmons, 1990). That is, objectives support the goals—these immeasurable, generalized ends or directions—by naming the number and kind of activities that will need to be completed in order to assume that the respective goal has been met. This figure or model of objectives as activities such as producing "X" number of press releases, radio spots, or column inches in a newspaper or magazine, is most often presented through the framework of the Management by Objective model (MBO) drawn from business management theory (Baskin & Aronoff, 1988; Grunig & Hunt, 1984; Rayfield et al., 1991; Simmons, 1990).

I want to give up, completely, this notion of an objective as an activity or as a measurable effect which facilitates a goal. Instead, I define an objective as information-based, as the delineation of what kind of and how much information should be presented to the audience in support of the respective goal. An objective names the content or information found in the messages and the amount of information found in the messages—*neither an activity nor a desired effect on the audience*. Several objectives should support each goal. (Explanations on how to determine activities related to choices of media or personal communication selections would come with the decisions on communication selections. See Chapter 5, "Communication Selection Strategies.")

My reading of others' definitions of goals and objectives and my teaching of these concepts in my campaign courses have been a struggle to develop a more concrete, more adaptable and detailed guide for laying out the basic strategies that are unique to every campaign. Each and every kind of campaign—given its unique crisis or project situation, the particular qualities of the organization, and the respective characteristics of each potential population—demands special, tailor-made basic strategies. I define basic strategies as goals and objectives, but I offer very specific, almost narrow, definitions of each concept.

A goal is any desired change or effect attempted in each targeted audience.

An objective is the number of pieces and the kind of information given to an audience to achieve each desired effect.

THE BOTTOM LINES

The purpose of this chapter is to explain the process of conceptualizing and choosing the basic strategies of goals and objectives, which are unique to the particular kind of campaign being planned and to explain how to organize and write them. But first you, as a campaign professional, must have an understanding of exactly what you are trying to do in this step of deciding basic strategies, or goals and objectives. You need to know the *bottom lines* involved in the conceptualization process of basic strategies. There are three.

Receiver-Based Strategies

First, remember that your client or your "boss" is an organization that wants you to persuade several audiences to think, feel, or behave in certain ways toward the organization. The campaign professional is obliged to create unique messages tailor-made to each of these audiences and, more important, to get the audiences *to pay attention* to these messages and, hopefully, then *be persuaded* to accept their content.

The first bottom line, then, is to think of choosing basic strategies as a kind of matching exercise. Your task is to create messages that match the interests of the audiences so that they will, first, pay attention to them and, then, be persuaded to accept them. Much research has been done in communication that confirms that receivers of information will pay attention to messages that are consistent with their currently held beliefs and interests. Dissonance theory (Festinger, 1957, 1964) and selective perception theory (Davison et al., 1976; Freedman & Sears, 1965), in particular, explain this phenomenon of audiences' attention to messages that agree with their knowledge, attitudes, and behaviors (selective perception) and that might be directly contrary to present beliefs (cognitive dissonance).

This is how it works: the campaign specialist's responsibility is to represent the organization to each one of its audiences. You attempt this through the process of communication and through the delivery of messages to the relevant audiences. In order to deliver messages to the populations, you need to create messages that will get the attention of the populations' members. Assume that your research into the targeted audiences has identified across each population the unique knowledge, attitudes, behaviors, demographics, and other images possessed by each and every relevant audience toward your organization. Your task is simple.

Consider how you would want to enhance or change these currently held "knowledges," attitudes, behaviors, or other images to be more favorable or more supportive of your organization. Think of the kind of changes or desired effects you would want to have in each population. Since you have a good idea from your formative research where each population is now in terms of images, opinions, demographics, needs, and behaviors toward your organization, you will want to decide what images, opinions, behaviors, or knowledge you might want to enhance or change.

Perhaps it would fit the organization's interest to have some images made stronger. Maybe it would benefit the organization if some of the current negative images could be made more positive or at least neutralized. All of these desired changes or effects decided for each population are your goals of the campaign. It is a matching exercise—the organization's desired effects based on the audiences' current interests and attitudes.

Next, think of the kind of information you will need to communicate that will achieve each goal. For each desired change—for each goal—for each audience, you will need to decide what kind of information and how much information will lead to the particular goal/effect/change you want to achieve. This twofold process is both an identification of information that will hopefully lead to a change and a quantification of how much information will most likely lead to the goal being accepted by the audience. This information is tied to the attempted goal in that the information is about the goal, but it is also tied to or related to the audience's interests and beliefs so that it gets their attention and, hopefully, has a persuasive effect on them. Again, it is a matching exercise—the information decided and delivered by the organization to match each audience's interests, beliefs, needs, demographics, and so on.

Assume, for example, that you are planning a campaign for your organization that will, hopefully, give your corporation a stronger image in the community. This community relations—public relations—campaign is designed to address and neutralize a crisis situation in which the organization was accused of circumventing zoning laws and illegally dumping hazardous materials in the groundwater and in illegal garbage dumps. Your formative research suggests that your community population is relatively conservative, possessing strong family values, with strong ties to school activities, to church activities, and with especially strong support of sports activities. Perhaps you have created *a goal:* that one or more of your populations will have a stronger image of the organization as a charitable organization, as an organization that cares about the children in the community.

Some objectives that could support this goal might be:

- fifteen pieces of information about how the organization supports Toys for Tots at Christmas time;

- twenty pieces of information about how the organization supports little league soccer and little league football in the community; and

- ten pieces of information about how the organization's employees use their flex-time to serve as coaches and umpires and referees for various youth sports leagues in the community.

Notice that these objectives relate to family values, school, sports, and church interests of the community while, at the same time, supporting the goal that the community will consider the organization as a charitable organization that supports the community's children. The matching of desired effects (goals) and of message content (objectives) to the feelings, images, lifestyles, behaviors, demographics, and knowledge of the audiences is what gets the audiences' attention, facilitates persuasion, and accomplishes the intentions of the organization to inform and persuade audiences. The good news for the campaign professional is that she/he is not obligated to focus on creating dramatic, perfect messages that get people's attention and, consequently, persuade them to the organization's position. The good news is that all the good work done on researching the feelings and images of the audiences is what directs the goals of the campaign and the content of the messages.

A campaign strategist cannot and should not pull messages out of thin air just because they are clever and entertaining. Messages can certainly be clever and entertaining, but these approaches are not necessarily persuasive and most probably are not designed to generate certain knowledge, attitudes, behaviors, and images in the respective audiences. It does not follow that cute, shocking, or sexually suggestive messages get the immediate attention of the audience and, necessarily, in turn persuade the audiences via their content. Your dramatic, clever, or entertaining message might draw the attention of an audience member, but the attention is most probably temporary, momentarily based on a shocking or cuteness factor.

This brief attention time does not presume that receivers will automatically be persuaded by the content of the message. You have achieved a kind of surface-perception attention but most likely not an in-depth attention or understanding of the message content. Have you ever seen an outrageously funny or clever commercial and you could not even recall what was being advertised after it was over?

If, however, your message matches the receiver's current lived experiences, demographics, interests, or images, your message has a chance to have a greater impact on the receiver. This is because the information processing function is stimulated when the message content matches the perspectives of the receiver. Remember your intention is not only to get persons to pay attention to your message—this is only surface perception based on cuteness or entertaining value—but to get persons to process the information in the message in order to ultimately be informed or persuaded.

Even though I discuss how similar campaigns should match similar belief structures of the audience, there are theories that contend that some persons are also occasionally reached or influenced by messages that are directly contrary to their beliefs. The principle here (cognitive dissonance theory) is that persons, while naturally attracted to similar messages, will, nevertheless, also be encouraged to process information that runs contrary to their accepted opinions so that they can sort out both sides and choose what to believe (Davison et al., 1976; Freedman & Sears, 1965). Given this, the campaign strategist can also consider that in addition to planning consistent and matching goals, that, for some political or social issues, some opposing goals might also be included to raise the interest of the audiences on both sides of the campaign issue. Further, this allows the campaign strategist, for some volatile or controversial issues, to present opposite messages to the same audience throughout the course of a campaign. If a population possesses an attitude or image directly opposed to the organization, messages presenting the other side, or the organization's position, could be appropriate and even necessary.

Considerations of the Image-Public Collapse Model

This next bottom line also informs general considerations of receivers and suggests how to conceive goals and objectives to attract and persuade an audience. The Collapse Model's conceptualization of image and public position as any singular contrasting and ever-changing opinion or behavior toward an organization means that more basic strategies will most likely have to be created. This suggests that more messages and more communication selections will have

Basic Strategies 89

to be included in the campaign. Every dominant image that is prevalent in the members of a population will need to have a goal and respective objectives to address it.

For example, if an audience possesses across its membership a peculiar negative attitude about one facet of the organization, a unique positive attitude about something else, some undesirable behavior toward the organization, some erroneous knowledge of the organization, then one or two goals should be created to address each one of these images: the negative attitude, the positive attitude, the undesirable behavior, the erroneous knowledge. You can see that breaking the constructs of image and public position into singular attitudes or images necessarily dictates more goals and objectives to address each image-public position that results in a more thorough communication of relevant messages to the entire population(s).

Thus, this new model of image and of public position conceptualizes both functions as similar entities where both are actually the same concepts. For example, a member of an audience who holds an image of the organization as treating their employees well holds this positive image and shares this public position with other individuals who also feel that the organization is good to its employees. Recall that when "image" is considered as any one opinion, attitude, need, knowledge, or behavior that a person holds toward an organization, then any individual has the potential for multiple and changing images and public positions within himself/herself toward any corporation or business. Further, if we assume that any corporation will have multiple, positive, neutral, and negative images held toward it by every audience member who knows the corporation and relates to it, then every person will have many, ever-changing opinions or images of the organization, depending on what is the topic of conversation at hand about the organization. To explain, let me refer again to my research findings about image that found that persons can have negative images of an organization in their opinions of the organization's treatment of their employees but, at the same time, have a very positive image of an organization in their opinions of the organization's community charity activities. The image/opinion shifts according to the particular facet of the organization considered at the time.

In terms of the concept of "public position," this proposed Collapse Model envisions any singular population as made up of persons who hold multiple images, rather than a population that is segmented into publics based on shared similar images. The proposed Collapse Model envisions each population as a group of individuals who individually possess multiple similar and contrasting images and (possibly changing) public positions herself/himself.

The earlier figure of dividing a population into segments of individuals based on demographics, psychographics, needs, shared knowledge or attitudes or behaviors, or images dictated that messages should then be created to target each segment of persons within the population; that is, one or two messages for each major demographic appeal, messages for each dominant psychographic finding, messages for identified needs, messages for each prevailing knowledge or attitude or behavior, or one message for each dominant image. This established, traditional method for segmenting populations and targeting messages to the segments or publics fails to account for two crucial facts that the Collapse Model includes. The earlier model rests on the notion that, first, audience members have only one or a few prevalent images of any corporation and, second, that these images are relatively fixed and unchanging within the persons who hold them. In contrast, the Collapse Model accommodates many more images toward an organization. If multiple images are within each person, then there are many more images and public positions—images and publics that can be changing literally moment to moment—of an organization than previous models can explain.

The Collapse Model's figure of image and public position as similar constructs has crucial implications for the conceptualization of basic strategies. Assume that you have conducted formative research on your targeted populations for a crisis management campaign to counter false allegations of selling contaminated food products. Your research has identified some dominant demographic findings in each population, some strong needs per population, some principal knowledge, attitudes, and behaviors for each population, and other various central images for each population.

Say, for example, that out of five or six major targeted populations for your campaign, each population has at least three dominant demographic classifications. Your community population has multiple socioeconomic and age classes. Your employee population has multiple positive and neutral attitudes and multiple strong and weak needs toward the company. Your media population has disinterested and negative images of your organization. The environmental activist group that monitors your organization has intense negative images for several issues surrounding the corporation's business operations. Your consumer population has no knowledge of the issues that the environmental activist group protests but has important sales behaviors toward your organization.

The campaign strategist who is setting out to plan this crisis management campaign to prove that the allegations against the product are false will have to address each one of these images or public positions in each population. This means that every population receives for each important principal image across it—for each relevant and significant demographic classification(s), for each attitude(s), for each need(s), for each image(s), for each knowledge(s), and for each behavior(s)—a goal and supporting objectives.

Just for the employee population, for example, the following goals and objectives could be identified. The campaign strategist might need to have four goals on demographics for the population of employees, a goal for each of the four main demographic findings revealed through the formative research such as gender, marital status, age, or level within the organization. The strategist might need to have three goals on needs for this employee population: one goal to address the employees' need for job security, another goal to satisfy the need for information on the future of the company, and a third goal to address the need for retirement and health benefits. Further, each primary behavior toward the organization by the employees, each positive, each negative, and each neutral attitude or behavior held of the organization by the employees will need to be addressed in the respective goals and objectives.

Using the Collapse Model means including detailed and comprehensive basic strategies—goals and objectives—for each dominant image, or prevailing public position, held by the members of each relevant population. This attention to each image accommodates the multiplicity of images held across a population and accommodates the changing nature and flexibility of persons to go in and out of different images of the same organization.

Organization-Based Strategies

The third bottom line complements the first two bottom lines. Think of basic strategies as a two-prong message attack on the targeted audiences. Your first prong is the matching operation just explained in the first two bottom lines, whereby you take into consideration the experiences and images of the audiences in designing message content to match or to counter the receivers' images. Your next prong is not audience-based but organization-based. That is, this third bottom line suggests that message content can also be decided by the organization and delivered to the targeted audiences, without direct consideration of audience beliefs, attitudes, or images. This third bottom line contrasts with the initial, matching operation of the first and second bottom lines to contend that the organization, nevertheless, also has the power to determine goals and objectives and create its own messages *and images* independent of the audiences' positions.

The campaign strategist must include for every campaign that leaves her/his office an image goal (or goals) of the organization desired by the organization in all its relevant populations. This goal or goals might be similar or exactly the same for every campaign conducted by the organization or slightly different from one campaign to another, but, in any case, corporate image goals must be included. The organization is obligated to consistently present its desired images to all the relevant audiences relating to it. This is, indeed, an organization-based goal since it is the organization's decision to present the images it wants of itself to all its relevant populations.

Just as any organization has a consistent logo or graphic design included on its letterhead and on all its other messages, any organization needs to make a decision on what are the desired corporate images it wants to portray in all its messages in all its campaigns. The Metropolitan Life Insurance campaigns feature Peanuts cartoon characters presented with a round and playful font for the "Get Met, It Pays" campaign slogan; this is consistent with their desire to present a warm and fuzzy, approachable image for their company.[1] The Mountain Dew soft drink commercials and Nike shoe commercials are permeated with a youthful, playful, "cool" image desired by these corporations.

---

[1] Reprinted with permission, Metropolitan Life Insurance Company.

Corporate images are decided and delivered by organizations, but they can be decided and created from any number of sources. Even though technically the organization is the source of its own corporate image, an intended corporate image can, nevertheless, be modified or changed by what the audiences have experienced of the organization or of the product/service it sells. That is, any member of an audience receives several corporate images—intended by the organization or not intended by the organization. For example, images can be developed from knowledge into the various facets and traits of the organization itself, or from knowledge of the particular characteristics of the product or service sold by the organization, or from information about the organization's competitive businesses which, in turn, reflects on the organization's images.

The goals and objectives framework of basic strategies is retained for organization-based images and messages. Given a campaign situation, the organization can consider each of its targeted audiences and decide what goals (that is, changes or desired effects) it wants to stimulate in each audience throughout the course of the given campaign. The formative research can possibly suggest these independent, organization-informed goals, or the goals can simply be decided by the organization as desirable changes in the audiences that would foster better relations between the audiences and the organization. In addition, objectives (that is, number and kinds of information) can be decided by the campaign strategist and her/his staff to support each of these "independent" or "organization" goals.

For example, let's return to the campaign situation where an organization is planning a campaign to strengthen its image and community relations by reacting to a crisis situation of allegations of polluting the local environment. An organization-generated *goal*—separate from other, audience matching goals—might be to present a corporate image of environmental concern by informing the population/community about procedures the organization follows before releasing wastewater into the local environment.

A few representative *objectives* to support this goal might be:

- twenty-five pieces of information about the purification steps the water passes through from use to release into the environment;

- fifteen pieces of information about how the water is tested and determined to be safe days and weeks after release into the groundwater sources;

- ten pieces of information on how improved inspection methods will avert accidental dumping of unclean water in the future.

Notice how the two sample goals presented in this chapter are very different from each other—the audience-based goal on contributions to youth sports programs and the organization-generated goal on nonpollution of the environment—even though they are basic strategies from the same campaign. For this sample campaign situation of enhancing community relations after a crisis involving allegations of damage to the environment, two radically different goals nevertheless support the campaign's efforts to enhance corporate image in the community population. When strategies are conceptualized as goals and objectives, as desired effects in the population, and as number and kinds of information to support each goal, the campaign strategist has much more leeway to create both *broad-based* goals and objectives as well as *detailed* and *focused* goals and objectives on one subject area.

To conceptualize basic strategies in this new, relatively narrow sense, as effects and as kinds of information, rather than the earlier definitions of goals as "generalized ends" and objectives as "day to day activities," tends to lead to many more goals and objectives for any campaign. This new model encourages much more attention to particular subject areas, certain knowledges, specific attitudes and behaviors, and any number of images that the organization wants to encourage or change in its various targeted audiences. In effect, this new, proposed model for basic strategies encourages each goal with its respective, supportive objectives to be a detailed, thorough presentation of one or more related content areas. In the example, it was a knowledge goal of the organization's support of community youth sports and a knowledge and attitude goal about the organization's efforts to avoid water contamination in the community. And finally, the campaign professional chooses basic strategies: to respond to the audience members' images and to present those additional images the organization has decided to present to the targeted audiences.

THE GOAL: HOW TO CREATE IT AND HOW TO WRITE IT

I have already offered a general definition of a goal as any desired change or desired effect that the organization wants to affect in a targeted audience in the course of a campaign. This general definition does not offer, however, the practical, hands-on suggestions for exactly how to create or make up the appropriate goals for a given campaign, and it does not offer the specific directions for writing the goals (and eventually objectives). This section suggests methods for conceptualizing goals for most kinds of campaign situations and offers, as well, practical suggestions for writing the goals.

The Conceptualization Process: How to Begin

Conceptualizing campaign goals is not a difficult operation. The process of conceptualizing and writing goals is an informed operation, dependent on your research findings done on the targeted populations and dependent on those specific intentions and messages that the organization wants to deliver to its relevant populations. Goals are not decided or chosen by the campaign strategist out of thin air as simply cute or clever goals or content areas that will get the attention of the audiences and, hence, "automatically" persuade them. Rather, the formative research done on the targeted populations and the findings and information gained from the targeted populations dictate directly what some of the goals for the given campaign should be. Additional goals are those image goals that the organization decides should also be communicated to these same targeted populations. You will notice that this framework parallels the fundamental guidelines and bottom lines detailed above—that some goals are designed according to the audiences' interests and that some goals are designed according to the organization's interests.

To begin conceptualizing basic strategies for the campaign, first consider each population separately and create goals appropriate only to the one population under consideration. Every population is an autonomous entity, separate from all the other populations. The campaign strategist decides on the basic strategies for one population and then starts all over choosing the appropriate basic strategies for the next population. The campaign manager might decide to duplicate some goals across two or more populations, but, nevertheless, she/he considers each population's interests and images separately.

This framework will be followed in decisions on the messages and communication selections as well. That is, one population is examined and decisions made on messages and communication selections. Then, the next population's messages and communication selections are decided separately.

As the campaign planner considers and analyzes each population separately, he/she will decide exactly to what degree the population relates to the organization. These decisions on degree of importance for the campaign and for the organization have significance for choosing which populations will be addressed and for deciding the respective basic strategies for each targeted population. For example, some populations will be absolutely crucial to the given campaign situation, such as an activist environmental population for an organization's campaign to manage false allegations of polluting the environment. For another campaign, for example, answering accusations of selling contaminated products dictates that the consumer population is one of the most important populations to be contacted.

On the other hand, in both these same campaign situations other populations may not be quite as important, for example, the industry population for the campaign about false accusations of environmental pollution or the stockholder population for the product contamination campaign. Thus, the campaign planner does not treat every population as equally important; decisions about which populations are more important than others dictate that a prioritization of populations needs to be done in the conceptualization stage of planning a campaign—especially when money concerns might dictate how many populations can be communicated to in the course of one campaign (see Figure 3.1).

In addition to the process of prioritizing populations, another decision needs to be made concerning each population. The campaign strategist, based on considerations of the kind of campaign being planned and the needs and interests of the organization, makes a decision on what degree of change should be attempted by the organization on each population. Following a framework of knowledge, attitudes, behaviors, and other images, the strategist determines, for each population, whether only knowledge goals should be attempted, or know-

Figure 3.1
Conceptual Model of Importance of Some Populations

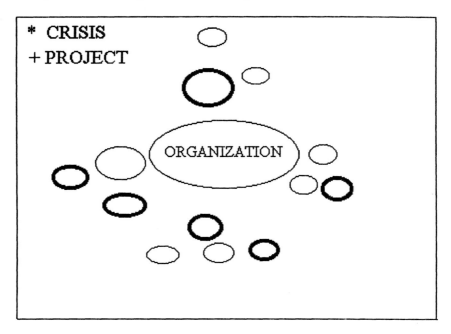

ledge and attitudes goals attempted, or only behavior goals, or other different image goals, and so on (see Figure 3.2).

Consider another example. In the campaign about false allegations of environmental pollution, the environmental activist population has been actively demonstrating against the organization through public demonstrations and through a media campaign. Since this population has knowledge, attitudes, and behaviors against your organization, your goals for this population should be knowledge, attitude, and behavior goals, with perhaps some extra information or image goals, in hopes that your information can offset their currently held opinions, information, and actions (see Figure 3.3). However, with another population affected by this same campaign issue, for example, your employees who have knowledge of (and no significant attitudes or behaviors toward) the false allegations, the goals might only need to be knowledge goals in order to address the currently held knowledge of the employees.

Therefore, in the conceptualization process of the campaign, each population is analyzed separately according to importance and each analyzed individually according to whether it possesses knowledge of the crisis or project situation prompting the campaign; knowledge and attitudes toward the crisis/project; knowledge, attitudes, and behaviors; or possibly knowledge, attitudes, behaviors, and additional information about the crisis/project or about the organization

Figure 3.2
Sample Campaign Goals Relative to Knowledge, Attitude, Behavior, and Other Desired Images

---

Campaign situation: the first campaign targeting employees to inform them of new benefits packages available from the organization
    Knowledge goal
    Knowledge goal
    Knowledge goal
    Knowledge goal
    Additional image goal

Campaign situation: another campaign (the second) targeting employees to have opinions that participating in benefits packages of the organization is good for their current finances and retirement
    Knowledge goal
    Knowledge goal
    Attitude goal
    Attitude goal
    Attitude goal
    Additional image goal

Campaign situation: another campaign (the fifth) targeting employees to participate in some of the benefits packages available to them by the organization
    Knowledge goal
    Attitude goal
    Attitude goal
    Behavior goal
    Behavior goal
    Behavior goal
    Behavior goal
    Additional image goal
    Additional image goal

---

opinions, information, and actions (see Figure 3.3). However, with another population affected by this same campaign issue, for example, your employees who have knowledge of (and no significant attitudes or behaviors toward) the false allegations, the goals might only need to be knowledge goals in order to address the currently held knowledge of the employees.

Therefore, in the conceptualization process of the campaign, each population is analyzed separately according to importance and each analyzed individually according to whether it possesses knowledge of the crisis or project situation prompting the campaign; knowledge and attitudes toward the crisis/project; knowledge, attitudes, and behaviors; or possibly knowledge, attitudes, behaviors, and additional information about the crisis/project or about the organization that will have to be addressed. Your formative research on the targeted populations and on the organization itself can help you here to determine the level of interest of each population—knowledge, attitude, actions, or other information—which, in turn, informs the kind of goals appropriate for each population.

Figure 3.3
Sample Campaign Goals Relative to Knowledge, Attitude, Behavior, and Other Images With Different Populations

Campaign situation: a campaign targeting an environmental activist population and the employee population denying false allegations of organizational pollution of the environment

Environmental Activist Population:	Employee Population:
Knowledge goal	Knowledge goal
Knowledge goal	Knowledge goal
Attitude goal	Knowledge goal
Attitude goal	Attitude goal
Attitude goal	Image goal
Behavior goal	
Behavior goal	
Behavior goal	
Image goal	
Image goal	

A word of caution is needed here. Do not think of the basic strategies of goals and objectives as the exact words or the visuals or graphic designs of the messages. *Goals are not messages; messages are the exact words and visuals of a message.* A goal is simply the statement of the desired change or appeal made to an audience. A goal and, for that matter, an objective, does not include any reference to what exact words or visuals should be included in a message. Also, goals and objectives do not include any reference to what communication selections—media channel or personal contact—are most appropriate.

Do not get ahead of yourself in your decisions on what the basic strategies should be. Just focus on what changes you want to make in your intended audiences and what kinds of information would best support each of these changes. Fortunately, if you do a thorough and detailed job of laying out all of your goals and supporting objectives for every important audience related to a given campaign, the messages and communication selection choices will naturally flow from the basic strategies. Try not to anticipate what your messages should be or what are the best communication selections to deliver the messages. Your decisions on what the basic strategies should be will directly inform the next campaign steps of construction and creation of the messages and of choices of appropriate communication selections.

Two Kinds of Goals: Change and Appeal Goals

Two fundamental kinds of goals are available for any campaign situation: change goals and appeal goals. The *change goal* is a relatively direct statement of the particular change desired in the populations by the organization. The *appeal goal* functions more or less as a two-step operation in the audience; first, the goal gets the attention of the audience through an appeal to an image or lived experience present in the audience membership, so that, next, the desired change can be suggested to the audience.

Change Goals

The *change* or *effect* kind of goal parallels the four general classifications noted above. A change goal is a proposal or suggestion of (1) a particular kind of knowledge, (2) an attitude or opinion, (3) a behavior or action, or (4) any other images desired in the audience. These kinds of goals are direct statements of the intended changes hoped for in the targeted audiences throughout the course of a campaign.

A change goal (obviously) proposes a change or desired effect in the audience. The desired effect might be to maintain and strengthen a certain level of knowledge, attitude, or behavior in a population or to maintain other images at the current level experienced by a population. Another example of a change goal is to counteract a neutral or negative image present in a population with a positive, alternative opinion. Another kind of change goal is to move a population from a knowledge level to an attitude/opinion level toward a particular issue; the issue might be the subject—project or crisis—of the campaign or any other issue related to the campaign under consideration. Another change goal might be to move a population from an attitude level (holding a particular opinion) to a behavioral level where the population is encouraged to take specific actions toward an issue. And, finally, a campaign professional can simply propose extra change goals of additional kinds of knowledge, attitudes, behaviors, or other image(s) desired in the population but not presently held by the targeted population.

Your inspiration for these four kinds of change goals of knowledge, attitudes, behaviors, and other images flows, first, from the research you did on those targeted populations most important to your intended campaign. Generally speaking, you can create a goal for every substantial piece of knowledge, each strong attitude or relevant opinion, each crucial behavior, and every other image revealed in the formative research and that you want to address through the campaign.

In fact, one way to begin conceptualizing your changes goals is to go back to the survey, interview, or focus group instruments themselves and the respective research findings. Examine your first population and from your research findings determine all the major pieces and kinds of knowledge that are shared across the membership of the population. Next, look for any significant attitudes or opinions toward the campaign project/crisis or toward the organization that are shared by the members of the population. Then, look for any significant behaviors or actions that the persons in the population have and which might be important for the campaign. And finally, find any other images—information, opinions, positions toward the organization—that might not be typically classified as a knowledge, attitude, or behavior (see Figure 3.4).

Figure 3.4
Sample Campaign Goals Relative to Knowledge, Attitude, Behavior, and Other Images

> (Hypothetical) campaign situation: The American Red Cross (ARC) is conducting a campaign to get more persons to donate blood since the ARC and small communities face a shortage of blood donations. This is a result of an increasing number of for-profit blood banks and blood donor decisions to donate to a blood bank instead of the ARC. For the blood donor population, sample goals are:
>
> - knowledge goal: that the blood donor population know all the services the ARC provides as a not-for-profit agency
>
> - attitude goal: that the blood donor population have the opinion that donating blood to the ARC is more charitable to society and small communities than selling to a blood bank
>
> - behavior goal: that the blood donor population be prompted to tell others of the ARC and its blood services
>
> - image goal: that the blood donor population know that the ARC provides only safe, well-tested blood

Labels taken from the Grunig Typology on kind of publics found within a population can be very informative here, especially in findings of how many persons are of nonpublic, latent, aware, and active status (Grunig & Hunt, 1984). Generally speaking, persons who have active public positions toward the organization have knowledge, attitudes, and behaviors toward the organization. Any persons with aware public positions will have mostly attitudes and knowledge but little or no behaviors toward the organization. Persons who share latent positions have no knowledge, attitude, or behavior *yet* toward the organization but have the potential for any or all of these; latent positions have the potential to be moved to aware status with knowledge and possibly attitude information. And finally, nonpublic positions have no knowledge, attitude, or behaviors for an organization and probably never will.

If you find through your research that one of your populations has a significant number of persons with nonpublic positions and if this population is extremely important to reach given the campaign situation, you can create a goal(s) that attempts to move the nonpublic public positions to latent status. This is accomplished primarily with knowledge goals and objectives since the nonpublic persons have no significant knowledge, attitudes, or behaviors toward the organization or toward the crisis/project yet.

In another situation, if you find a large number of latent public positions across a population that is important to the organization, you can create a goal or goals and objectives that move the latent positions to an aware status. This is achieved primarily through knowledge and attitude goals and objectives since latent persons have little knowledge or opinions of the campaign situation but have the potential to be informed of it.

For a significant number of aware public positions in a given population, the campaign planner has two choices. She/he can maintain the aware persons at the aware level if the organization needs no pivotal actions or behaviors from them or attempt to move the aware persons to an active status with several attitude and action goals if the organization desires specific actions from them.

If the campaign planner finds a large segment of active positions in a population, only one kind of strategy is appropriate. Several behavior goals will maintain the active members at active status since they share important behaviors toward the organization. If you do not provide a lot of information on the campaign issues and the organization, those holding active public positions will seek their information elsewhere—possibly from sources contradicting your views. Remember, an active public position means an individual who wants to act and wants to seek information; if your organization does not provide enough information, the individual will seek it from other sources.

Refer to Figure 3.4 again for examples of knowledge, attitude, behavior, and other image goals. Given the variety of campaign situations and the vast differences among populations relating to any organization, it is possible to have only knowledge goals going out to a population with mostly nonpublic or latent public positions. In another campaign situation, a population with significant numbers of aware and active public positions across its membership will need to receive attitude and behavior goals. And, what can happen in particularly large populations, all four kinds of goals—knowledge, attitude, behavior, other image—will have to be created, given the variety and breadth of public positions across the entire population.

From this inventory of major findings on kinds of public positions, or images, shared across the population, the campaign strategist selects those images that are most significant and important to the campaign's purpose. For each knowledge image, attitude image, behavior image, and other image deemed important across the audience membership, a goal is created respective to each one. These goals are audience-centered goals, respective to the lived experiences of the audience.

Another inventory is also conducted on the same population, this time to identify the knowledge images, attitude images, behavior images, and other images that the organization wants, independent of the audience research, to deliver to the population. Ideas for these organization-centered goals, or desired changes, may come from the research findings but, just as often, they come from the organization itself, as those desired changes in knowledge, opinions, actions that the organization wants to foster in its related audiences. The campaign strategist, together with his/her staff and with his/her superiors simply chooses those images that they want to suggest and encourage in the various audiences. Just as with the audience-centered goals, the organization goals can be knowledge, attitude, behavior, or other, independent image goals (see Figure 3.5).

Basic Strategies 101

Figure 3.5
Sample Campaign Goals Based on Targeted Audience and Based on Organization Intention

---

Campaign situation: a manufacturer of building supplies and windows plans a campaign to involve its employees in a fund-raiser to benefit muscular dystrophy

Sample audience-centered goals:
- knowledge goal: that the employees have information on how organization will give release time to participate in fund-raiser

- attitude goal: that the employees will feel that the organization cares about those afflicted with muscular dystrophy

- behavior goal: that the employees will want to participate in the fund-raiser

- other image: information on how to sign up for the fund-raiser

Sample organization-centered goals:
- knowledge goal: that the employees know how the company once struggled financially and now wants to share its success with the community

- attitude goal: that the employees feel that muscular dystrophy is a worthy charity for the organization to support

- behavior goal: that the employees will solicit other persons in the community to also participate in the fund-raiser

- other image: information on how the company will raise and give money to charity

---

Appeal Goals

The second kind of goal, the *appeal* goal, is very similar to the change goal but with a slight twist. Whereas a change goal makes a direct statement of a change desired in the targeted population—a change in knowledge, attitude, behavior, or other image—the appeal goal makes an initial statement that is a reference to some lived experience in the targeted audience so that the audience will pay attention to the content that comes later or is contained in the objectives that support the goal. The appeal goal is structured as a more or less two step-process. First, information is presented, which, hopefully, gets the attention of the members of an audience because it matches some lived experience of the audience, so that, additionally, information is presented that contains the intended image hoped for in the audience.

Any appeal goal can be viewed as relating to a lived experience in the receiver. That is, every individual experiences on a day-to-day basis unique personal *and* socially dictated lived experiences. All of us experience various demographic classifications; we are female or male, we are married or single, or we are a certain age or at a certain level of income. Additionally, each of us experiences certain personal and social needs. We also can possess certain psychographic distinctions such as high achievers or inner-directed persons. Another, interesting lived experience that can inform appeal goal creation is the model of cognitive schema that each person possesses: learned social behaviors and attitudes toward stereotypes, various settings, and occupations. And once again, appeal goals can also match any kind of knowledge, attitudes, behaviors, or other images that are significant across the population. Let me examine now each of these various lived experiences one at a time.

First are *demographic appeals*. Given your formative research on the targeted populations, any significant findings on a demographic classification can be turned into an appeal goal. For example, if you find from your survey research or from other kinds of research on your audiences that a substantial number of persons in any of your targeted audiences are female and are important to the campaign's purpose, you might want to create a goal that is an appeal toward females, in hopes that they will consequently pay attention to information on the organization, the organization's product or the campaign issue.

Let me offer another example of a demographic appeal goal. Assume that one of the important populations for a campaign you are planning is community residents. Suppose that you know from research findings that a dominant demographic trait of this community is that the residents are mostly from a high socioeconomic level; the population's level of income is relatively high, mostly upper class, mostly white collar. If you plan to run a social issue campaign in this community to raise money for disadvantaged children throughout the state, you might include a goal or two that has an appeal to wealthy families helping out disadvantaged families. In principle, for this community residents population, a goal with a direct appeal to lower income, financially troubled families will not match their socioeconomic level and might not get the attention of this community as much as an appeal to their social needs and the upper socioeconomic lived experience that the greatest segment of the population lives.

As you plan your appeal goals as part of your basic strategies, think through any demographic appeals that would match demographic information you know about every targeted population: information such as gender, socioeconomic level, geographical area, urban or rural area, level of income, racial makeup, ethnic background, age, level of education, religious preferences, or marital status within a population (see Figure 3.6). Findings on significant demographic classifications can come from the survey you administered to the populations or from interviews, focus groups, content analysis, or experimental research findings as part of your formative research or from any secondary research about your populations from other sources. Look for any significant demographic factor(s) in each of your relevant populations that might make good appeal goals.

A couple of very good sources for gaining secondary research on the demographics of potential audiences are the *U.S. Bureau of the Census Reports* and the *Standard Metropolitan Statistical Area (SMSA) Reports* (Simmons, 1990, p.

Figure 3.6
Sample Demographic Goals

- Level of income and geographic area goal: To appeal to persons in high income levels in urban areas

- Geographic area goal: To strengthen the appeal of Major League Soccer on the West Coast and the East Coast

- Gender and age goal: To appeal to males and females from the early teens to the mid-twenties

- Level of management and family status goal: To appeal to lower level managers who are married with children

21). Almost every library will have these references for investigating a geographical graphical region as to demographics. For example, if you are planning a campaign for the Chicago area and the Chicago suburban area, you can look in the records of the *Census* and the *SMSA* reports for the latest on demographic information gathered at the last census for the inner-city Chicago residents and the Chicago suburb residents. You will find information on almost every demographic classification: socioeconomic levels for each region, family size, marital status trends, religious preferences, age classifications, gender ratios, and so on for both geographic areas.

Another very common kind of appeal goal is *needs appeals*. If your research or prior information on a population identifies some strong needs present in the audience, you can match these needs in one or more appeal goals to get the audience's attention. The most common framework for exploring and identifying needs in individuals is Maslow's Hierarchy of Needs (1943, 1970). Maslow identifies five sequential or hierarchical levels of needs and contends that one level of needs usually needs to be satisfied in a person before the next level of needs can be addressed and satisfied. His five levels are needs for physical sustainment, safety, social acceptance, self-esteem, and self-actualization. Maslow and others have found, however, that persons can go up and down the hierarchy; that is, a person can experience physical needs, then safety needs, then social needs, then perhaps go back to a need for safety or perhaps even skip some needs going up or down the hierarchy.

His first level of needs is physical needs; each person has basic physical needs for food, water, and shelter. If you find an important population has a strong need for any of these basic physical needs across its members, you might very well consider an appeal goal matching any of these primary physical needs.

Maslow's second level of needs is a person's need for security or safety. Maslow argues that a person, with physical needs met, secondarily needs to feel safe and secure in the environment. This need, unfortunately, is revealed in several facets of our society today. Dysfunctional homes, unsafe neighborhoods, crime and drug settings, gangs, unsafe schools, and troubled children and adults are just a few examples of settings and persons who live their lives every day experiencing and craving a need for safety and security. Given a population living in these unsafe and threatening situations, appeal needs goals and objectives could be created to match these safety concerns if a significant number of persons in a population are experiencing an insecure and unsafe environment.

Maslow's third level of needs is social needs. That is, a person needs to feel she/he fits into the society and that she/he has friends and acquaintances. In other words, a person needs to feel that she/he can communicate well in a group situation, relate properly to others, and be accepted by other persons.

The fourth need for self-esteem is more personally directed in that it is a need for the individual to feel respected and appreciated by others, and even admired by others. The final and ultimate need experienced by people is the need for self-actualization; this is an experience that "I have reached the goals that I am capable of reaching." It is the realization by persons that they have realized their full potential and accomplished what they set out to do; it is the feeling that they are capable of doing worthwhile things and that they have used their capabilities to achieve the things they set out to do. Should the campaign strategist recognize through research findings any of these five needs to any major degree in any of the targeted audiences, the strategist should consider whether an appeal goal targeting the respective need(s) might be appropriate for the campaign being planned.

Pfau and Parrott (1993) have added to considerations of needs appeals and suggested two additional ways to conceptualize needs in populations. They contend that individuals have both personal and social needs. Given this binary model, the campaign planner can investigate the degree of personal needs and of social needs in the relevant populations and prepare appeal goals accordingly. For example, if a population is found to have very strong personal needs—of any kind, related to the organization or to the campaign or of a general nature such as Maslow's five needs—goals could be included to appeal to any or all of these personal needs. At the same time, if a population is found to have very strong social needs—either to be part of a certain group or organization or to help society at large in some way—goals could be included to appeal to any or all of these social needs found in the population(s).

Another interpretation of needs appeals is to consider the differences between a rational need or appeal and an emotional need or appeal (Pfau & Parrott, 1993). Considerations and research findings on the targeted audiences can suggest to the campaign planner whether an appeal based on logic or rationality would match the interests and lived experiences of most of the audience or whether an emotional appeal would more closely get the attention of and match the lived experiences of the audience under analysis.

It is also completely proper to construct multiple appeal goals that target several kinds of needs (see Figure 3.7). If a population cannot be neatly segmented as to one or two of Maslow's needs, it might be necessary for the campaign planner to construct several need appeal goals and objectives, to target multiple

Figure 3.7
Sample Goals Targeting Needs

- Physical and safety needs goal: To appeal to the homeless in the inner city that shelters are now safe and secure

- Social needs goal: To appeal to blood donors that giving blood to American Red Cross benefits society at large

- Self-esteem and social needs goal: To appeal to employees that donating time and money to muscular dystrophy makes them feel important and respected and helps others in need

- Self-actualization needs goal: To appeal to potential stockholders that making investments in an organization will provide them with financial advantages worthy of their upper socioeconomic level and their other financial achievements

- Personal needs goal: To appeal to environmental activists that allegations of organizational pollution of the environmental are false and that they have not been personally affected or hurt

- Social needs goal: To appeal to environmental activists that allegations of organizational pollution are false and that the environment and community residents have not been hurt

- Rational needs goal: To appeal to consumers that buying low-fat foods is good for the body and a natural way to pursue good health

- Emotional needs goal: To appeal to consumers that buying low-fat foods will make you feel disciplined in controlling how you eat and give you a more positive outlook on life

needs, according to the Maslow framework. A campaign planner, given a population with both personal and social needs or with both logical and emotional leanings, would be obliged to construct goals and objectives that match both personal and social needs and to both rational and emotional perspectives.

Another framework for sorting out appeal goals for your audiences is to reference *psychographic appeals*. Several psychographic models have contributed to campaign communication primarily through the fields of advertising and marketing (Clark, 1988; Schultz, 1990; Schultz & Tannenbaum, 1989; Schultz et al., 1984). Psychographic information refers to the general psychology of your populations, to their personality types, to their lifestyle practices, to their leisure activities, to how they want to be regarded by others, and even to their preferences for how they spend their money. If the campaign professional can determine to any significant degree any of these psychographics of a given population, making up appeal goals to match these psychological leanings, personality types, leisure practices, lifestyle behaviors, or spending preferences can be very effective in catching the attention of the audience membership.

Your own research on your targeted audiences will probably suggest some psychographic information on your pertinent audiences, but other, secondary sources of information are also available for discovering the psychographics of your related audiences. Library research from books and periodicals might offer insights into audiences in certain professions or in certain geographic regions of the country. Be sure to read the *U.S. Bureau of the Census Reports* and the *Standard Metropolitan Statistical Area (SMSA) Reports* again for any clues to psychographic information on your targeted audiences. But today, also, new technology forms have revolutionized ways of doing secondary research. World Wide Web pages and other Internet sources can provide instantaneous information (and free!) on groups of persons and their respective interests, leisure practices, and lifestyle behaviors.

One particular psychographic model has laid the foundation for most of the methods and models for how to investigate and categorize psychographic information on an audience. The VALS typology was developed in the late 1970s, and categorized four kinds of people (Clark, 1988). The typology is a hierarchy that begins at the lowest level with needs-driven persons; these are persons who are driven primarily to satisfy their physical needs rather than other lived experiences. The next level is outer-driven persons who buy things and live generally to impress others in society around them. The next level is inner-driven persons who purchase commodities to satisfy themselves, with little or no thought to impressing those around them. The final level is integrated persons, who have both elements of outer-driven persons and elements of inner-driven persons.

The VALS model was first introduced by the marketing and advertising fields and had value to campaign planners in that it isolated and labeled personality types and persons' lived experiences so that commercial messages could be designed to appeal to consumer groups with these dominant characteristics and personality types. It has since been modified and adapted to define additional types of persons and consumers. The VALS 2 typology identifies eight more classifications of personality types: strugglers, experiencers, makers, strivers, achievers, believers, fulfilleds, and actualizers—labels that are essentially self-explanatory (Russell & Lane, 1990). Another example of an adaptation of psychographic classifications was developed by Schultz, Martin, and Brown (1984) a decade ago; they suggest there are self-made businesspeople, successful professionals, devoted family people, frustrated factory workers, retiring homebodies, contented housewives, chic suburbanites, elegant socialites, militant mothers, and old-fashioned traditionalists. Aside from the fact that these are dated and stereotypical gender labels, this model demonstrates how various images and public positions can be identified according to multiple lived experiences and psychographic orientations.

Given these various efforts to segment and identify public positions within populations according to psychographic distinctions, your project as a campaign strategist is to identify or "guesstimate" how the targeted populations you have identified for your campaign situation fall within the various classes of the VALS, VALS 2, or other psychographic models. You can base your psychographic positions on answers to survey questions or interview or focus group questions (or the other research methods of content analysis and experimental design) gathered in the formative research on your relevant populations. Or, you can gain additional information on your populations from the U.S. Bureau of the Census or the SMSA reports from any good library or from Internet sources.

From your original and secondary research findings and from your identification of various psychographic elements within your audiences, you can now fashion goals and objectives respective to each major psychographic classification you believe exists. These are psychographic appeal goals and objectives that identify and match each psychographic categorization in hopes of catching the attention of various segments of the related audiences. My caution here in considering psychographic categories for creating appeal goals comes from my understanding of the Collapse Model of corporate image. Keep in mind that any individual can go in and out of images, or experience any of the various psychographic classes, from moment to moment. The campaign planner cannot assume—as these established psychographic models implicitly do—that the psychographic distinctions of any audience are relatively fixed and unchanging. Consistent with the Collapse Model, a person be outer-directed on one day or at one time during the day and on another day, or at a different time of the day, be an inner-directed personality. I may be a frustrated factory worker *and* a contented housewife *and* a militant mother *and* a successful professional all in the same day! The campaign solution to this principle that persons may be basically one kind of personality but experience multiple, possibly changing psychographic types is to prepare multiple appeal goals to match the major psychographic types present in an audience, in hopes that the psychographic appeal goals will match most of the psychographic types across the audience (see Figure 3.8).

A final framework from which to conceive appeal goals is to use *schema appeals*. Schema are cognitive processes, or cognitive structures, that all persons have learned throughout their lives (Salomon, 1979, 1981, 1987). These experiences are learned from the media, friends, and family, and all other experiences and stimuli surrounding us in our environment. We are not born with schema. They are learned reactions to the environment around us. Perhaps the best way to understand schema is to define the three kinds.

One kind of schema is event schema: we know how to act or to behave in certain settings or places from our experiences in these settings. We have learned throughout our lives the typical and correct behaviors in church, in school, in a doctor's office, in our place of work, in our best friend's house. These situationally based behaviors and attitudes are formed from lived experiences, not from behaviors and attitudes we are born with.

Another kind of schema is role schema: we have learned what a person in a certain occupation or performing a particular job will most likely act like or should act like from all our experiences of different occupations. We have a pretty good idea of how the typical professor talks and behaves, how a physician

Figure 3.8
Sample Goals Targeting Psychographics

- Inner-directed goal: To appeal to inner-directed persons that supporting the fund-raiser will give them self-satisfaction

- Outer-directed goal: To appeal to outer-directed persons that supporting the fund-raiser will give them recognition and respect from their peers

- Needs-driven goal: To appeal to employees that planning for retirement will benefit their personal finances at retirement

- Outer-directed and big money spenders goal: To appeal to potential consumers of luxury automobiles that an automobile purchase will signify their high social status to others

- Strivers goal: To appeal to lower management workers that the organization provides many opportunities for job advancement

- Experiencers goal: To appeal to high school students that avoiding drugs is "cool" and socially acceptable with peers

- Contented housewives goal: To appeal to at-home mothers that pursuing personal fitness makes them more efficient and productive around the house

- Chic suburbanites goal: To appeal to upwardly driven socialites that pursuing personal fitness will make them more attractive and socially accepted by their peers

acts and reacts to patients in his office, how a junk dealer might act or might dress in his junkyard, or how a minister or priest walks and talks in the church and on the street.

The third kind of schema, person schema, is those learned experiences and stereotypes that some people have toward certain types of persons—not stereotypes of occupations but, more particularly, cultural stereotypes of kinds of persons. For example, schema exist that suggest that blondes are "spacey" or "dumb," that college professors are absent-minded and eccentric, or that Southerners wear flannel shirts and have no manners and are "rednecks." Of course, these stereotypes and humorous references to certain kinds of persons have no basis in truth for all persons who happen to be blonde, who happen to teach at a university, or who happen to live in the South.

If the campaign planner can identify through formative quantitative or qualitative research or through outside, secondary sources any schema most likely held by the targeted populations, then another avenue exists for creating appeal goals. Once again, as with psychographic and need and demographic findings, for any population that might experience multiple schema, multiple schema ap-

Figure 3.9
Sample Goals Targeting Schema

- Role schema goal: To appeal to college students that recycling their soda cans and wastepaper is consistent with the role of college student as concerned with the environment and leaders in social concerns

- Event schema goal: To appeal to college students that recycling their soda cans and wastepaper is correct and appropriate behavior in the dorms, houses, and classrooms

- Person schema goal: To appeal to college students that recycling their soda cans and wastepaper demonstrates that college students are responsible and socially conscious and not self-centered and careless persons

peal goals will be necessary to match the various schema. In addition, any singular audience might not only hold one dominant role, person, and event schema, but audience members might also hold contrasting or differing role schema, person schema, and event schema. Given the possibility across an audience of prevalent but differing role schema, dominant but contrasting person schema, and multiple event schema, then multiple, contrasting schema appeal goals will be necessary to the entire audience (see Figure 3.9).

One very curious and real phenomenon occurs in relation to appeal goals and must also be noted. So far, the discussion of appeal goals has assumed that appeal goals will reach audiences when the appeals imbedded in the goals and objectives are consistent with the currently lived experiences of the intended audiences.

The notion of appeal, and goals and objectives that appeal to lived experiences, also work another way. In fact, we are exposed to this alternative notion of appeal every day in advertising messages. As many of the goals already presented in this chapter implicitly suggest, appeal goals can also be designed to target the *ideal lived experiences that the audience member wants to match, not only the real lived experiences felt by the audience member.* Makeup and clothing advertisements and all kinds of commercials pushing luxury products are excellent examples of goal-directed messages that appeal to an ideal, rather than to the real or actual experience of the receiver. These can be very influential and simple in their persuasive impact. Goals and objectives present an ideal physical or personality type or a coveted commodity, in hopes that the receiver will be induced to buy the product to match social ideal.

THE OBJECTIVE: HOW TO CREATE IT AND HOW TO WRITE IT

Each singular objective names the number of pieces of information and the one subject area or nature of information to be delivered to the targeted population. Each objective has two parts: a statement of the number of pieces of information and the subject area or content area covered by the respective objective.

Sample objectives that could support a hypothetical goal of strengthening the image of the American Red Cross (ARC) by demonstrating its partnership with hospitals would be:

- fifteen pieces of information regarding the history of the ARC and its partnership with hospitals;

- twenty pieces of information concerning the current amount of blood that the ARC provides to hospitals; and

- ten pieces of information to support the opinion that the ARC has responded to blood needs of hospitals around the nation.

Recall that this proposed model of objectives does not, in any way, relate an objective as an activity that supports a goal. An objective is only about kinds and amount of information.

And simply put, you cannot justify a goal unless you can provide a listing of objectives that contain the number of pieces of information and the content of these pieces of information. The basic strategies are a unique combination of the two factors of goals and objectives that are dependent on each other—the goal that states the desired change in the population(s) and the objectives that name the kind of information that will accomplish and reach the goal. To state a goal, the desired effect, is not enough for a campaign. You must provide the information that will allow the goal to be successfully reached and the audiences to be informed and persuaded. The statement of a goal without sufficient objectives to support it is like a gun with no ammunition. The objectives are the proof, the support, the ammunition that allow the goal to be sufficiently attained.

Audience-Centered and Organization-Centered Objectives

One of your first considerations as you begin to conceptualize and create objectives for your stated goals is that objectives fall into two general classifications that parallel kinds of goals stated above. Objectives can be audience-centered or organization-centered. Objectives can be created and written to directly appeal to the lived experiences of the audience(s): their demographics, needs, psychographics, schema, knowledge, attitudes, behaviors, and other images. Or, objectives can be written from the organization's point of view, as those kinds of information, opinions, and behaviors that the organization wants its targeted populations to hold, in addition to and outside of the currently held experiences of its related audiences.

While it is a fact that audience-centered objectives and organization-centered objectives *can support any of the various kinds of goals*, usually, it works out that audience-centered objectives will more naturally support appeal goals while organization-centered objectives will more naturally support direct change goals. This makes sense. An appeal goal is directed at particular lived experiences of the audience members, and audience-centered objectives contain information that directly relates to lived experiences of the audience. At the same time, organization-centered goals state the information that the organization wants its audiences to have, and organization-centered objectives contain the amount and kind of information that will support the goal.

Knowledge, Attitude, Behavior, and Image Objectives

Another way to classify objectives is to determine if they are knowledge objectives, attitude objectives, behavior objectives, or other image objectives. If an objective names a certain kind of knowledge or information to be communicated to an audience, it is a knowledge objective. If an objective suggests an opinion or an attitude for the audience to hold, it is an attitude objective. If an objective suggests a behavior or action, it is a behavior objective. Or, an objective can simply name another image that makes it a general image objective.

The value in recognizing the difference in knowledge, attitude, or behavior objectives is that certain kinds of goals will necessitate more of one kind of objective than another. For example, if you have planned a knowledge goal or an image goal for a certain population, then, typically, the objectives supporting this goal will be mostly knowledge objectives. If you have an opinion or attitude goal planned for a population, then you will want to include both knowledge and attitude objectives to adequately support the goal. If you plan a goal that states a desired behavior or action in the targeted population, then you will want all three kinds of objectives—knowledge, attitude, and behavior—to sufficiently support the goal. For any of the direct change goals—knowledge, attitude, behavior, other image—and for any of the appeal goals—demographic, psychographic, needs, schema—you can plan audience-centered objectives *and/or* organization-centered objectives naming knowledge, attitude, or behaviors that will support the respective goals.

However, when you are constructing objectives for active, aware, latent, and nonpublic goals, some extra considerations come into play. Recall that I noted above that if a population has a large number of nonpublic and/or latent positions, the appropriate goals are knowledge. With a large number of aware positions across a population, knowledge and attitude goals are appropriate. With a large number of active positions, knowledge and attitude and behavior goals are proper.

When you are planning objectives for these goals, both the number of pieces of information and the content according to knowledge, attitude, and behavior are crucial. Some general guidelines can suggest the kinds of objectives for the active to nonpublic goals. With a large number of nonpublic positions, fewer numbers of pieces of information are necessary, and only knowledge objectives are appropriate since these persons sharing the nonpublic status are not interested in the organization or the campaign issue. With a significant number of latent positions, only knowledge objectives are again suitable since persons with these positions do not have knowledge of the organization or campaign issue although they have the capacity and receptability to be informed in the future.

With a population of aware positions, you have one option of maintaining them at aware; if keeping these persons at aware serves the organization, you will want to plan for higher numbers of pieces of information and objectives that are both knowledge and aware. With the second option available for aware positions, if you want to move the aware positions to active status or if you have active positions that you need to maintain at the active status, you will need relatively larger numbers of pieces of information and all three kinds of objectives since these persons are most likely predisposed to have opinions and actions toward your organization and your campaign.

And, finally, once all your goals are determined and all the supporting objectives written for each goal, a few sentences or a short paragraph is written for each goal that presents the rationale for the goal and supporting objectives. These rationale statements accompanying each goal are critical for your client (if you work for an agency) or your superior or manager (if you do in-house campaign communication). Then the organization has a statement of each goal with an explanation of why the objectives adequately support the goal; and for each goal, an explanation of why each goal is important to the respective population and the campaign at large. For the following sample goals, after samples of knowledge and attitude objectives have been presented, I will merely name "knowledge objective," "attitude objective," rather than write out samples at length again.

Figure 3.10 presents a suggested framework for active, aware, latent, nonpublic goals for one population. Notice that both organization-centered objectives and audience-centered objectives are included to support each of the Grunig goals. In addition, the number of objectives and the number of pieces of information increases as the positions move from nonpublic to latent to aware to active status. Remember also that not every population will get all of the active, aware, latent, non-public kind of goals. You might have a campaign situation where one population receives only a latent goal and perhaps an aware goal whereas another population receives only active goals and supporting active objectives. The active to nonpublic goals are all relative to the findings on the positions present within a population.

Note also that Figure 3.10 is the framework for only the active to nonpublic goals. In an actual campaign situation the basic strategies for one population would include active to nonpublic goals, the change goals (knowledge, attitude, behavior, image), appeal goals (demographics, needs, psychographics, schema), and other separate image goals.

IN SUMMARY

Hopefully, this intensive explication of basic strategies for each population targeted in the course of a campaign demonstrates how in-depth and detailed the

Figure 3.10
Sample Grunig Goals with Respective Supporting Objectives and Rationale Statements

Campaign situation: a manufacturer of exercise equipment is facing a crisis since defective machines were shipped to consumers, and angry consumers are returning their machines and some even getting hurt on the defective machines.

Nonpublic goal: To move the nonpublic positions to latent status
- Knowledge objective: ten pieces of information about the parts used in the manufacture of the equipment
- Knowledge objective: eight pieces of information about the testing procedures for new equipment
- Knowledge objective: five pieces of information about the kind of materials used in the manufacture of the equipment

Rationale for nonpublic goal: Since a significant number of persons in this consumer population share the nonpublic position, a nonpublic goal with supporting objectives is appropriate for targeting them. Individuals with a nonpublic position have very little or no interest in the organization or the campaign. As a result, only knowledge objectives with relatively low numbers of pieces of information are appropriate and reasonable for them to process.

Latent goal: To move the latent positions to an aware status
- Knowledge objective: ten pieces of information on how manufacturing process contains multiple inspections
- Knowledge objective: fifteen pieces of information on the efforts to correct the defective parts and replace with correct parts
- Knowledge objective: fifteen pieces of information on the causes of the defective parts
- Knowledge objective: twenty pieces of information on the importance of physical fitness for weight loss
- Attitude objective: fifteen pieces of information to foster the opinion that this exercise machine is better than all the competitive products
- Attitude objective: twenty pieces of information that the organization is a socially responsible company that places the safety of its consumers in high priority
- Attitude objective: ten pieces of information so that consumers will believe that this exercise machine is made out of the best, state-of-the-art materials
- Attitude objective: seventeen pieces of information about how the manufacturer will resolve the crisis promptly

Rationale for latent goal: Since a significant number of persons in the consumer population share latent positions, a goal and supporting objectives are necessary for this population. Latent positions indicate a current lack of interest in the organization and the product but a potential to process information about the product and organization. Hence, both knowledge and attitude objectives are appropriate for this goal and the persons in the latent positions; these suggest the knowledge and opinions that the population should hold. A larger amount of information is also appropriate for this position, which dictates that more objectives and higher numbers of pieces of information are proper.

Aware goal: To maintain the aware positions at aware status
- Knowledge objective:
- Knowledge objective:
- Knowledge objective:
- Knowledge objective:
- Knowledge objective:
- Attitude objective: fifteen pieces of information so that consumers will have the opinion that machine is dependable and will not break down with regular use
- Attitude objective: twenty pieces of information to convince consumers that they have purchased the best exercise equipment on the market
- Attitude objective: eighteen pieces of information indicating that this machine works the body more effectively than other machines
- Attitude objective: twenty pieces of information to foster belief that manufacturer will be in business for years to come and is not a new, short-lived organization
- Attitude objective: thirteen pieces of information convincing the consumers that the design of the machine is superior to all others for total body workout

Rationale for aware goal to maintain at aware status: Since a significant of aware positions were indicated in this population, it is necessary to maintain the aware positions at aware status. Also, since the organization does not desire significant actions from these persons, the goal strategy is to maintain the aware positions at active status, not move to active status. As aware positions, more pieces of information and more objectives in both the knowledge and attitude areas are needed than in the latent positions.

Aware goal: To move the aware positions to active status
- Knowledge objective:
- Knowledge objective:
- Knowledge objective:
- Knowledge objective:
- Attitude objective:
- Attitude objective:
- Attitude objective:
- Attitude objective:
- Attitude objective:
- Behavior objective: fifteen pieces of information that would convince the consumers to buy other products from the company
- Behavior objective: ten pieces of information to suggest that the consumers tell their friends and acquaintances about the corrections to the equipment
- Behavior objective: ten pieces of information to suggest that the consumers tell their friends about the merits of the exercise equipment
- Behavior objective: fifteen pieces of information to indicate how the consumers can replace their machine at local retailers or through contact with the manufacturer
- Behavior objective: eighteen pieces of information to encourage the consumers to regularly and faithfully use the exercise equipment

> Rationale for aware positions to move to active status: Since a significant number of aware positions are indicated in the population and since the organization needs to solicit particular actions from the population, it is necessary to include this goal of moving the aware positions to active status. Since there is a significant number of aware positions who can hopefully be moved to active status, all three kinds of objectives are necessary, along with larger numbers of objectives and larger numbers of pieces of information.
>
> *Active goal:* To maintain the active positions at active status
> - Knowledge objective:
> - Knowledge objective:
> - Attitude objective:
> - Attitude objective:
> - Attitude objective:
> - Behavior objective:
> - Behavior objective:
> - Behavior objective:
> - Behavior objective:
> - Behavior objective:
> - Behavior objective:
>
> Rationale for active goal: Since a large number of active positions are indicated across the population, a goal suggesting knowledge, attitudes, and behaviors is appropriate. Since persons with active positions have solid knowledge and attitudes already, a larger number of behavior objectives is proper. Persons with active positions have established interest, knowledge, and opinions toward the organization, as well as the predisposition to act in significant ways. If the persons with active positions do not get a large amount of information on opinions and behaviors from the organization, they will get their information from other sources, such as the competitors, the media, their friends, and so on.

creation of goals and objectives should be. For the campaign professional and campaign strategist, this proposed model of multiple goals and supporting objectives targeting many and contrasting images, demographics, needs, psychographics, schema, knowledge, attitude, behaviors, and other knowledge indicates how detailed and thorough the planning process is for basic strategies. If done correctly, the extensive basic strategies framework for each population will clearly indicate the message strategies and the communication selections strategies to follow that are appropriate for each targeted population.

One final principle needs to be stressed here. Sometimes we get so overwhelmed with the details that we lose sight of the big picture. Basic strategies set the goals and objectives for each population. However, we as campaign planners cannot direct a particular goal and its respective objectives to deliver information directly to some persons out of a population and not the other members of a population. This is where the theories of selective perception and cognitive dissonance come into play again; remember that these principles recognize that a person will be inclined to pay attention to information that is consistent with their currently held lived experiences (selective perception) and, at times, pay attention to contrary information in order to sort out and even strengthen their opposing positions (cognitive dissonance).

What happens when all kinds of diverse information are communicated to a population in the course of a campaign is that, in principle, even though all the members of a population might be exposed to multiple messages, each individual in the population will be inclined to selectively pay attention to messages that are consistent with her/his own values and not be inclined to process those that are not. For sure, each person will be exposed to other demographic, psychographic, or organization-generated images and information targeting other positions and held images, and she/he might even pay attention to them, but that person might not be as inclined to process and assimilate and be persuaded by that information and those opposing messages.

Now here is some good news for the campaign professional. We set out to saturate each audience with multiple kinds of information in hopes that most everyone in each of our targeted populations will receive *and pay attention to and process and be persuaded by* at least some of the messages. We hope that sooner or later, in the course of a campaign, the population membership will be attracted to some of the messages and process them. What most certainly happens, though, is that overlap occurs: persons not even targeted will, nevertheless, be affected and persuaded by our messages. There is no way to plan for unintended targeted persons to be reached, but it certainly happens. So, some persons whose lived experiences and current images are not consistent with the organization's position will, nevertheless, hopefully be persuaded by some of the campaign's information.

Another overlap phenomenon occurs. Information directed to one population is often received by other, unintended populations. A campaign targets multiple populations throughout the course of a campaign, and information directed to certain audiences is often received and processed by other populations. This is good for the campaign and good for the campaign professional directing it.

How can you, as a campaign professional, know when overlap within the population and among several populations occurs? You do summative or evaluation research after the campaign is finished. You survey, interview, discuss the campaign with and research each population to measure how much information they were exposed to, what information they paid attention to, and where they got the information. The good news is that the campaign planner can document for the client or for their department manager that campaign messages reached not only the intended but even some unintended audience members who were nevertheless influenced by it.

Concluding this chapter are several figures that provide sample messages which have been analyzed and interpreted to uncover the basic strategies imbedded in them. Examining these messages allows the campaign strategist to see how basic strategies are operationalized into a message and further, how basic strategies can be similar and different depending on the kind of campaign. Figure 3.11 presents the basic strategies in a marketing campaign message for the Nissan pathfinder sport vehicle. Figure 3.12 contrasts to the Nissan *market-*

ing message presented in Figure 3.11 in that it presents an analysis of the basic strategies in an *advertising* message, also for the Nissan Pathfinder. Figure 3.13 is an analysis of a message from a *political* campaign waged by the Christian Coalition during the last national election. Figure 3.14 is also a sample message from a *political* campaign; this campaign message is taken from the Al Salvi campaign for the U.S. Senate also conducted during the last national election. And the final sample message, Figure 3.15, is from a social issue campaign that warns children of the dangers of fire.

IMPORTANT THINGS TO REMEMBER

- Basic strategies are goals and objectives.

- A goal is a desired change or effect in an audience, primarily in knowledge, attitude, behavior, or other desired image.

- Several objectives should support any goal. An objective is the number of pieces of and the kind of information communicated to achieve the respective goal.

- Selective perception is a theory that says that audiences tend to pay attention to messages that are consistent with their already-held beliefs.

- Cognitive dissonance is a theory that states, on the other hand, that persons will often pay attention to messages that contradict already-held beliefs, in an effort to sort out or reinforce their attitudes.

- Receiver-based strategies are efforts to match message content to the audience's various lived experiences in order to, first, get the audience's attention so that, second, the audience will process the message; these are mostly appeal goals.

- The Collapse Model of Corporate Image claims that an individual often possesses many, momentarily changing images or public positions toward an organization, political, or social issue. This means that messages are targeted to groups of images/public positions shared throughout an audience.

- Organization-based strategies are the goals and objectives that the organization wants the targeted audiences to hold; these are mostly direct change goals.

- Audiences who are interested in the organization or campaign should get more information and get knowledge, attitudes, behaviors, and other images as content.

- Less interested or uninterested audiences should get less textual copy and more visuals and creative designs and get primarily knowledge appeals.

- Appeal goals can relate to knowledge/attitudes/behaviors, demographics, needs, psychographics, schema, level of public position (active, aware, latent, nonpublic), or intensity of information processing and information seeking in the targeted population.

PATHFINDER

Demographics
Median Age: 34
 under 35 — 52%
 35-44 — 20%
 45-54 — 17%
 over 55 — 6%
Marital Status: Married — 64%
Median Household Income: $60,200
 under $35K — 16%
 $35K-$75K — 41%
 $75K-$100K — 13%
 over $100K+ — 15%
Sex: Male — 67%
Education: College Graduate+ — 55%
Career: Professional/Executive — 48%

Psychographics
Profile: Upscale couples seeking adventure/escape to the outdoors. Very career-oriented and successful, but want their vehicle to project image that they are also active, smart consumers. They come from the ranks of Accords, Legends, Maximas and performance/luxury sedans with correspondingly high expectations from their vehicles.

Interests
Skiing, hiking, water sports, mountain biking, etc.

Vehicle Preferences
Reliability, well-made vehicle, value for money, manufacturer's reputation, 4-wheel drive availability, fun to drive, styling, riding comfort.

Positioning Statement
The Nissan® Pathfinder® is the rugged on-road/off-road sport-utility vehicle, while providing uncompromised comfort and style.

Tonality
Parallel NMC's overall marketing strategy by stressing quality beyond expectations. Focused on rugged/tough with sedan-like handling, exceptional comfort and amenities. Sophisticated, intelligent tone best communicates to these educated buyers.

Primary Competitors
Toyota 4-Runner
Ford Explorer
Jeep Grand Cherokee
Honda Passport
Isuzu Rodeo
Chevy S-10 Blazer

Marketing
Promotions/regional tie-in merchandising will emphasize sponsorship of the forthcoming Warren Miller Ski Film Tour.

669915

Copyright Nissan (1997). Nissan, Pathfinder, and the Nissan Pathfinder logos are registered trademarks of Nissan. Reprinted with permission.

Figure 3.11
Identifying Goals and Objectives in Sample Messages in Commercial Campaigns: A Case Study of Marketing

Campaign situation:

- Organizational source of message: Nissan
- Kind of campaign: marketing
- Target populations: Nissan dealers, auto salespersons, potential customers
- Message: two fact sheets about Nissan Pathfinder sport utility vehicle included in marketing press kit given to dealerships by Nissan

Direct change goals and objectives:

- Knowledge goal: that dealers and salespersons know demographic profile of potential customers

    Knowledge objective: five pieces of information on age
    Knowledge objective: one piece of information on marital status
    Knowledge objective: five pieces of information on household level of income
    Knowledge objective: one piece of information on sex
    Knowledge objective: one piece of information on career

- Knowledge goal: that dealers and salespersons know psychographic profile of potential customers

    Attitude objective: twelve pieces of information on leisure preferences
    Attitude objective: four points of information on hobbies and leisure practices
    Attitude objective: eight pieces of information on qualities of vehicle preferences

- Knowledge/attitude goal: that Pathfinder is best sport vehicle on market

    Knowledge objective: four pieces of information on positioning in the market
    Behavior objective: eight pieces of information on tonality or on how the   salesperson should discuss vehicle
    Knowledge objective: six pieces of information on competition
    Knowledge objective: two pieces of information on promotion sponsorship

PATHFINDER

Product Highlights

Pathfinder XE-V6 4x2
The versatile XE-V6 4x2 includes as standard:
3.0-liter SOHC V6 engine
Sequential multi-point fuel injection
Power vented front disc/rear drum brakes
Rear-wheel Anti-lock Braking System (ABS)
Double wishbone front suspension w/stabilizer bar
5-link coil spring rear suspension w/stabilizer bar
P235/75R15 mud-and-snow steel-belted radials
Center high-mount stop lamp (CHMSL)
Opening glass hatch with intermittent rear wiper
Split fold-down rear seats with adjustable head restraints
Reclining rear seatbacks
Center console CD or cellular phone compartment
High-output 130 watt AM/FM stereo audio system with
    8 speakers and diversity antenna, w/auto-reverse casssette
Optional Sport Package

Pathfinder XE-V6 4x4
In addition to or in place of equipment on the XE-V6 4x2,
    the rugged, economical XE-V6 4x4 includes:
4-wheel drive
Optional Sport Package w/limited-slip rear differential
Integrated fender flare/splash guards
Rear heater ducts

Pathfinder SE-V6 4x4
In addition to or in place of equipment on the XE-V6 4x4,
    the sportiest Pathfinder, the SE-V6 4x4 includes:
Dual heated power mirrors
Fog lamps
Step rails
Integrated fender flares/mud guards
Luggage rack
Outside spare tire carrier w/cover
Privacy glass: rear door, quarter windows and liftgate
7JJx15 3-spoke argent alloy wheels with 31x10.5R15 mud-and-
    snow steel-belted radials
Rear wind deflector
Chrome grille, front/rear bumpers, mirrors and windshield
    moldings
Multi-adjustable driver's seat with 3-position lumbar support
Rear-seat fold-down side armrests
Cloth seat trim
Optional leather trim w/heated front seats
Optional CFC-free air conditioning
Flip-up/removable glass sunroof
Power windows
Power door locks
Keyless remote entry with vehicle security system
Cruise control with steering wheel mounted controls
Illuminated visor vanity mirrors
Cargo net
Optional Off-Road Package
Optional Leather Trim Package

Pathfinder LE-V6 4x2
Includes as standard vs. the XE-V6:
4-speed automatic overdrive transmission
Power heated outside mirrors
Fog lamps
Running boards
Luggage rack
Privacy glass: rear door, quarter windows and liftgate
6JJx15 six-spoke polished alloy wheels with 235/75R15
    mud- and-snow tires
Chrome grille
Chrome upper bumpers
Unique badging and graphics
Leather trim and seating surfaces
CFC-free air conditioning
Flip-up removable glass sunroof
Power windows/locks
Remote keyless entry with vehicle security system
Cruise control with steering wheel mounted controls
Dual-illuminated visor vanity mirrors
CD player

Pathfinder LE-V6 4x4
In addition to or in place of equipment on the LE-V6 4x2,
    the LE-V6 4x4 includes:
Power 4-wheel disc brakes
Limited-slip rear differential
Leather seating surfaces w/heated front seats
Rear heater ducts

Copyright Nissan (1997). Nissan, Pathfinder, and the Nissan Pathfinder logos are registered trademarks of Nissan. Reprinted with permission.

Knowledge goal: product highlights on various Pathfinder vehicles

>Knowledge objective: fifteen pieces of information on XE-V6 4X2
>Knowledge objective: fifteen pieces of information on XE-V6 4X4
>Knowledge objective: twenty-five pieces of information on SE-V6 4X4
>Knowledge objective: nineteen pieces of information on LE-V6 4X2
>Knowledge objective: four pieces of information on LE-V6 4X4

Both fact sheets make up the marketing message targeted at two primary populations: dealers and salespersons of Nissan Pathfinder sport vehicles. These are *direct change* knowledge goals and objectives rather than *appeal* goals and objectives because the fact sheets are information, or pieces of information, delivered to the dealers and salespersons from the Nissan organization. Although demographics, psychographics, and needs are presented on the fact sheet, this information is for the benefit of dealers and salespersons to use in their attempted sales rather than as a direct influence on the potential customers.

This two-part message of two fact sheets contains mostly organization-based images as pieces of information about the product. Again, audience-centered images are presented but primarily as information for the salespersons to use on the potential customers population.

These fact sheets are an excellent example of a message targeting active populations: dealers and salespersons. The numerous pieces of information and few visuals demonstrate a message targeting populations with mostly active public positions and with high information seeking and information processing public positions, not surprising for dealers and salespersons trying to sell automobiles.

And finally, this message illustrates that multiple images—knowledge, attitudes, and behaviors about and toward the Pathfinder—are suggested to these two populations, in this case, exclusively positive images about the Nissan product.

Copyright Nissan (1997). Nissan, Pathfinder, and Nissan Pathfinder logos are registered trademarks of Nissan. Reprinted with permission.

Basic Strategies   125

Figure 3.12
Identifying Goals and Objectives in Sample Messages in Commercial Campaigns: A Case Study of Advertising

Campaign situation:

- Organizational source of message: Nissan
- Kind of campaign: advertising
- Target population: potential customers
- Message: two pages from a brochure on Nissan Pathfinder given out to potential customers at dealerships

Direct change goals and objectives:

- Knowledge goal: that vehicle can travel over rough terrain

    Knowledge objective: one visual of car parked in mountain
    Knowledge objective: one visual of car not parked on a road

- Attitude/behavior goal: that vehicle is fun to drive because it can travel over any kind of rough terrain

    Knowledge objective: one visual of car parked on rough terrain
    Knowledge/attitude objective: one visual of pristine, untouched, untraveled setting surrounding the vehicle
    Attitude objective: one piece of information that "tread lightly" is a worthwhile environmental program
    Behavior objective: one piece of information that drivers should support this environmental program through actions

Appeal goals and objectives:

- Demographic appeal goal:

    Knowledge objective: upper socioeconomic level, in order to afford this car
    Knowledge objective: relatively young or persons who see themselves as youthful

- Psychographic appeal goal:

    Knowledge/attitude objective: VALS of integrated, or persons who are both inner-directed and outer-directed
    Attitude objective: persons who like rugged outdoors and nature
    Behavior objective: persons who will fight to protect nature and environment

Certain settings – where man's imprint is barely evident – DEEPEN OUR RESPECT

for what is natural and untamed. They are places that we seek out as much FOR THEIR SOLITUDE

as for their beauty. And, certainly, the Pathfinder is designed to take you there.

More important, IN THESE SURROUNDINGS, *we're reminded of our responsibility*

to future generations. That is, to help ensure they will be able to share our wonder and appreciation. In

that spirit, let's recall the thinking behind the "TREAD LIGHTLY!" *program: the most welcome guests*

are those who leave behind NO TRACE OF THEIR STAY.

Copyright Nissan (1997). Nissan, Pathfinder, and Nissan Pathfinder logos are registered trademarks of Nissan. Reprinted with permission.

- Needs appeal goal:

    Behavior objective: for drivers who like to explore nature
    Attitude objective: to enhance self-esteem and self-actualization through protecting the environment

- Grunig appeal goal:

    Knowledge objective: to appeal to latent public position through creative visuals and little copy
    Knowledge objective: to appeal to aware public position through creative visuals and little copy

- Schema appeal goal:

    Behavior objective: to appeal to event schema, to protect the environment

These are mostly *appeal* goals and objectives rather than *direct change* goals and objectives because the message is targeting consumers by appealing to them to purchase the product. Taken together, the appeal goals attempt to match the demographics, psychographics, needs, latent and aware public positions, and schema of the potential customer population.

In contrast to the fact sheets message to dealers, that contained mostly organization-based images, this message contains primarily audience-centered images. Also, in contrast to the Nissan organization fact sheet message which contained numerous pieces of information appropriate for active public positions, this message's large and creative visuals and few pieces of information reveal that the targeted audience is considered latent or aware by the organization. This message also suggests that relatively fewer images are necessary for the consumers.

128   Campaign Strategies and Message Design

'96 Christian Coalition
VOTER GUIDE

PRESIDENTIAL
Election

Bill Clinton (D)	ISSUES	Bob Dole (R)
Opposes	Balanced Budget Amendment	Supports
Opposes	15% Federal Income Tax Cut	Supports
Opposes	Banning Partial Birth Abortion	Supports
Supports	Taxpayer Funding of Abortion	Opposes
Opposes	Voluntary School Prayer Amendment	Supports
Opposes	Public and Private School Choice	Supports
Supports	Homosexuals in the Military	Opposes
Opposes	Term Limits for Congress	Supports

ILLINOIS
U.S. Senate

Dick Durbin (D)	ISSUES	Al Salvi (R)
Opposes	Balanced Budget Amendment	Supports
Supports	Raising Federal Income Taxes	Opposes
Opposes	Banning Partial Birth Abortion	Supports
Opposes	Voluntary Prayer in Public Schools	Supports
Supports	Homosexuals in the Military	Opposes
Opposes	Term Limits for Congress	Supports

★   **Vote on November 5**   ★

Reprinted with permission, Christian Coalition.

Basic Strategies 129

Figure 3.13
Identifying Goals and Objectives in Sample Messages in Political Campaigns

Campaign situation:

- Organizational source of message: Christian Coalition
- Kind of campaign: primarily political (although could also be argued to be a social-issue campaign)
- Target populations: voters in 101st district in Illinois, voters in 103rd district in Illinois, and persons who attend church in these districts
- Message: two pages from a brochure/fact sheet handed out in front of churches in Bloomington, Illinois, weeks before national election, November 1996

Direct change goals and objectives:

- Knowledge goal: that voters know persons running for elected offices

    Knowledge objective: two pieces of information on persons running for office
    Knowledge objective: eight pieces of information on voting record on selected issues

- Knowledge goal: that voters know persons running for U.S. Senate

    Knowledge objective: two pieces of information on persons running for office
    Knowledge objective: seven pieces of information on voting record on selected issues
    Knowledge objective: seven pieces of information naming the issues

- Knowledge goal: that voters know persons running for the House in the 101st District

    Knowledge objective: two pieces of information on persons running for office
    Knowledge objective: seven pieces of information on voting record on selected issues
    Knowledge objective: seven pieces of information naming the issues

- Knowledge goal: that voters know persons running for the House in the 103rd District

    Knowledge objective: two pieces of information on persons running for office
    Knowledge objective: seven pieces of information on voting record on selected issues
    Knowledge objective: seven pieces of information naming the issues

- Knowledge goal: that voters will know about The Parental Rights Amendment

    Knowledge objective: six pieces of information about tenets of The Parental Rights Amendment

IL House of Representatives - 101st Dist.

	Jerry (R) Stocks	Julie (D) Curry
Abortion on Demand	Opposes	Supports
Taxpayer Funding of Abortion	Opposes	Supports
Special Rights for Homosexuals	Opposes	No Response
Parental Choice in Education (Vouchers)	Supports	Opposes
Parental Rights Amendment[1]	Supports	No Response
Expansion of Gambling	Opposes	No Response
Injecting Government Services Into Daycare[2]	Opposes	Supports

IL House of Representatives - 103rd Dist.

	Rich (R) Winkel, Jr.	Naomi (D) Jakobsson
Abortion on Demand	Opposes	Supports
Taxpayer Funding of Abortion	Opposes*	Supports
Special Rights for Homosexuals	Opposes	No Response
Parental Choice in Education (Vouchers)	Supports	Opposes
Parental Rights Amendment[1]	Supports	Undecided
Expansion of Gambling	Opposes	Opposes
Injecting Government Services Into Daycare[2]	Opposes	Undecided

* Candidate "opposes" except in cases of rape, incest, or to save the life of the mother.

[1] The Parental Rights Amendment reads: "The right of parents to direct the upbringing of their children shall not be infringed. The General Assembly may provide by law for the enforcement of this section. Nothing in this section shall be construed to permit the abuse or neglect of children."

[2] A bill was introduced last year that proposed setting up a new government program for the purpose of injecting state-defined educational, health, nutritional, and social services into ALL daycare centers. Although the program was voluntary, the Illinois Christian Coalition opposed this effort because it allowed the state to take over the roles and responsibilities of parents.

Reprinted with permission, Christian Coalition.

- Knowledge goal: the voters will know about daycare center bill introduced last year

  Knowledge objective: six pieces of information on what the daycare center bill proposed
  Knowledge objective: three pieces of information on why the Christian Coalition opposed the bill

Appeal goals and objectives:

- Demographic appeal goal:

  Knowledge objective: persons who are old enough to vote
  Knowledge objective: persons who reside in the 101st and 103rd districts, Illinois
  Knowledge objective: persons who attend church in these districts
  Knowledge objective: persons who are mostly pro-life

- Psychographic appeal goal:

  Behavior objective: outer-driven persons who will fight to support life of unborn fetus
  Attitude objective: inner-driven persons who see pro-life as personal choice of fetus
  Attitude objective: social activists who see abortion as murder
  Attitude objective: persons who believe and uphold other, related tenets of the conservative right, such as balanced budget, voluntary school prayer, no homosexuals in the military, parental rights
  Attitude objective: persons who see themselves as religious, in particular, in holding to issue of the conservative right

- Need appeal goal:

  Attitude objective: six pieces of information that support the physical need of saving the life of the fetus
  Attitude objective: four pieces of information that support the social need that homosexuality is unnatural and against God's word
  Attitude objective: four pieces of information that support the safety need of protecting heterosexuals from homosexuality activity
  Attitude/behavior objective: four pieces of information on social need for balancing national budget and federal income tax cut
  Attitude objective: six pieces of information on safety need that parents have the right to protect their children in daycare centers and in lack of school prayer
  Attitude objective: two pieces of information on social need that gambling hurts society at large

- Schema appeal goal:

  Attitude objective: twelve pieces of information on event schema that parents have the right to decide behaviors in school and in daycare centers

Behavior objective: all pieces of information support role schema that elected offi cials should vote according to voting constituencies in daycare centers

Attitude objective: five pieces of information that support the person schema that those against God's law should be opposed

This political message—two pages taken from a brochure handout—contains direct change goals and supporting objectives and appeal goals and supporting objectives. As such, the suggested images are both organization-centered and audience-centered. The image of the organization is very implicit, almost hidden, but extremely strong. Beneath the very "objective-like" listing of issues and corresponding voting records is an enormous implicit and suggested corporate image that presents the major tenets and images of this conservative right organization. The Christian Coalition can do this and be subtle, since their positions on these major social and personal issues are well-known within the conservative right and without, in the liberal left positions.

The pieces of information are presented as knowledge, but implicit in all of these "listed" issues is the moral stamp of the Christian Coalition that suggests that abortion, gambling, state-supported daycare centers, and homosexual rights are wrong, and a balanced federal budget, a federal tax cut, term limits for Congress, prayer in schools, and parental rights are correct and make good policy. Also revealed in this message is that the Christian Coalition considers its targeted populations to be active. The multiplicity of pieces of information and scarcity of visuals suggest the organization's assumption that the targeted populations possess knowledge, attitudes, and behaviors and have, therefore, mostly active positions and that they are interested in their messages and are high on information processing and information seeking.

Figure 3.14
Identifying Goals and Objectives in Sample Messages in Political Campaigns

Campaign Situation:

- Organizational source of message: citizens for Al Salvi
- Kind of campaign: political
- Target population: voters in Illinois
- Message: yard sign stuck in residents' yards

Direct change goals and objectives:

- Knowledge goal: that Salvi is running for political office

    Knowledge objective: one visual that Salvi is a Republican
    Knowledge objective: one piece of information that Salvi is running for U.S. Senate

This political message is very limited in basic strategies. One one direct change—a knowledge goal—is contained in it. No appeal goals or other images are present. The message, with its primary visual components and limited pieces of information, is directed at latent and nonpublic positions across the targeted population.

Reprinted with permission, Al Salvi.

TM & © 1997 Marvel Characters Inc. All rights reserved. Reprinted with permission.

Figure 3.15
Identifying Goals and Objectives in a Sample Message for a Social Issue Campaign

Campaign situation:

- Organizational source of message: Marvel Entertainment Group, Inc.
- Kind of campaign: social issue
- Target populations: parents, grammar school children, community residents
- Message: two pages taken from a comic book passed out in schools by local fire departments

Direct change goals and objectives:

- Knowledge goal: that fire can hurt you

    Behavior objective: visual showing not to touch gasoline can
    Knowledge objective: visual that fire can destroy your house
    Attitude objective: comic book hero "Daredevil" will save children from fire
    Knowledge objective: that fire can spread quickly

- Attitude goal: that fire is bad

    Attitude objective: fire is a danger to avoid
    Attitude objective: Daredevil is a good hero who protects children from fire
    Attitude objective: Vapora is an evil fire figure who destroys through fire
    Attitude objective: mixing fire and gasoline is dangerous and can start fire
    Attitude objective: a fire can ruin your house and your belongings, leading to tears

- Behavior goal: be careful to avoid fire

    Behavior objective: do not mix gasoline and rags
    Behavior objective: run out of your house if it is on fire

Appeal goals and objectives:

- Demographic appeal goal:

    Attitude objective: children are especially in danger if there is a fire

- Need appeal goal:

    Attitude objective: you can lose your life in a fire

- Psychographic appeal goal:

    Behavior objective: do not be adventurous and try to play with fire
    Behavior objective: be cooperative when an adult helps you get out of a fire

TM & © 1997 Marvel Characters Inc. All rights reserved. Reprinted with permission.

- Schema appeal goal:

    Behavior objective: appeal to event schema in that when there is a fire, get out of building immediately
    Attitude objective: appeal to role schema in that there are good people and bad people; Vapora is dangerous fire, and Daredevil is a hero who saves children from fire

This social issue message is directly aimed at children, with parents and community residents as less relevant audiences. As such, this message demonstrates some unique twists on concepts of goals and objectives. The direct change goals are simple and direct: fire is dangerous. Appeal goals are also fewer but very direct.

All these message images are audience-centered, all with reason of a child's understanding. Fire is the prominent image, captured in the figure of Vapora. The comic book art is very attention-getting for a child reader, indicating the assumption that the child audience has latent and nonpublic positions toward fire.

4

Message Strategies

Once your basic strategies are conceptualized and written, you have already begun your messages. The goals and objectives conceptualized as basic strategies have laid the foundation and framework for the messages. The objectives that name the number and the kinds of information also indicate the amount of text and the nature of the information that should be contained in the campaign's messages. The campaign strategist should consider the messages as, actually, the manifestation of the basic strategies and, in particular, the objectives.

The objectives are transformed directly into the messages. Messages are the text material and the photos, graphic designs, or sound material that appear in the communication selections. That is, the words of a newspaper article written from a press release are the message while the newspaper itself serves as the communication selection. In another example, in an advertisement paid for by an organization that is also placed in a newspaper, the words and visuals in the advertisement are the message, but the newspaper is not the message nor even part of the message; it serves only as the channel of communication. Words and visuals on a billboard are a message even though the billboard itself is not, technically, a message; again, the billboard is the communication channel and the communication selection.

The campaign professional has to be very clear on the difference between messages and communication selections. Messages are words and visuals, but the source or channel of the message (newspaper, billboard, magazine, radio, television, campaign button, speech, protest demonstrations) is not the message or even part of the message. The communication selection is separate from the message. It contains its own guidelines and principles and its own respective strategies, which will be discussed in the next chapter.

Do you see my point here? Be careful in defining a message and a communication selection. When we refer to messages, we are only considering the words and the visuals contained in a message, not the channel that the words and visuals are contained in. This chapter will define messages as only words and visuals and, as such, will present only those strategies that are suitable for choosing the most appropriate messages to match each of the targeted audience's lived experiences and to deliver in the most efficient way the images desired by the organization in each of its targeted audiences.

Aside from this rather precise definition of messages, I want you to consider how broad the concept of messages can be, especially relative to campaign communication. Organizations have become very creative today in getting their product or their cause before the public's eyes in sometimes very subtle and very unconscious ways, even though they are strategic messages placed intentionally by the organization. It has been a common practice in recent years for corporations to put their names on football bowl games, professional golf tournaments, tennis matches, and professional races and the race cars. Names of products appear on fences behind baseball games or tennis matches.

More recently, however, more subtle ways to present products to the public have been designed. Major deals are struck between organizations and movie productions to use their products in a movie, for example, the automobiles driven in them, the soft drinks consumed in them, and even the candy used to lure an extraterrestrial, such as Reeses Pieces in the movie *E.T.* All of these efforts by organizations are messages (and communication selections), as surely as if their design department sat down and designed an original and specialized message to be placed through media or personal channels.

Another dimension to messages that this chapter will examine is that in a campaign situation, each population receives its own, original and specialized messages. When conceptualizing and executing the design of messages for a campaign, you want to retain the figure of each population receiving its own, uniquely designed, messages. Just as the basic strategies were conceptualized separately for each population, so also are the messages designed specific to each population.

This chapter, then, will first define and explain words as message components and visuals as message components. Next, strategies for selecting the appropriate words and appropriate visuals for each population will be detailed. And finally, some sample messages will be examined to demonstrate how basic strategies inform the proper messages to match the unique lived experiences of each population.

WORDS AS MESSAGE COMPONENTS

Messages are defined through two components. Messages are either the words or the visualization factors. Parts of messages that are words include both written words and spoken words, depending on whether the communication channel is a print or broadcast or personal communication selection. Parts of messages that are visualization factors are, simply put, all the unspoken dimensions of a message that are not the words, such as the size of the message, or the length of time a message takes, any colors used, any celebrities, the font of the print, the kind of paper, any sound effects, any background music.

Most messages contain both components in a singular message. However, a message can be primarily words, or a message can be only visuals. Given the constraints of the communication selection used to contain the message, a selection or channel such as a newspaper article or a speech might rely almost exclusively on words as the message, with very limited visualization factors at play. However, it is possible, as well, for a message to have only visualization factors—for example, a popular kind of advertisement message found today, the Nike television commercials that feature young people playing sports and then the shot of the Nike "swish" logo at the end or the print messages of just one Nike shoe. [1] Think of words and visuals as your *tools for creating and designing messages*. They are the design components that link the objectives (number of pieces of and kind of information) to the eventual message contained in the communication selection.

Copy Points

What I want to turn to, now, is a closer definition of how words are used in messages. I want to begin by defining in greater detail the words component of messages. Following Simmons (1990), I divide messages into two broad classifications, copy points and copy platform.

Quantifying Copy Points

A copy point is one piece of information. It does not necessarily correspond to a sentence although in some message situations, a sentence contains one copy point. Nonetheless, one sentence taken from a message can contain several copy points. For example, a sentence such as, "The hiking boots are made of all leather uppers, with composition soles and steel inserts for durability and long wear," contains three copy points that correspond to the three pieces of information of leather, soles, and inserts.

In terms of message definitions one of the first considerations of the campaign strategist is to consider that a copy point is only one piece of information, which can be a word, a phrase, or a sentence. A copy point directly corresponds to the objectives that were named as part of the basic strategies. That is, a basic strategy objective that names, for example, "fifteen pieces of information about the history of the organization," has, in essence, named fifteen copy points that are actually the fifteen pieces of history about the company. The process of choosing copy points to be used in the messages is simply to look at the number of

---

[1] Reprinted with permission, Nike, Inc.

pieces of information indicated in the objectives and to look at the subject area from which the pieces of information are taken.

In one respect, converting objectives into messages is a "numbers game." If you look at all the goals and, especially, all the supporting objectives you have planned for one population only, you have a rough idea of how many copy points will need to be contained in your messages that go out to that population in the course of one campaign. Let's work a hypothetical campaign situation. Say you have one targeted population for which you have eleven goals—an image; two Grunig; three direct change which are one knowledge and two attitude; five appeal that are one demographic, one need, two psychographic, and one schema. Totaling up all the pieces of information contained in all the objectives gives you a grand total of 1,400 pieces of information. You know that you have allowed for 1,400 pieces of information—*1,400 copy points*—to be communicated to this population over the course of several months of the campaign.

Do not let the rigidity of this formula turn you off. In the actual writing of the copy points and in the adaptation of selected copy points to particular messages, some of the copy points will not be used. And, for sure, some copy points will most appropriately be repeated across several messages because of their importance. In the listing of the hundreds of copy points, the campaign strategist will need to prioritize the copy points so that there is a cataloging of which points are most important and must be communicated and those that could be omitted if no room nor time allows their inclusion in any of the messages. What the recording of number of pieces of information offers the campaign strategist is a rough idea of how much information is appropriate to be adapted to the message formats.

I hope that my "numerical" model of goals and objectives and the consequent copy points offers a more concrete monitoring of message content and a more precise approximation of how many copy points are needed for each population. This process of conceptualizing message content, first, as respective copy points at the very least provides a framework for a more thorough dispersal of information to targeted populations. And it bears repeating that knowing you have allowed for 1,400 copy points to be communicated to a population over several months does not mean you have to use every copy point once. When it comes down to the actual message designs, some copy points will not be necessary, and many more will probably be used repeatedly.

This initial, conceptualization process is not designed to be a mathematical exercise in that the exact number of objectives correspond directly to how many copy points must be written into all the population's messages. But the preliminary exercise of creating objectives as numbers of pieces of information offers a very thorough and in-depth *inventory* of all the precise kinds of information that support the goals, the changes desired in the populations. At the very least, the campaign strategist can look to the objectives as sources of the amount of and the kind of information that should be communicated to a particular population in order to work toward a saturation of the population with appeals to most lived experiences and with information considered important to know by the organization.

Considerations of the Collapse Model

If this process of using the basic strategies objectives to "write" the copy points seems lengthy or unnecessary, remember the Collapse Model (Moffitt, 1994a, 1994b; Williams & Moffitt, 1997) that this book is based on. If we accept that all the members of a population have multiple and changing images and public positions within them personally, then it makes sense that multiple copy points targeting the various positive, negative, or indifferent images will need to be communicated to the population membership to insure a more thorough saturation of the population with the organization's messages. For a campaign to be successful you need to communicate, as best you can, to all the dominant images, needs, knowledge/attitude/behaviors, psychographics, or appeals present across an audience's members. And do not forget, either, that in addition to targeting the audience's lived experiences, the strategist will need to communicate the organization's positions and desired images to the same audience. This necessitates *a lot of copy points.*

Creating an Inventory of Copy Points

I want to give you some good news now about how simple it is to begin to operationalize your message designs. In this stage of the campaign, you need only provide the copy points that should or could be used in the messages. The campaign manager compiles a detailed prioritized listing of all the actual copy points that could be used in the campaign and does not begin, yet, to worry about placing them in message formats. If we return to our example above, the campaign strategist creates an inventory of the 1,400 copy points that would be available to be used in the messages. *You are not designing message formats yet—only listing the available copy points.* Do not anticipate and do not worry in this stage about creating the actual message formats yet.

The intention here is to break the initial considerations of design of message formats into two steps. First, an inventory or record of all the available copy points is created. *Then,* in the second step, the campaign strategists take what copy points they want to put in each selected message format. I firmly believe that this step in creating campaign message formats has for too long been collapsed into one operation. What usually happens in campaign communication today is that the campaign planner sits down to create messages and decides the copy points to use at the same time as she/he chooses the communication selections.

This method does a disservice to both procedures. The choice of what copy points to use as pieces of information is crucial. But, the actual placement of copy points (and visualization factors) within the actual communication selection format is also critical. These two decisions deserve separate and careful consideration. Today's campaign professional must consider message format design as a two-step process: decisions on all the available copy points (and appropriate visuals) and decisions on how to format the finished messages within the parameters of the chosen communication selection.

When it comes to deciding the copy points, then, your only responsibility at this point is to provide a cataloging of all the available copy points to draw from in the next step of putting together the message components relative to the communication selections. Having done this at the outset of the message strategies does not mean you never return to this task again. In truth, you will, during the course of the actual campaign, periodically examine and reexamine your communication selections and copy points. The campaign strategist should after the campaign is launched and running a period of weeks, want to do some interim research to measure the reception of the messages so far.

I have a colleague who planned and managed a recycling campaign for the university student body, faculty, and staff. After some beginning weeks of the campaign he ran some focus groups to get an assessment of the effect of the messages to that point. The focus groups with the students revealed that the messages were perceived as rather simplistic, with little information in them. He realized that the messages that were being aimed at latent students should really be aimed at active students. As a result, more detailed and informational posters and fliers were created. The ongoing, periodic research conducted during the course of this campaign was a critical tool for fine-tuning the copy points and messages and for assurances that the messages were received as they were intended.

Copy Platform

I turn now to another kind of message that deals with words. The copy platform is a slogan—word or phrase or even sentence—that is found on all a campaign's messages. It is a slogan or phrase that serves as an identifying tactic for the campaign. The Nike athletic shoe campaign's well-known copy platform is "Just Do It." Some copy platforms have been maintained by corporations for years: Zenith's "The quality goes in before the name goes on"; Lay's potato chips' "Bet you can't eat just one." Some platforms are very short: Ivory soap's "It floats"; or Metropolitan Life Insurance's "Get Met. It Pays." or Cellular One's "The Wireless Phone Company." The Atlanta Braves call themselves "America's Team." [2]

In addition to the three kinds of commercial campaigns, political and social issue campaigns almost always have copy platforms as well. The Armed Services are technically a social agency that has its respective copy platforms. The Army's is "Be all that you can be," and the Marines' is "We're looking for a few good men."

Copy platforms are not usually changed from campaign to campaign. Once a corporation or politician or social agency has identified and used a copy platform with its product or service, its candidate, or its social cause in one cam-

---

[2] All of the above slogans are reprinted with the permissions of Nike, Inc., Zenith Electronics Corporation, Frito-Lay, Metropolitan Life Insurance, Cellular One, and the Atlanta Braves, respectively.

paign, it will want to use it for several, if not all, of its campaigns. This is a solid and reliable way to help the audience to remember your organization and your product.

In some very ingenious cases some companies have used more than one copy platform for a campaign's messages. The organization might have a very well-known copy platform that is established in the audiences' minds but then create another copy platform, a subslogan, that fits another campaign run by the company, usually for one product. This use of two copy platforms is often employed for those companies that support the Olympics. Xerox, for example, has an established copy platform of "The Document Company", but for the 1998 Olympics in Nagano, Japan, for campaign messages Xerox added "Official Sponsor of the XVIII Olympic Winter Games." [3]

A good copy platform is a phrase that relates to the organization's purpose and/or to the product. In some cases the copy platform will relate directly to the particular campaign being waged. If you are conceptualizing a copy platform for use in a campaign, think of a general theme that captures the image of the organization you are presenting or the image of the organization's product. A commercial campaign creates a copy platform consistent with the product or service sold or with the organization as a whole. A political campaign creates a copy platform that captures the identity of the candidate and even implies what the candidate stands for. A social agency wants to develop a copy platform that suggests the social cause that the agency is working toward.

A final dimension of a copy platform ties into the logo of the organization. Even though the logo, or graphic design, of an organization is a visualization factor, it is effective when the copy platform is consistent with the logo. This creates a kind of "double whammy," whereby the audiences receive a written or spoken copy platform that supports or is supported by a visual image. The campaign strategist must appreciate the power of a copy platform and a logo to succinctly and compactly call up in people's minds their organization. The copy platform (and logo) are powerful memory tools to use on targeted audiences. A good copy platform can identify an organization in only one or two words. The Nike copy platform is so renowned in the general public's eyes that only hearing or seeing the phrase "Just Do It," or the logo of the swish, for most persons, recalls the Nike corporation to them.

Within all of campaign communication, the copy platform is one of the most powerful message tools. It can provide a bit of familiarity to unknowledgeable or unreceptive audiences. A well-known, catchy, and clever copy platform can influence persons to think positively about the organization's product, the candidate, or the social issue contained in the messages. Additionally, the cleverness of a copy platform not only catches people's attention with its familiarity, but it encourages the audience *to process the messages* that are associated with the slogan. A good copy platform can catch people's attention and also lead to information processing or persuasion (See Figure 4.1).

---

[3] Reprinted with permission of Xerox.

146 Campaign Strategies and Message Design

Figure 4.1
Samples of Copy Platform (slogan) and Subcopy Platform (subslogan)

The Nissan copy platform on the left is the long-standing copy platform found on most messages of Nissan products: It's time to expect more from a car.

The Xerox long-standing copy platform is: The Document Company. The subcopy platform for the Xerox Olympics campaign is: Official Sponsor of the XVIII Olympic Winter Games.

VISUALIZATION FACTORS AS MESSAGE COMPONENTS

Visualization factors are the other component of messages. These are all the other features of a message outside of any words contained in the message. Visualization factors include all the physical and/or auditory properties of a message, whether communicated on broadcast or print media or through personal communication. Just as conceptualizing the words components of your messages begins with an inventory of all the available copy points, so also are the visualization factor components conceived first as a comprehensive list. That is, all the possible visualization factors that would be appropriate for each and every targeted population are cataloged for possible use in the respective population's messages. And again, as with the copy points, perhaps not every visualization factor will get into the eventual campaign's messages, but in this initial step, decisions on all the available and appropriate visualizations factors—for print and broadcast and personal channels—are listed for consideration for each population, separately. Do not at this point of listing visualization factors be concerned about how to design them into the message formats. The design of the message formats comes after the inventory is completed.

I want to stress also with the visualization components that the concept of visual messages needs to be broadened to include not only the obvious and accepted visualization factors but other perhaps more subtle and unexpected visuals available to campaign strategists today. Let us turn now to the definitions of the various kinds of visualization factors. It is important to appreciate first what visuals are available before you can choose and strategize the correct visuals for each of your populations.

Visualization Factors for Print Media

In order to consider what print media visualization factors are available for your campaign, you must first consider the logistical constraints of the print media. Even though I have stressed throughout that you must divorce the design of message content from the selection of communication selections, you need to, in a general way, acknowledge the parameters of print media and how they constrain the visualization components put into them.

To begin, consider that typical print communication selections are newspaper articles written from press releases, paid-for newspaper messages, magazines, brochures, fact sheets, newsletters, annual reports, letters, billboards, e-mail, internet pages. I state the obvious here, but it is important to remember that inherent characteristics of print media are that they are "flat" media, fixed messages that allow the receiver to search the message format usually at her/his leisure, and almost exclusively without any moving parts to distract or change focus of the eyes. In other words, generally speaking, print media are regulated and processed actively and intentionally by the receiver since the printed text is fixed and unmoving. On the other hand, broadcast media, as we all know, are moving, full of sound and color and multiple shots, which necessitates that the receiver keep up with the message, in a sense be at the mercy of the message, in order to process it.

As is done in identifying possible copy points, the campaign strategist lists all the appropriate visualization factors that would be appropriate *for each population*. This comprehensive listing of every visual which is proper and fitting to use in any campaign message targeted to the respective population allows the campaign strategist to pick and choose from this listing any visual(s) for any message(s). Notice that the unique characteristics and qualities of each of these visual message options are obvious, but stating the obvious about each one forces the campaign strategist to consider the diverse and multiple visual options available for designing message formats.

The dimensions of the message are one of your first decisions on your visuals. Think of whether you want to place messages in print media that take up the entire page or half a page or a quarter of a page, such as considerations of paid-for newspaper or magazine messages. Of course, money is a consideration here, but, as much as you can, make decisions about the appropriate sizes to draw sufficient attention to the campaign messages. Bigger does not always mean better or more successful communication. A full-page message with inappropriate appeal content for the audience or with ineffective organizational information is ineffective, no matter what the size. A smaller message with good audience appeal and/or with relevant organization images can be just as or even more persuasive to the targeted population.

For some channels size is a given, such as annual reports, Web pages, letters, or fact sheets. Interestingly, though, even these print media can be changed in size for a persuasive effect. Companies are becoming very creative in their annual reports or fold-out fact sheets cut to interesting shapes or sizes.

Blank space as a visualization factor is another decision related to size or dimension of messages. You have the choice to use a lot of blank or empty space in your messages if you want to emphasize other message components within your various message formats. Consider the use of blank space as much a choice of message design as the choice of copy points or other visuals to use within a given message format.

Sparse or *crowded message components* also relate to dimension of messages. You will need to decide, as a visual factor, whether you want your words and visuals for each population's messages to be sparsely arranged or intentionally crowded. I am reminded of how crowded the messages are on many music videos today; their designs are intentional efforts to make the receiver's eye constantly move over multiple images contained in one format, in order to disrupt the normal ways of leisurely information processing. Sparsely designed messages can also be very dramatic. One of the first companies to employ this and blank space, Bayer aspirin, used an entire page of a newspaper with only two aspirin in the middle.

Color placed in messages can be a strong, even commanding, visual. Color is one of those visualization factors that is played out in other visualization factors, such as graphics, photography, print, or paper. Your choice of loud *or* unobtrusive color in your prominent message elements and in your background areas is a critical factor that can have an impact on the general feeling and theme of campaign messages.

The kind of paper is a conscious choice for some print media. Newspapers offer a limited choice in paper, unless you want to use a message insert placed within the regular pages of the daily or Sunday newspaper. Magazines have a little more choice, either their regular paper or the more expensive, thicker, or shiny paper that sets off messages from the other pages in a magazine. Annual reports, fact sheets, newsletters, brochures, and especially letterhead are print media that are wide open to the kinds of paper you might want to use. You can help visualize your organization's or your product's image through the choice of paper.

Font and size of print are powerful visuals that can help you relate messages to the image of your corporation. For a businesslike and traditional organizational image, a classic font such as Times New Roman or Old English can match this desired image. For other, more easygoing corporate images or product images a more relaxed or playful font can suggest a casual image, for example, the round and almost childlike letters used by Metropolitan Life Insurance in their copy platform "Get Met. It Pays."

The size of the letters employed in your message design is another careful decision consistent with the dimension of the message. You will need to decide what words or visuals are enlarged and what can be smaller in size.

Other graphic designs such as lines, arrows, dots, borders, or bullets are also considerations related to font and size. These extra graphics can be consistent with the font of your print or the visuals. Or, they can intentionally be designed as different, as contrasting, from the print font and other visuals in the message formats in order to dramatize or call attention to something. Larger graphic designs such as cartoon characters or handdrawn or computer-generated background scenery are other choices for visualization factors.

Photography placed in message formats is a common visualization factor. Obviously, your choices are wide open here, with possibilities such as background scenery, a smaller visual of any photo used as only part of the larger message format, or adults or children who enhance the message components. Photography has powerful communication properties to frame a message or to readily create a mood or tone for the message, for example, in photos of mountains or pristine forests, in photos of cruel and dirty inner-city urban areas, in photos of the happy traditional family in their average middle-class home, or in photos of attractive or unattractive people or places.

Celebrities and other persons used in message design are crucial decisions. If you choose a celebrity to represent your product, all the traits of the particular celebrity are embraced by your organization as consistent with the organization's own. If you want your product identified by older persons, then an actor or entertainer representing that generation helps appeal to your mature targeted population. The converse is also demonstrated in messages where young, carefree celebrities advertise products for the younger generation.

Primary choices for celebrities are either entertainers from movies or television or athletes from all kinds of sports. The use of a celebrity is one of those powerful and commanding visualization factors that totally capture and enhance the image(s) the message presents to its targeted audience about its organization. For example, if your product or your organization wants to communicate an antisocial or deviate image of the product, you might want to choose Dennis Rodman as your spokesperson celebrity. If you want to go with a mainstream and uncontroversial spokesperson, you could consider James Garner. You want to be very careful in your choice of a celebrity as visualization factor since it is a visual that immediately attaches all the person's qualities to the image of the organization.

As far as choosing other kinds of persons to use in your messages, the same kind of principles apply. If you choose attractive and socially acceptable or even socially desirable individuals, then you are naming your product and your organization as such. If you want to convey a controversial, unusual image for your client or organization, then the persons used in your messages should also reflect this. Some of the most interesting examples of the power of spokespersons as visuals are found today in products targeting the young generation. The Calvin Klein advertisements intentionally create controversy in their scantily clad models, in suggestive or erotic body positions. The Benetton advertisements have created even more attention in their portrayals of such antisocial images as a priest and a nun kissing. The very controversial nature of these persons as visuals communicates images to these organizations' targeted consumer youth populations that the product is for them, for the unconventional, and for the independent thinking youth of today—images not accepted or understood by most adults.

Exaggerated and unexpected images are conspicuous and obvious visualization factors that can present distinct images and strong appeals to targeted populations. As receivers, we all have expectations for what reality is and how it is presented in messages. Whenever a message "plays with accepted codes," the receiver is inclined to pay attention to the message. For example, a current advertisement for Coors beer portrays young people playing in the mountains which are about knee-high to them. Other product messages that are some of the most ingenious plays on reality are the Miller Lite advertisements with the copy platform of "Tastes Great, Less Filling";[4] in these messages they show football players playing golf and professional wrestlers wrestling with beauty queen contestants. However, any message can draw attention to itself through illogical factors, through enlarging or diminishing an image, by placing something sideways or upside down, or by placing something in an unexpected setting such as an elephant in a house.

Emotional or rational appeals represent the final visualization factor to consider. This is another factor that can be suggested through other visual factors. An emotional appeal is an effort to raise an emotion through the message, be it erotica or sexuality, romantic love and affection, or the more negative themes of anger, hatred, danger, or fear. You can manipulate colors, the physical appearance of your message spokespersons, graphics, exaggerated elements, or photography to create a general emotional appeal for a message.

Rational appeals, obviously, contrast to emotional appeals in that they portray a message logically, as an accepted and unquestioned situation. An example would be a message explaining all the reasons for why a computer has better features than other computers on the market or a message that spells out the reasons why one automobile is safer to drive than other automobiles. The theme and tone of the message is very matter-of-fact, with little reference to feelings or emotions associated with the product.

As you consider and choose the visualization factors that might be appropriate for the messages targeting your respective populations, keep in mind what I have advised in terms of copy points. You have many options to consider in choosing your visualization factors for print media. You might not and probably cannot use all of them. You might even list some as appropriate and later decide not include them. You most certainly will use some visualizations repeatedly

---

[4] Reprinted with permission of Miller Brewing Company.

across most of the messages within a certain population and among all the targeted populations in a campaign. In any case, this very important first step in designing the visualization factors for the campaign's print media is to know all the possible visualization factors that are available, so that you can choose which of them are proper and appropriate for the messages targeting your designated populations. You, as the campaign professional, need to know that visuals as message components are just one of the kinds of tools available to you for message design.

Visualization Factors for Broadcast Media

As with the print media, broadcast media also have their own unique logistical characteristics and message constraints. Given the inherent characteristics of all the various broadcast media, some identical and some different considerations go into the definitions of each visualization factor that can be used in broadcast media.

I state the obvious again but consider this. Broadcast media are processed differently by the receiver than print media are. Their movable qualities, the dynamics of color and motion and the energy that sound and voices can bring to a broadcast message make the visualization factors of broadcast significantly different from those of print. In other words, an audience member processes a broadcast message in different ways from a print message; the relatively fixed qualities of print allow the receiver to actively process a message in his/her own way whereas the receiver for a broadcast message must keep up with the ever-changing broadcast message in order to process and understand it.

Since the rules for processing and understanding a print or a broadcast message change from one to the other, the campaign strategist must keep these differences in mind when listing the respective inventories of appropriate print and broadcast visual factors. Visualization factors appropriate for broadcast media, then, are sometimes slightly different and sometimes radically different from print visualization factors. In any case, first, the campaign strategist must understand the possible visualization factors available for broadcast message design so that, secondly, she/he can create an inventory of broadcast visuals to eventually create appropriate messages for each of the targeted audiences. Your most common broadcast communication selections are the mainstream media of television, radio, movies, and other, more peripheral broadcast channels such as billboards that move, video movies, video games, internet pages, or CDs and cassette tapes.

The good news for the campaign planner is that most of the visualization factors identified in the print media are also available for broadcast messages, albeit with different adaptations to broadcast situations and broadcast messages. In any case, let me emphasize again that you will make an inventory of each and every visual that would be appropriate for each and every population. This is the same operation that you did for copy points. Consider your individual lists of visuals for every population only a possible inventory of visuals that would work and would be desirable and appropriate for the respective population. This does not mean—just as it did not mean with the inventories of copy points—that you will use every visual that you have named; when you get down to the business of creating the message formats, some visuals might not be used at all, and others will be used repeatedly.

The length of the message corresponds to the dimensions of a print medium. One of your possible visualization considerations is how many seconds or how many minutes long will the most appropriate messages be. Generally speaking, you can approximate in seconds for television, radio, or movie trailers what a good length should be for the message spots. For longer messages contained in videos or in moving internet pages, your visualization factor of length is most likely measured in minutes.

Movement from shot to shot and the print visual of sparse or crowded message spots are two related considerations for visual effects. For the visual broadcast media such as television or videos you will have to decide how long you want each message frame to last before moving on to the next frame. A leisurely, relatively lengthy "stay" on each frame allows the receiver to process completely each shot. At the other extreme, a message with numerous shots, or frames, forces the receiver to quickly attempt to process the shots. The strategist can, in a sense, manipulate how completely the receiver processes the video message—through few and lengthy frames or through multiple, rushed shots.

Related to this is the print visualization factor of sparse or crowded message formats. In a video message as well, the strategist can place elements in the shots to create a sparse and simple format or a crowded format. This factor can be added to the factor of amount of time on the frame so that sparse frames can go together with lengthy amounts of time on the frames, *or* crowded frames can be put with short amounts of time on the frames for much more rapid, quickly moving message images.

Celebrity figures and other persons also figure into the broadcast message designs. However, in the use of famous entertainers, well-known athletes, or other persons as visualization factors, the additional elements of vocal quality and movement of the persons are introduced. Whether television or radio, the vocal quality of the persons speaking in the messages is an important visualization factor to consider. The use of James Earl Jones' deep and resonant voice is a powerful visualization factor in only three words: "This is CNN." In broadcast messages, it is also important to remember that your celebrities and other persons will talk and will walk in them; this might affect your decision on whom to choose if you desire certain movements like dancing, walking, or playing a sport.

Music and sound effects are exclusive to broadcast visualization factors. The choice of background music can create a mood or theme consistent with the desired images of the message. The use of sound effects also has measurable impact when drawing attention to some element in the message. There is a movement today to use well-known songs and lyrics to support the product or organization presented in the message, such as Bob Seger's song "Like a Rock" in the message advertising the Chevy trucks.

Exaggerated and unexpected images, along with emotional and rational appeals can also be dynamic visualization factors in broadcast messages. That is, a campaign strategist can adapt these effects in moving messages. Broadcast message formats can include an exaggerated visual or unexpected image; the additional element present here is that it is almost always moving. Any illogical image—or a completely rational image—can add to the emotionality or the rationality of the message. The exaggerated images can be consistent with the theme of the message, or they can play against it for effect or for an interesting appeal; I am thinking of the message presented on the weather channel of a woman hanging sideways to a pole on a windy day. Computer technology today can do amazing effects in exaggeration of visual images; witness, for example, the facial expressions, body shapes, and movements of Jim Carrey in the movie *The Mask* and the remake of *The Nutty Professor* with Eddie Murphy.

Color, graphic designs, photography, and print font and size are all print visualization factors that are also adapted to broadcast messages. The same considerations of the impact of these in print messages apply when the broadcast messages contain color, graphic designs, printed words, and photography. The additional consideration here is that these will be moving images now, shifting and changing with each frame. The strategist will have to consider the movement patterns of these colors, graphics, photos, and printed words.

The logo of an organization's message is a graphic design or visualization element that is present on all the messages of a campaign. Much like a copy platform, the logo can identify the organization in a dramatic visual way and in a consistent way on all the messages put out by an organization. In some campaign situations specially designed, different logos can identify the messages for just one campaign or the organization or a specially designed logo can be used in addition to the more well-known established logo. It is one of the most important visualization factors an organization can use on its messages. It is a visual tool that readily identifies the organization and the organization's product to its audiences.

Generally speaking, a logo can be designed in two ways. It can be a graphic design that is separate from the name of the organization but that is usually placed close to the name of the organization or close to the copy platform. Or in many cases, the name of the organization takes the form of a logo. That is, a unique color, shape, or size of the name of the organization serves as a visualization factor. In fact, it is an extremely common means for visually identifying a corporation—through the unique design of the name of the organization. On many messages today, organizations employ both a separate logo and the name of the organization as a logo. Organizations work hard to establish their unique logos and, to protect their image, copyright or trademark their logo(s); they do not usually change them very often (See Figure 4.2).

At the top is the logo of Nissan found on all campaign messages in which the name Nissan is also the logo. Below that is an example of a logo and sublogo—

Figure 4.2
Examples of Logos and Sublogos

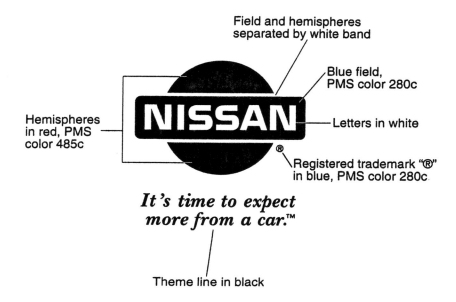

Copyright Nissan (1997). Nissan logo is a registered trademark of Nissan. Reprinted with permission.

Reprinted with the permission of Xerox.

of the Olympics—to demonstrate Xerox's sponsorship of the Olympics. The name Xerox acts as a logo, but the Olympics sublogo has both the traditional Olympic rings as a logo and, just for the Nagano Olympics, another logo of the Olympic colors in a kind of "flower" design.

Visualization Factors for Personal Communication

Personal communication in a campaign involves a person representing the organization communicating directly and usually in-person to targeted populations. Examples range from very casual interpersonal conversations or group conversations between organization officials and audience members to more formal, structured interviews, organized focus group discussions, speeches, business meetings, annual stockholder meetings, and professional conferences or seminars. The distinguishing characteristic here between media messages and personal messages is that the constraining elements are slightly different; each media channel necessarily frames the messages contained in them according to their respective logistics whereas personal communication dictates different constraints on the messages contained in the communication setting.

In a personal communication setting the messenger, the speaker, representing the organization is as important as the message. More than a "celebrity" or "spokesperson" visualization factor in the sense of print media messages, the organization representative serves as a primary and dominant visualization factor.

As with copy points and visuals, you will also create an inventory of desirable traits you want in the personal communication utilized for each targeted population. Do not assume that the same spokesperson is appropriate for communication to all the populations. Perhaps, given the unique lived experiences of each population and given the differing corporate images you might want to send to these same populations, you should represent the organization to these various populations with different spokespersons and different personal communication. Again, make a list for each population so that the message designers can have an inventory of traits to draw from in the design of personal communication for the respective campaign.

The physical appearance of the spokesperson who represents the organization is a primary visualization factor delivered to the targeted audiences. The organization chooses a person whose physical appearance is consistent with the desired image the corporation wants for itself and/or for the products it markets, perhaps a traditional businesslike image, or a casual relaxed image, or a youth-oriented "hip" image. Very fundamental considerations such as clothing, hairstyle, makeup and jewelry for a women or clothing and facial hair for a man are the physical traits that identify the speaker's (and the organization's) image.

The personality of the spokesperson is another visualization factor adding to the image of the speaker. The way the person handles herself/himself while speaking and listening, the way any humor is delivered in the remarks, the way any serious points are made in the message, and the quality of his/her voice all help define the personality of the speaker and, in turn, the image of the organization.

The reputation of the speaker is another message element attached to the speaker's personality and also to the speaker's credibility in the eyes of the audience members receiving the organization's message. Obviously, if the audience is receptive to the fact that the speaker is a famous celebrity, athlete, or powerful figure in the organization, the audience might be more inclined to listen and process the messages. If the speaker, however, has no demonstrated reputation before meeting the audience, she/he is obliged to create a credible and responsible persona as she/he goes along.

The language of the speaker is an unusual visualization factor in that it connects directly to the words of the spokesperson. Even though we have defined words as a separate message component from visuals, the choice of words, the vocabulary, the phraseology, and the general delivery of the speaker serve as visualization factors.

The physical and emotional setting for the communication act is a powerful visual that is, nevertheless, not focused on as a prominent visualization factor. If you are conducting casual conversations with employees about an issue affecting the organization, the setting is not as emotional as an interview between management and line workers over a pending labor strike. The physical location for the meeting helps to define the organizational messages. A seminar at a posh hotel adds a unique kind of visualization to the personal messages whereas a business meeting on site in a cluttered and crowded room adds another visualization element to the personal messages delivered there.

My intention throughout the detailed listing of the various kinds of visualization factors is to emphasize that the campaign strategist has, at her/his disposal, multiple kinds of visuals to include in message formats. Some of these are well-known and used by many campaign planners today. However, other visual considerations may not be appreciated as visualization factors, even though they can be used in this way.

Your in-depth inventory of all the visualization factors that would be appropriate for each targeted population serves as a foundation as you choose the correct visual factors to include in the respective populations' messages. As with the copy points, in the actual execution of the message designs you might not use some of the visuals you originally determined, and you will most probably use some visualization factors repeatedly in several messages. I am sure, even as I attempt a somewhat comprehensive listing of the visualization factors available for design of message formats, that I have missed some visual elements that you can think of. I hope you let your imagination explore other, suitable visuals for your campaign's messages. Simply knowing and being aware of the most commonly used visualization factors for print, broadcast, and personal communication does not automatically lead to the design and the choosing of message components. Very specific design strategies must understood for the placement and arrangement of the various print, broadcast, and communication message components.

STRATEGIES FOR CHOOSING MESSAGE COMPONENTS

Creating a message design is choosing words and visuals and arranging these into a message format to be delivered via a communication channel to a targeted population(s). It seems a simple process. It is not.

We have laid the foundation for the consideration of messages strategies by defining the various choices available for words in messages, for visuals in messages, and for personal communication as messages. But when it comes to actually designing and formatting messages, it is not enough to know simply what are the possible choices or components, in order to place them in message designs. General guidelines and principles can inform and suggest how the campaign strategist arranges, fashions, and designs message formats for different audiences.

At the same time, a really exciting and challenging facet of the creative process of making message designs is that no hard-and-fast rules absolutely govern the process. Ingenuity and creativity also rule, as well as common sense. Campaign message designers are artists, creators, given freedom to choose message components and fashion them as precise communication to certain audiences. Let the fun begin.

In this discussion of message strategies it will be more efficient to distinguish between a message and a message format, also known as a message design. I want you to consider a "message" as any word(s) or visual component(s) that makes up the larger, total, finalized "message format" or "message design." Consider a copy point, a copy platform, visualization factor as a message, or company spokesperson, as a "tool," as a building block for building the finished message format.

Creating message formats suitable for a campaign's purpose—the organization's purpose—and suitable for the campaign's intended audiences can be an inductive or a deductive process. The campaign strategist can use a deductive strategy to create messages by beginning with a general tone or theme desired in the campaign's messages and, hence, campaign as a whole, and then choosing the messages that fulfill or are consistent with the identified and desirable purpose and theme. OR, the campaign planner can identify the appropriate words, visuals, and personal effects and consider these as building blocks that will collectively identify or suggest the proper theme and tone for the campaign.

Either strategic direction is appropriate—inductive or deductive—but some campaign situations seem to be more suitable for one direction or the other. For example, if you are planning a crisis management campaign where you have an intense crisis situation that prompts a campaign to reassure the organization's populations, it seems more feasible to use a deductive strategy since your crisis dictates a strong theme and purpose to guide the eventual campaign's messages. In another situation, where a campaign is planned as a more-or-less general image campaign that necessitates corporate image management in relatively nonhostile populations, you might want to use an inductive strategy where you rely on information about the lived experiences of the populations and about the desired images of the corporation to dictate the general theme(s) most appropriate for the campaign.

For either an inductive or deductive strategy, the following steps will help you plan and arrange your message designs. The following steps in message decision-making demonstrate an inductive model, but for a deductive approach, the steps need only be reversed. First, the inductive model relies on the basic strategies for precise information on isolating those words, visualization factors, and personal factors that are the appropriate inventories for each of your targeted populations. Second, based on your inventories of messages, the amount of copy needed in the various campaign's messages is suggested by the Grunig model of nonpublic, latent, aware, and active kinds of public positions. And, finally, the grand theme(s) of the campaign, along with related topics or motifs, can be more easily identified and utilized in the message components and in the eventual message designs incorporated into the campaign; decisions on these major theme(s) might necessitate some rewriting and reworking of message components and message formats to reflect this theme(s).

Building on Basic Strategies

Consistent with an inductive strategy of identifying individual message components first, in order to later arrive at a general deduction or theme or purpose of the campaign, this first step in the inductive strategic design of messages begins with another look at the basic strategies selected for the campaign. One of the first considerations available to the campaign strategist as she/he begins to conceptualize and compose message formats is to reflect on the basic strategies that have already been laid out for the respective campaign. Remember that the campaign planner creates goals (and, afterward, supporting objectives) for targeted audiences that follow a two-pronged attack: to appeal to the lived experiences of the audiences *and* to deliver information that the organization wants the audiences to know, believe, and/or act on. This framework is retained for creating message designs.

Message formats parallel this two-pronged attack in a couple of ways. For each intended population, some message formats will appeal directly to certain lived experiences of the audience, and other messages will contain content the organization wants them to know, content reflecting the image of the organization as a whole, or content reflecting the image of the product or service sold by the organization. Or another possibility is that one message format can contain message components that both appeal to the audience *and* reflect the organization.

Words as Strategic Decisions

Recall that the basic objectives set out goals and objectives: goals as either appeals to lived experiences in the audience or direct changes desired in the targeted audience and objectives as the numbers and kinds of information that support each respective goal. The copy points (message components) that you have written from the objectives (basic strategies) are already, inherently, a manifestation of message strategies that both appeal to the audience or reflect the organization's image or organization's product's image. That is, any copy points identified as numbers and kind of information supporting appeal goals inherently serve as message components that will appeal to lived experiences of the targeted audiences. The campaign planner who chooses copy points from appeal goals is, in effect, targeting the audience's lived experiences in some way. Any message format containing copy points from appeal goals is, indeed, facilitating one strategy (one "prong") of appealing to the audience.

If the campaign strategist chooses copy points to include in message designs that are from the direct change goals, then, consequently, these chosen copy points act as message components attempting to directly change the knowledge, attitude, behavior, or other images of the targeted audience. *The campaign strategist plans messages based on the copy points chosen from the two respective kinds of goals—which can either appeal to audiences or reflect the organization or both.*

All the in-depth and detailed "lists" which have preceded the actual designing process of the message make the designing of messages, initially, a "choosing process"—an efficient and thorough creative process of choosing from appropriate and available message components. The message designer has before him/her a detailed listing of objectives for each goal intended for each targeted audience. The message planner has, from this, a detailed listing of the copy points manifested in the objectives. The campaign planner also has in mind all the possible message components available for designing campaign message formats: words components of copy points and copy platforms (and visualization factors) appropriate for print, broadcast, and personal communication. You can see that one of the first steps in creating message designs is choosing your words, as messages, from your established inventories.

I do not want to given the impression that each message designed for a campaign is a separate and distinct format from all the other message formats. Rather, the message designer (and the design and production staff) need to identify some messages to retain across message formats, in order to establish consistencies among messages. The obvious message components to provide consistency are the use of a copy platform and/or subcopy platforms (and logos). Typically, copy platforms (and logos) are used for all or most messages to all the populations for one campaign.

But words, or copy points, can establish themes and consistency also throughout a campaign. That is, the planner can choose certain copy points to include among many messages. The campaign planner can unify message formats *within a targeted population* by repeating copy points. Or, the campaign planner can *identify one campaign* by unifying message components throughout all the campaign's messages to all the targeted populations.

The choice of what precise and particular unifying message components to use is the artistic choice of the campaign strategist. In addition to identifying a population's messages or an entire campaign's messages through common message components, any copy point(s) or copy platform(s) can also serve as constant message components along two other parameters, the two-prong attacks mentioned above: to establish which messages appeal to the audiences' lived experiences or to reflect the organization by establishing those messages that reflect the organization's image as a whole or identify a product of the organization.

Visuals and Spokesperson Traits as Strategic Decisions

By their very nature, visualization factors are more elusive and suggestive as message components. Words as messages are relatively concrete and fixed, through the words of the copy points and the copy platform. Visuals, however, by their very logistics, are graphics, cartoons, photos, music, sound effects, colors, paper, celebrities, or physical appearance or the language of a spokesperson. For the campaign message planner, simply put, visualization factors as messages offer many more different kinds of message possibilities and more range in message components.

Just as with words message components, visuals factors are the building blocks of the eventual message decisions. Similar to word messages, you also have various lists to draw from in choosing appropriate visuals for your message designs: the campaign's goals and objectives, the respective visuals marked as suitable for each population, and the whole inventory of visualization factors possibilities.

Also analogous with words, any visualization factor(s) can be utilized as a unifying procedure. Any visual factor or all the visual message components that are included in messages sent to a particular population can unify or identify this population. Any visual or visuals included across all the messages of a given campaign also serve as a unifying procedure for the whole campaign. These visuals can be subtle or obvious. They can be as much in the background as a kind of paper or a background color or as prominent as a logo, striking graphic design, or well-known or unusual spokesperson.

And, similar to the use of words as messages, visuals are additionally utilized to appeal to audiences' lived experiences or to reflect the organization's image or organization's product image. However, according to this function of messages serving this two-pronged attack, visual factors' unique and inherent qualities as message components make them operate a little differently from words as components. It is in this function of visualization strategy that the campaign message planner emerges prominently as an artist and creative designer of communication.

Whereas words as messages obviously and inherently flow from stated copy points and objectives, visual factors *do not flow directly* from any stated objective. Words as messages are decided through the statement of copy points, which are, in turn, drawn from respective basic strategy objectives. Visual factors do not have this more or less direct link to basic strategy objectives.

In fact, visuals are more adept at facilitating goals—especially appeal goals—rather than objectives. Think about how appeal goals are worded. Demographic goals might state "an appeal to single, career-minded females" or "an appeal to upper socioeconomic married couples with children." Demographic appeals are easily identified through visual components included in the message formats, for example, in visuals that typify single career women or suggest upper-class living conditions.

Visual message components, in fact, can facilitate all kinds of appeal goals by indicating and identifying surroundings consistent with the psychographics, leisure practices, needs, or schema of a intended population. The visual component might fulfill a need or psychographic appeal goal and be *as subtle as* a luxury automobile or expensive home in the background of a message appealing to a psychographic variable of achiever or outer-driven personality type. Or, another visual manifesting appeal goals or schema might be *a very obvious and prominent* visual that alludes to a physical need such as emotional photos of starving children or an event schema of a well-known celebrity/athlete who wears a certain brand of shoe when playing basketball.

While visuals are especially important for identifying and framing goals and messages to populations, visual messages can also, however, along with copy points, deliver information contained in objectives. Graphics, photos, music, color, persons, celebrities are all typical visual message components that help identify content areas (objectives) and desired changes (goals) in any population. Witness, for example, the use of children as visuals to identify a product as child-intended or the use of fast-paced rock-and-roll music and multiple and crowded shots together in one message to appeal to the MTV generation or letterhead with very traditional font and logo on conservative, business paper to identify an organization's image as a traditional, conservative business.

This inherent feature of visuals to serve as subtle background messages or as primary, obvious message components dominating a message format demonstrates their flexibility and power to deliver goals and deliver objectives for a campaign. These qualities of visuals provide the campaign planner with decided advantages in utilizing visual messages in message designs. The creative use of visuals in any message design marks real artistic processes in designing message formats for specific lived experiences of an audience or for precise images desired by the organization in an audience.

Strategies for Quantifying Message Copy

The selection of the exact words and visuals to fashion all a campaign's messages that you have just completed marks the first step in strategic decision-making of a campaign's messages. These initial choices and decisions initiate the creative and artistic process of fashioning message formats. So, you should have before you now, at this point in time, the tentative message components and message designs that are appropriate for each of your intended populations.

These tentative message formats reflect the words, visuals, and spokesperson traits that are appropriate for each population. These same messages' words and visuals, additionally, follow the two-pronged strategy of appealing to the audiences and/or reflecting the organization. These same messages' words and visuals grow out of and are the manifestation of the basic strategies drawn up for each population.

Now, the campaign strategist is ready to enact another critical decision relating to the campaign's messages. As part of the inductive pattern of creating campaign messages, this step builds on the detail and decisions made first in order to lead into the next step or level, which entails more general decisions on the campaign's messages and designs. The next strategic decision relates to the inventory and choosing of message components chosen in the first step, but the campaign planner now needs to consider *how many copy points and how many visuals should be included in the tentative message formats*, respective to the audiences the campaign will target.

Information gathered in the formative research on the populations and in your research on the organization directly informs these decisions. More particularly, information on how many public positions exist across each population and across all the intended populations helps to identify and quantify the amount of message copy that is appropriate for each population's messages.

The Grunig Typology's findings on kinds of publics (what I would call public positions) and on intensities of information processing and information seeking present in your targeted populations informs the quantity of copy that is appropriate for each of these targeted populations (Grunig & Hunt, 1984). Let me explain, first, the general strategies suggested by the Grunig Typology. According to the kinds of public positions identified, individuals who belong to a population can be primarily active, or aware, or latent, or a nonpublic in how they relate to the organization. Additionally, each member of an audience will most likely possess one or two or even more of these public positions within himself/herself toward any number of issues: their image of the organization, their image of the campaign issue, or their image of the product or service sold by the organization.

An active public position will necessitate more information and, hence, more copy in the form of copy points and possibly visuals, because, generally speaking, persons sharing an active position toward the organization are interested in the organization or interested in the product. This *active* position also suggests that these individuals already possess knowledge, attitude, and behaviors toward the organization, which, in turn, indicates that message formats aimed toward an active contingent in a population should have copy that includes knowledge, attitudes, behaviors, and other desired image content. Additionally, given that the active individuals have this relatively intense interest in the campaign's issue or in the organization itself, they need to receive a relatively large amount of copy points and be exposed to those visuals that contain a lot of information. If the persons with active positions toward the organization do not get their information from the organization, they will naturally seek the information wherever they can get it; this might prove disadvantageous or even disastrous if they pursue information from those who might oppose the organization's intent or actions.

In sum, an organization who has found that its targeted population(s) possesses a significant number of active public positions is obliged to communicate a relatively large amount of information and message content to them. This information, additionally, should be knowledge-based, opinion-based, and suggested behaviors since the very term "active" indicates that the individual has an active interest in, strong opinions of, and behaviors toward the organization.

If your research finds that you have a strong contingent of *aware* public positions within or across your intended audiences, then the amount of message copy lessens a bit and the emphasis on behavior content is relaxed. In contrast to active public positions, persons possessing aware public positions have primarily knowledge and attitudes toward the organization but little or no behaviors toward the organization. The message content reflects this with its emphasis on suggested knowledge and opinion-based copy points and visuals in the intended audiences.

At the same time, the amount of copy can be less than in the active messages. These persons possessing aware public positions are not as interested and committed to the organization and its issues, so the strategist needs to include fewer numbers of copy points and an increase in visuals in the respective messages. The reduction of copy points and the increase in visuals appeals to the aware public positions since these persons have less interest in the organization than those with active public positions. This means that the campaign strategist is obliged to catch the attention of those with aware public positions through the increased use of visuals and, at the same time, maintain and enhance their knowledge and attitude positions through a substantial number of the copy points and copy platform(s).

For those *latent* public positions, message shifts to primarily knowledge-based, and, at the same time, visualization factors are markedly increased. The latent positions are those persons who have the potential to be informed about the organization but, at the current time, they know little or nothing about the organization and the campaign issues. This dictates that message content is appropriately only knowledge, with little or no reference to suggested opinions, attitudes, or behaviors toward the organization. The quantity of message components is reduced by decreasing the number of copy points even more (than active and aware) and by increasing the amount of visualizations even more (than active and aware). In principle then, the increase of visuals will more readily capture the attention of the latent positions so that, hopefully, they will be inclined to process at least the lesser amount of message copy.

For those persons who share a *nonpublic* position, or a noninterest in the organization, the only strategies available to the campaign planner are to ignore them or to try to move them to a latent position. Your decision on what tact to take—ignore or attempt to move to latent—rests on how important the targeted audience is to the organization and the campaign. Say, for example, your campaign needs to target the organization's employees, but your formative research reveals that they are mostly in a nonpublic position toward the organization and the campaign issue. You can never ignore the interests and feelings of your employees, so you will need to at least attempt to move them to a latent position through messages that capture their attention and through copy points that increase their knowledge of the organization and the campaign. If, however, one of your targeted populations is not crucial to the campaign's interests, such as the other competitive organizations within your industry, then it might be wise to ignore them, at least in the current campaign.

These considerations and findings based on the Grunig Typology can help the strategist further refine and fine tune the messages by informing the amount of word and visual components most appropriate for the active, aware, latent, and/or nonpublic positions held by those audience members most important to the organization and the campaign. You can see that this is not a "cut and dry" operation. The campaign strategist also borrows from notions of the Collapse Model and takes the findings on how dominant or prevalent each of these positions is in each audience and then fashions message formats containing the proper and respective amount of words and visuals to match the public positions. If you find all four public positions present across an audience's membership, then you will be obligated to create messages to target all four public positions. In another case, where only two or one of the public positions are dominant, then the messages, in turn, will be designed for only those respective public positions.

Keep in mind one thing here. You are *not interested in assigning or determining how many persons might be* active or latent. You are not interested in assigning so many individuals to one segment of active or another segment of aware, latent, or nonpublic. What *you are interested in is how many total public positions are held throughout the population,* that is, how many active positions are most likely in the population, how many aware positions, and so on by all members of the audience. The Collapse Model suggests that any particular individual can possess one or more public positions, so the exercise of segmenting a population according to active, aware, latent, or non-public publics will not work. You need, instead, to determine within the entire audience how many active public positions are experienced throughout the entire membership, how many aware public positions throughout the entire membership, and how many latent and nonpublic positions throughout the audience's members. These numbers of total public positions in the four areas more accurately suggest the correct and proper amount of copy and visuals appropriate for the respective audience's campaign's messages, rather than the number of persons assigned to an active public, aware public, latent, or nonpublic.

Another finding from the Grunig Typology can also inform the quantity of message components suitable for a targeted population. Findings on information processing and information seeking also indicate a degree of willingness to pay attention to messages. Information processing measures how likely a person is to pay attention to a message when the message is provided to her/him; that is, if a person comes across a message in a newspaper or while watching the television, how willing is the person to pay attention to the message and process the content in it. Information seeking defines a more intense interest in a message; information seeking measures how likely a person is to go out of his/her way to seek a message. Information seeking individuals would buy a magazine to read a message they believed was in it, or they would make a point of tuning in a television show to see a message that interested them.

These findings are also consistent with the active, aware, latent, and nonpublic kinds of public positions. A person who is active toward a subject or toward an organization will, most likely, also be strong in information seeking and information processing. And, with every kind of public position, from aware status to nonpublic status, in principle and in theory, the intensity of information seeking and of information processing will lessen. So, you have two measurements from the Grunig Typology that can help you in determining the quantity of message components, each complementing the other.

IN SUMMARY

With your initial decisions on message content and on determinations of quantity of copy, you can now more easily identify a theme(s) for the campaign. The advantage of the inductive process just demonstrated is that now you can take cues from the established content areas across all your message copy to determine and brainstorm any possible themes or approaches for the campaign being planned.

In other words, the copy points, copy platform, visuals, and logo you have already identified can point you in the direction of a general theme or focus to reiterate throughout most or all of the message components. This identification of a theme and related motifs might necessitate some reworking and some rewriting of messages you have tentatively formatted. This is to be expected. But the entire strategic process, broken into separate steps with respective strategic decisions guiding each level, makes your final decisions on the campaign's messages more thoroughly thought out and, hopefully, more in tune with the audiences and with the organization.

Possible themes for a campaign might be as diverse as using an entertainment approach. Other themes can use fear, shock, romantic love, or "warm and fuzzy" feelings. The possibilities are endless. For example, in a campaign to support a research fund-raiser against child leukemia, if you already have before you basic strategies and message strategies that suggest optimism for finding a cure, then you can decide that your general theme is optimism and demonstrated success in fighting this disease. Having established this theme(s), drawn from your preliminary message decisions, you can now go back to the tentative messages and emphasize them even more.

There is another example of the inductive process of choosing campaign themes. If you are planning a campaign to manage a crisis of false allegations of product tampering against your organization, say that your basic strategies and message strategies so far indicate that the allegations can be proven false, that the tampering would be impossible at the organizational level, that certain competitors would gain from your damaged images, that your product is superior and always has been, and that no one has ever been hurt by any product sold by your organization. Your available themes could be product superiority or false and unfounded allegations or the strong and established reputation of the organization. In your capacity as an artist and creative writer, you and your staff can elect any one or all of these themes to emphasize even more in your tentative message designs.

The entire inductive process, from the goals and objectives, to the choice of message components, to decisions on message quantity, to the general focus of the campaign has been, in a sense, only steps in choosing one strategy or a few unifying strategies. All the considerations and strategies used to inform every step also inform the final decision of campaign strategy, which is the final theme or themes most appropriate for tying the campaign messages together as a whole. Were you to use a deductive process—because you already know at the outset what theme and focus should guide the campaign's message strategies—you would simply let the general theme inform the goals and strategies, inform the choice and design of message components, reflect the audience in quantity of copy, in order to, in turn, reflect the chosen campaign focus. Throughout both directions, inductive or deductive, considerations of messages appealing to the audience and reflecting the organization are included and built into each step.

IMPORTANT THINGS TO REMEMBER

- Message strategies are choices of actual words and visualization factors that are placed in the various message formats.

- The objectives detailed as basic strategies become the copy points in messages.

- Message components are only choices on words—spoken or written—and visuals—broadcast, print, and personal—not the communication or media channels.

- A copy point is one piece of information presented in a message.

- A copy platform is a slogan—word or group of words—that is present on all the messages of an organization or an organization's campaign.

- Visualization factors are all the other components of a message's design that are not words: broadcast, print, and personal visuals.

- A logo is the primary visualization factor, the graphic design accompanying the organization's name on every message in a campaign.

- The first step in designing message formats is creating an inventory of all the possible copy points that would be appropriate for the various audiences targeted by a campaign.

- The second step is creating an inventory of all the visualization factors that would be appropriate for the various audiences targeted by a campaign.

- Creating a message format is bringing together the words components of copy platform and copy points and the visual components of logo and other visualization factors in each unique message design.

- Messages can be audience-based content, organization-based content, or both.

- Audiences interested in the organization or the campaign issue should receive messages with more copy points and less visuals.

- Audiences with little interest or no interest in the campaign should receive more visuals and less copy.

- Identifying themes or consistent images throughout the campaign's messages can come from the organization itself or from the prominent lived experiences of the audience's members, or both.

Just another Avon Lady

who runs, jumps, hurdles and throws javelins and shot puts just for fun (and gold medals), Jackie Joyner-Kersee can pretty much do it all.

Kind of like Avon's **Skin-So-Soft Suncare Plus.** It's the bug and tick repellent with a moisturizing waterproof **SPF 30** sunblock. (Also available in SPF 8 and SPF 15.) So when you can't outrun mosquitoes like Jackie can, at least you can outsmart them.

Call your Avon Representative or
1-800-FOR-AVON
Visit Avon at http://www.avon.com

Reprinted with permission of Avon Products, Inc.

Figure 4. 3 (first page of a two page message)
Identifying Words and Visuals in a Commercial Message

Campaign situation:

- Organizational source of message: Avon Products, Inc.
- Kind of campaign: advertising
- Targeted populations: customers, potential customers, women
- Message: magazine page

Copy platform: none for Avon

Logo: the font and size of the word "Avon"

Copy points:

- Just another Avon lady
- Skin-so-soft moisturizing suncare (on tube)
- Mosquito
- flea
- deer tick repellent (on tube)
- SPF 30 (on tube)
- Paba free sunscreen lotion (on tube)
- Active ingredients...(on tube)
- Caution Keep out of reach of children (on tube)
- 118 ml   4 fl. oz. (on tube)
- who runs
- jumps
- hurdles
- throws javelins
- shot puts
- just for fun (and gold medals)
- Jackie Joyner-Kersee can pretty much do it all.
- Kind of like Avon's **Skin So-Soft Suncare Plus.**
- It's the bug
- and tick repellant
- with a moisturizing waterproof SPF 30 sunblock.
- Also available in SPF 8
- And SPF 15
- So when you can't outrun mosquitos like Jackie can, at least you can outsmart them.
- Call your Avon Representative at 1-800-For-Avon
- Visit Avon at http://www.avon.com

Visualization factors:

- Graduated larger font of "Just" "another" "Avon" "Lady"
- Tube of product at angle
- Three "S" logo on tube
- Dimension of message is full page
- Sparse copy points
- Large lettering and visual product in center
- Regular magazine paper
- Top two-thirds of message is one copy point and tube
- Bottom third is mostly copy points
- 800 number is bigger and bold font
- Web address is relatively small

170   Campaign Strategies and Message Design

Reprinted with permission, Avon Products, Inc.

Figure 4. 3 (second page of two page message)
Identifying Words and Visuals in a Commercial Message

Copy platform: none

Copy points: none

Visualization factors:

- Celebrity is Joyner-Kersee, a woman
-   an African-American woman
-   very well-known and respected as Olympic athlete
-   known as nice and personable woman
- Dimension of message is full page
- Regular magazine paper
- Sky in top half of page
- Joyner-Kersee in center
- Photo is outdoors, on a rough road, with bushes in background
- Blue sky, nice sunny day
- Exaggerated and unexpected visual of her posture
- Has elements of emotion in her broad smile
-   In her body flexibility
- Direct gaze of Joyner-Kersee to the reader

    This message is composed of two messages. The left message, with the copy points and photo of the product, appeals to aware public positions and even suggests behaviors that would also include some references to active public positions. The right message illustrates an almost exclusively visual message that appeals to latent or even nonpublic public positions.

    I want to demonstrate that a message that at first glance seems to contain only a little or scarce information, in reality, can contain numerous copy points. The left message portion has copy points on the bottom third of the page, but these sentences are packed with copy points, as indicated above.

    On the other hand, the right message can also effectively contain a lot of information through its exclusive use of visuals. Because Avon has such a widespread name recognition and given the celebrity status of Joyner-Kersee as a woman and as an athlete, this right message can advertise Avon products effectively only through visualization factors.

    The copy points and visualization factors in this two-part message not only represent information that Avon wants to deliver to its targeted audiences, but these message components also embody the basic strategies that most certainly drove their conceptualization by Avon: goals and objectives of demographic appeals to gender, psychographic appeals to active women, physical need appeals for protection from mosquitos, physical need appeals for skin sunblock and moisturizers, and so on.

5

Communication Selection Strategies

With your initial determinations of basic strategies of goals and objectives decided and having further refined your campaign messages by arranging the words and visual message components into the finalized message formats, you are now ready to consider the communication selections that are best for carrying your message formats to the intended audiences. The placement of deciding communication selections strategies *after* the basic strategies and message strategies have been determined might be considered a bit "out of place," since many other campaign professionals determine communication selections. That is, for many campaign planners today, deciding the communication channels to use in the campaign is one of the first campaign decisions—usually because considerations of campaign costs limit what and how many communication selections (and message formats) should be used, or *can be afforded,* by the organization.

Hopefully, the arguments in this chapter, for this final step of the message design process, demonstrate that reserving decisions on communication selections for after message formats have been designed and completed is best for the success of the campaign and ultimately best for cost efficiency. The suggestion that the decision of which communication selection should carry a message to an audience is not a decision based primarily on cost. Rather, it is a strategic decision also based on determinations such as the inherent characteristics of the selection for enhancing the persuasive impact of the message, the capability of the channel to complement the other channels delivering message formats, and the ability of the selection to accommodate the words and visual components already decided and formatted.

This chapter's consideration of communication selections focuses on various frameworks for defining communication selections and on the advantages and disadvantages of each selection. As with the other strategies already discussed, strategic decisions on communication selections consider the lived experiences of the targeted audiences and the intentions of the organization. And finally, this concluding chapter will be able to advise you on how long your campaign should be, based on how many messages are needed for each audience and based on what communication selections are most appropriate for each and every intended population. Throughout, considerations of cost of the various communication selections is not ignored; indeed, the cost of a campaign is a critical bottom line for determining strategies throughout the entire campaign.

DEFINITIONS INITIATE CONCEPTUALIZATION OF STRATEGIES

Before we can examine some precise strategies for choosing the proper communication selections given a campaign situation, for correctly targeting the campaign's intended populations, and for reflecting the organization's interests, it is important to first offer some essential and fundamental definitions. Definitions and explanations of what is available to the campaign strategist directly inform later strategic decisions on choosing the correct communication selections for any campaign situation.

Two Broad Classifications

The definitions of communication selections begin with two broad classifications of communication selections: media channels and personal communication. Even though some campaign specialists recognize the media as the sole or at least primary kind of communication channel, I want to stress that personal communication is also a viable and valuable kind of communication selection in a campaign situation. In fact, my use of the label "communication selection" to name the use of both media and personal means of communication in a campaign is a conscious effort to include both the media and the personal as options for communication choices. Think of any kind of communication selection as just that—a communication selection—which can assume many forms, including any of the mainstream media forms or popular media forms or any of the personal kinds of communication.

Recognizing that these two broad classifications of communication selections are available is a critical beginning point for the campaign strategist to begin conceptualizing communication selections for a given campaign. This forces the campaign planner to open up considerations of communication selections to include all the media options available and all the personal options available for the campaign.

Media Communication Selections

A more detailed definition of each can separate what is considered a media communication selection from a personal communication selection. In a *mass media* selection, the organization places a message in a mass medium, which, in turn, delivers the message to the audience. To use a media selection is to employ a kind of two-step process of communication; first, the message is contained in the medium, and then it is sent to or made available to the intended audience in hopes that the intended audience will pay attention to it and process it. In a media selection situation, the organization hopes that the audience members will see and will process the message content contained in the mass medium, but, as is true with any kind of communication event, no real guarantee exists that the audience will see or hear it or will see it or hear it *and process the information in it.*

A mass medium form is just that—a mediated form of communication—where the message is placed in a medium that, in turn, is conveyed or made available to the audience. In a media selection situation, a direct transfer of information from the organization to the audience is not feasible, so the message is placed in a mediated communication form (mass media) so that, hopefully or in theory at least, the audience will receive and process the message from the respective mass medium made available to them.

A number of advantages and disadvantages exist in using the media as communication selections. Obviously, the media, by their very nature, can reach thousands or often millions of receivers with one message. The ability of the mass media to reach masses of people has to be acknowledged as their primary advantage. Other advantages exist as well, such as their inherent qualities of flexibility of designs. For example, radio has vocal and musical visualization factors, and television possesses visual design capabilities, as do the print media of magazines and newspapers, and so on. The innate qualities of the mass media lend themselves to a multiplicity of creative visual and verbal appeals, designs and appeals that can catch the attention of the audience members.

Nevertheless, the media also possess some limitations as communication selections. Because of this two-step, mediated process of reaching the audiences, some measure of personal contact may be missing. True, the message components can include content that is a direct reference to lived experiences of the targeted populations, but media messages cannot name or directly address the persons receiving the messages. Research into the power of the media and research into media effects establish that the media, by their inherent nature of serving as a channel from the organization to the audience, do not in general have the persuasive power of direct, personal contact with a receiver.

Personal Communication Selections

On the other hand, *personal communication* is a one-to-one, direct link from the organization to the audience membership and, as suggested by research findings into the effects of the media, typically has more persuasive impact on receivers. Examples of personal communication selections are interpersonal conversations with an audience member, or meetings, focus groups, seminars, or conferences with audience members.

Do not let the term "personal" mislead you, however. Personal refers to any direct communication to the audience members, so, technically, an organization's letter or direct mail that goes out to a population member is personal, even though it does not involve an in-person presentation of a message to a receiver. What is missing in a personal communication selection is the two-step procedure that a mass medium form inherently possesses. Any direct organizational contact made to an audience is considered a personal selection.

Now, this can get a bit complicated when there are some selections that can be both. For example, an annual report that automatically goes to a stockholder population is direct, so it is personal communication. If, however, this same annual report is sent to a stockbroker's office, and someone in the office picks it up to read it, it now serves as a mass medium; the annual report was sent to someone else but made available to others to read and process. Fact sheets or brochures are other examples of channels that can be either mass media or personal communication selections, depending on whether they are sent directly to an audience or whether they are made available for an audience in the hope that someone read them.

Media versus Personal Communication

In any case, it is important for the campaign professional to know the differences, limitations, and advantages between using a mass medium and a personal communication selection. I do not want to suggest that one is necessarily better than another, except to recognize that personal selections tend to have a slight advantage in their persuasive impact. For sure, there will be instances when the use of mass media will be more advantageous because of their visual, audio, or creative impact on an audience. And also, there will be occasions when, if you can organize and use personal communication, you can assume a more direct communication link to the audience and perhaps a more memorable and powerful message experience for them.

A point to remember about using media as communication selections needs to be repeated. As a campaign strategist and campaign professional, you need to appreciate that the mass media are not all-powerful and do not have "magical" persuasive powers over individuals. In fact, as I argued in an earlier chapter, those of us who buy media time and space and place messages in them know that the media—no matter how clever or creative—cannot automatically make a population process information, develop an attitude or opinion, or take on a behavior that is contrary to their lived experiences and current interests. As theories of selective perception, cognitive dissonance, and agenda-setting suggest, the media's power lay mostly in their capabilities to set agendas for what we should think about and to reinforce knowledge, beliefs, and actions we already possess.

A final word about cost and persuasive impact should be interjected here. Campaign professionals argue among themselves over whether the media or personal selections are more cost effective, or even more important, whether one is more persuasive than the other. Certainly, in a situation where tens of thousands or millions of persons must be reached by a campaign, the cost of using personal communication might be prohibitive, and using media is the only choice for even reaching the targeted audiences. However, given these same numbers, but a different campaign situation, and different audiences to reach (your employees, your stockholders, a governmental agency, an activist group), personal communication might be feasible and even more cost effective. In another campaign situation, for example a smaller scale campaign where only hundreds or thousands of individuals need to be reached (community residents, the industry or competitive companies, consumers), media might still be the better choice over personal selections or a combination of both.

Campaign professionals have also argued over which kind of communication selection is more persuasive or has more audience effect. Again, given a certain campaign crisis or a project, unique characteristics of the corporation, and special considerations of the size and lived experiences of the intended audiences, arguments can be made for either kind of selection. Media are the better choice for communication channels for audiences who cannot be reached in any other way. Media are also the primary choice when considerations of the intended populations make affective, shocking, visual, or entertainment messages—messages best carried or only carried by certain media forms—more suitable and desirable. At the same time, personal channels should be considered primary communication choices when a certain campaign situation dictates that a personal touch is logistically and financially feasible and because this approach will be inherently more persuasive and effective.

To make a blanket statement as to whether either of these communication selection strategies is more advantageous in cost or in persuasive effect is a wasted exercise, since each campaign is so situation specific. Rather, the campaign professional, recognizing the limitations and advantages of each and after analyzing the precise campaign situation involving the crisis/project, the organization's purpose, and the audiences' lived experiences, should decide whether to use media or personal selections or what combination of both (I cover how to do this in the "Strategies for Choosing Communication Selections" section later in this chapter). Knowing the definitions and advantages/disadvantages of both kinds of communication selection options has been the beginning point for conceptualizing the choices for media channels or personal channels for the campaign being planned.

Anything/Everything Can Be a Communication Selection

Another initial step in the conceptualization of communication selections is to grasp exactly what kinds of communication forms can be regarded as campaign communication selections. In short, let me open up the definition of a communication selection and suggest that any artifact that references or *names the organization or the campaign* serves as a communication selection. This perspective adds to the typical and accepted definitions of media or personal communication selections as mainstream media forms of newspapers, magazines, radio, television, film and other alternative media forms such as posters, billboards, point-of-purchase displays, and subway and movie trailers as well as personal forms such as letters, flyers, fact sheets, in-person conversations, and business meetings.

Naming Ordinary Artifacts Creates Communication Selections

Consider that even the most seemingly insignificant reference to the corporation or to the campaign on an article or object, such as a pencil or calendar, functions as a communication selection. Any t-shirt or coffee mug with a company's name on it or the campaign's name or cause on it is a communication selection. Besides the name placed on the product sold by the organization, every day, typical objects representing the company name could be letterhead and envelopes, signs outside retail centers or offices, annual reports and company brochures, delivery trucks or company cars, or shirts or jackets with corporate emblems.

This seemingly "innocent" naming of the organization or the campaign on clothing or other objects is a conscious and deliberate practice very common in campaign communication today. Of course, this is not a new phenomenon. All kinds of commodities sold by the organization and other objects not sold but engraved by the organization—clothing, dishes, eyeglasses, toys, even building materials for the house—may contain the name/label of the company prominently or subtly displayed on it. The simple engraving or printing of a name on a pencil, mug, glass, cigarette lighter, piece of clothing, or even automobile or truck is an ingenious way to circulate your company's name, your candidate's name, or your social issue's cause.

Clothing as Communication Selections

Clothing manufacturers—from exclusive fashion labels such as Polo, Guess!, Gucci, or Nautica to other, less prestigious clothing labels—have utilized this practice of placing their logo or name on their own products of clothing. This functions both to circulate the name of the company for some measure of "free" advertising, which, in truth, the customer has paid for. It also functions as a way to designate the customer who purchased the certain label as having a lifestyle consistent with the cost and the image-factor of the item, whether it be Guess! jeans or Wrangler jeans. Note that this is consistent with psychographic labels of outer-directed or striver and serves demographic classifications of upper socioeconomic levels or "country" look.

Corporate Sponsorships as Communication Selections

Another, very popular communication selection used in all kinds of campaign situations today is to sponsor sporting events or social events. A corporation can sponsor a sporting event such as a tennis tournament, a golf tournament, an ice-skating championship, the Olympics, a car race, a college football bowl game. This allows the corporate name to appear prominently on an event that perhaps millions of persons will see. Placing messages on these events can even match the demographic or psychographic experiences targeted by the campaign in the intended audiences for these events: upper socioeconomic level and outer-driven persons in tennis and golf tourneys, males and rugged individualists in car races, age and education levels in college football games. Charity events or social events can also be corporate-sponsored, such as a local hospital's sponsorship of a "race for the cure for breast cancer" or State Farm Insurance's endorsement and support of MADD (Mothers against Drunk Driving) and SADD (Students against Drunk Driving) events.

In addition to sponsoring a major sporting, social, or charity event, an organization can also work with these kind of events to solicit name recognition on a smaller scale. A corporation can buy space on a backdrop behind the tennis players or the ice skaters, or on the race cars themselves, or on the t-shirts given out for participants in a race for a breast cancer cure.

Toy Giveaways as Communication Selections

Another, very recent but innovative example of how to create communication selections to publicize events is the movie industry's cooperation with fast food chains to give out little gifts in children's meals. McDonald's was among the first to explore this gold mine of publicity for Disney movies by including little figures from the movies in children's meals and by attracting parents and their children to patronize their restaurants. Today, numerous fast food restaurants, in cooperation with recent releases of children's movies, cater to the children with these gifts and support their own profits as well.

Communication Selections Can Be Subtle or Dramatic

The campaign professional needs to recognize the power of using any small OR huge object or commodity available to circulate the name of the organization, the political candidate, or social issue. A campaign strategist can use inexpensive or ordinary objects as communication selections for the organization. Or, the campaign professional can go for a dramatic and self-conscious effect by placing a corporate reference on a huge balloon floating above a building, or a message pulled behind an airplane, or on parachutists floating to earth, or on immense or towering banners or billboards.

You might be able to build up immediate name recognition with a dramatic and grand communication event, or you might build up name recognition by using modest channels as a constant reminder to those in your targeted populations, perhaps by labeling pencils or pens that these persons come into contact with on a regular basis. Or, you can use both grand and modest corporate reminders. Populations such as your customers, media contacts, or community residents can view your calendar or the packaging that your product was purchased in, drink out of your engraved mugs, wear or notice others wearing articles of clothing with the company name or logo on it, or watch the nightly local news and sports programming for stories on your promotions or company-sponsored events.

Keep in mind that you have two choices for creating communication selections for your organization and for your organization's campaign. The object that is engraved can be either the actual product sold by the organization or another artifact that contains the organization's or campaign's name. Remember also that the choice of objects to be labeled or choice of corporate-sponsored event should be consistent with the desired image of the organization. You would not want to engrave beer mugs with a Mothers against Drunk Driving message or, in another example, publicize a no-litter campaign by dropping thousands of flyers from a balloon floating over the city. Believe it or not, such publicity blunders have occurred; you might even know of some yourself. In any case, you would not want to go to the trouble and expense to create a publicity event and end up doing more damage to your corporate image than if you had done nothing in the first place.

Consider that any object—your actual product/service or another object—that has your company name, your company's product or service, or a campaign reference on it is, officially, a communication selection. The communication selection might not cost anything, if the name is on *the product* bought by the customer. Another example of a communication channel is *a gift* the corporation gives to customers or others exposed to the company or the company's product or service, such as a pencil, child's toy, notebook, calendar, or mug. Or a selection is any of the *paperwork* or *packaging* involved in the day-to-day company business, such as letterhead, memo pads, or boxes. Or the selection is a *dramatic event or promotion* designed to get news coverage or mass publicity. And, obviously, the traditional, more *mainstream media and personal communication* purchased by the organization are also communication selections.

Communication Selections Can Be Unobtrusive or Attention-Getting

A final word on considerations of what qualifies as a communication selection can further clarify and summarize these definitions. The campaign strategist needs to be aware of the range of communication selections available for campaign communication channels: mainstream media, alternative media, personal communication, subtle labeling, prominent sponsorships, or publicity events. The strategist needs to appreciate that any communication channel can be used in one of two ways.

The channel can serve as a subtle "relatively unobtrusive container" for the name of the organization or campaign, or the channel can be so dramatic that it "calls attention to itself" and becomes part of the communication event. For sure, a communication choice that one campaign planner might consider unobtrusive, another strategist might interpret as attention-getting. However, let me offer a broad generalization and suggest that a communication selection such as company letterhead or company delivery trucks or interpersonal conversations between management and staff might be interpreted as subtle channels serving the campaign communication needs of the corporation.

On the other hand, a sky-writing airplane or neon-moving billboard could be considered a dramatic attempt to include the communication channel as part of the message, perhaps an attention-getting "call attention to itself" kind of message for hard-to-attract or hard-to-reach audiences. The bottom line here for the strategist is to appreciate that a choice is available for how much attention can be brought to the message delivery system by the communication selection. A communication selection or channel can be efficient and unobtrusive, or it can draw attention to itself by its own dramatic logistics and add to the dramatics of the communication event.

Inherent Qualities of Selected Communication Selections

One more critical examination of communication selections is necessary before you can examine the strategies for how to use and when to use the various communication selections with different audiences. I want to discuss now the features of the various kinds of selections. Some of these features are advantages and some are disadvantages. Each communication selection option possesses its respective limitations and its positive qualities.

Rather than examining each selection in terms of its advantages and disadvantages, however, I would instead like to explore each form according to its "inherent qualities." This allows each selection to be critiqued on its own terms, on its unique qualities and characteristics.

Communication Selection Mix

The concept of *communication selection mix* is relevant here and a good point to begin with. As the campaign strategist sits down to plan what media and personal selections will best deliver the designed message formats to each relevant, targeted population, one principle frames and informs the strategist's decisions. You must acknowledge that because each personal and media selection has its respective benefits and weaknesses, a combination of several distinctive kinds of selections provides a mix of strong and weak features, a kind of offsetting of each other's limitations. A thorough communication mix can allow for the limitation of one selection to be offset by the strength of another in the mix.

For example, billboards are inherently limited in the amount of copy they can provide, yet they are dramatic, attention-getting selections when placed where targeted audiences will see them. Paid-for messages placed in newspapers can accommodate a lot of copy points, but they are often overlooked by readers who might be more interested in news stories or who are not drawn to seek one message out of many competing advertisements on the page. If both the billboard and the newspaper message will effectively reach your targeted audience, the attractive features of each compensate for the inherent negative features of the other.

Relying on a communication selection mix does not permit the disadvantages of one particular selection to dictate that it should not be used in a campaign. Always think in terms of what other selections, used in conjunction with this selection, will create an adequate mix of selections to reach the audience—communication selections that add to each other's strengths and that offset each other's limitations. When you consider each selection form for its relevance in a certain campaign situation and its relevant use for a particular audience, do not judge only on its own inherent qualities, but *always consider the communication selection mix that can allow many selections to be used.*

Reach and Frequency

One of your first considerations for creating your mix of communication preferences is whether the communication form operates on a principle of *reach* or *frequency* (Simmons, 1990; Pfau & Parrott, 1993). A communication selection that reaches each member or almost every member of a population at more or less the same time is operating on the concept of reach. That is, the communication selection carries the message to everyone at around the same time. Letters, newsletters, e-mail, faxes, direct mail and direct mail inserts, or business meetings where all the audience members are present are examples of selections with reach. You will notice that these examples that operate on reach are usually personal communication selections, communication that goes directly from the organization to the audience members.

A communication selection that operates on the principle of frequency relies on repeated messages to eventually reach all (hopefully) the members of a targeted population sooner or later. Some selections just do not have the capability of reaching the audience all at once. Media channels, especially, cannot reach everybody at once since they are inherently a two-step form of communication; messages are placed in media forms in hopes that the audience will be exposed to the messages and process them. Consider, for example, that a television message or a radio message could never reach an entire intended audience in one shot. Only through repeated messages, perhaps several times a day or week or month, could a radio spot or television message possibly target most of an intended audience.

These definitions of reach and frequency seem to suggest that selections with perfect reach are superior to frequency selections. This is not necessarily so. For example, we all get inserts in our utility bills, little newsletter-type inserts. How many people who open their utility ever pay attention to, read, and process the information in these "newsy" inserts? I would suggest that most persons just pull out the bill and toss the insert away. Now, in principle at least, the organization can feel that they have sent messages to all their consumer audience members and attained perfect reach in doing so. But, if only a few people pay any attention to the messages, how effective is a direct mailing that nevertheless has perfect reach?

In many instances, selections operating as frequency communications can actually have a greater persuasive impact on an audience. They can grab the attention of the audience members and bring forth a persuasive impact, even though frequency selections cannot possibly count on everyone in the audience receiving the media message at the same time. For the campaign strategist, a broad and varied communication selection mix that includes channels functioning according to both reach and frequency is desirable.

Each Communication Selection Possesses Distinguishing Qualities

Common sense and your previous experience of the inner workings of the various kinds of media and personal communication can help you distinguish the individual, discriminating qualities of each kind of communication selection. For example, you probably know that television and videos are good choices for dynamic messages that can be aimed at certain demographics and psychographics based on the viewers watching the programming. Cable television can be much less expensive than network programming, and local cable commercials can be extremely reasonable to purchase. Radio and magazine selections provide relatively precise demographic and psychographic targeting as messages can be placed on stations and in publications that have established and demarcated their markets.

Any computer selection—e-mail, home pages, electronic billboards, and so on—provide a no-cost way for the organization to reach populations that use the computer for information and an easy, accessible means for the audience member to access information about the organization. Newspaper press releases are also, of course, free to the organization, when they are accepted for publication by the editor. Billboards, transit displays, point-of-purchase displays, or dramatic communication events can, because of their nature to contain messages in "unexpected" places or along routine travel routes to other destinations, provide dramatic and unexpected places for messages.

In-person communication inherently contains an extra personal touch a persuasive appeal. Engraved artifacts and toys or other giveaways are unique and memorable selections. And selections used by the organization in the day-to-day business of the organization such as letterhead, pencils, signage, or delivery trucks provide constant and subtle reminders of the organization's name.

I have mentioned only a few selections and their respective distinguishing characteristics and advantages to demonstrate one principle. Any media and personal communication selection can be examined and analyzed according to its distinctive traits, to those inherent qualities that make it unique as a communication selection, and of its use to the organization in the mix of selections going out to targeted populations (see Figure 5.1).

Selections with Inherent Appeal

Having stressed the importance of selection mix and each selection's respective and unique characteristics, let me now turn to another examination of individual

Figure 5.1
An Inventory of Selected Communication Selections

• Broadcast communication selections	• Print communication selections

television
    network channels
    cable channels
radio
videos
movie trailers
computer pages
 	
• Personal communication selections
 	
interpersonal conversations
group discussions, focus groups
business meetings
seminars, conferences
direct mailings
brochures
fact sheets
inserts in billings, with purchases
 	
• Artifacts
 	
clothing
objects
toy giveaways
product or service container
dramatic staged event
packaging of product
delivery trucks
	newspaper
	    paid messages
	    press releases
	magazines
	annual reports
	computer pages
	letters and memos
	e-mail
	faxes
	inserts in billings, purchases
	billboards
	transit displays
	subway posters
	point-of-purchase displays
	product/service packaging
	letterhead and envelopes
	direct mailings
	brochures
	fact sheets
	press kits

selection's respective characteristics and the strengths and the weaknesses of each. An initial point of comparison to use to contrast selections, or to weigh one against another, is to consider the selection's capability to be visual or audible, to be dramatic in the way it carries a message and attracts the receiver. When the strategist is faced with sending messages to an audience with a multiplicity of negative or noninterested images or, at the least, neutral images toward the organization, she/he is obliged to turn to communication selections that, at the very least, will capture the attention of those persons with the negative, neutral, or noninterested images throughout the entire audience. The campaign strategist must include in the communication selection mix those communication selections that have inherent attention-getting qualities.

Some communication selections inherently have more power to attract a receiver through creative visual or audio messages or through qualities that allow it to be an affective or emotional channel. Television, both network and cable channels, can handle messages with striking or unusual visuals and graphics, novel spokespersons, creative dialogue, and almost unlimited visualization possibilities. Radio also has almost unlimited possibilities for various vocal qualities, dramatic copy, and varied sound effects. Direct mail videos (most sent on request of the receiver) have boundless opportunities for appealing and sensational visualization factors; designed as mini-documentaries or mini-movies, they can directly and thoroughly detail a product, candidate, or social issue. Recall, also, that my earlier examples of dramatic events such as parachutists or skywriting airplanes are communication selections with inherent attention-grabbing qualities.

Some print selections can offer unusual and special visual and audio appeals, although without the movement and sound that television, radio, or videos can offer. Computer home pages, magazine messages, annual reports, product packaging, point-of-purchase displays, billboards, brochures, direct mailings, and commercial newspaper inserts all offer color, photographs, dramatic print font and size opportunities, striking copy points, illustrations and graphics, and celebrities as their message components.

In-person communication selections can also be very striking as communication channels. Whether an interpersonal or group or public setting, whether a personal conversation or a focus group or a business meeting or seminar/conference, a sensational spokesperson who delivers a dynamic message can have a convincing and powerful persuasive impact on an audience. The message might be perceived as even more persuasive, given that it is communication delivered, in person, directly to the intended audience.

Selections That Accommodate More Message Components

At the other extreme, the strategist might face an audience with numerous positive images, positive knowledge and attitudes and behaviors toward the organization, and with multiple needs for information about the organization and/or the campaign situation. To accommodate these multiple positive, information seeking images, communication selections with a greater capacity to hold more copy points and to deliver a greater quantity of information are appropriate.

In the broadcast area, computer home pages offer pages and pages of information about the organization and current campaigns being waged by the organization. In the print media, annual reports, letters, faxes, e-mail, newspaper paid messages, newspaper and magazine press releases, fact sheets, brochures, and direct mailings can accommodate large numbers of copy points. For strong information seeking and strong information processing individuals, creative and visual appeals are not that necessary. Instead, the selection of print media with their capacity to deliver much more information in an accessible format is more important and suitable.

Personal communication selections can also deliver a multiplicity of message components—especially words—covering all kinds of information. Personal conversations, group meetings, business meetings, and professional seminars and conferences are occasions for the delivery of massive amounts of information on a multitude of topics.

Considerations of Audience Resistance

Once again a principle of communication channel choices should be emphasized again. Clearly, the campaign planner always has as her/his purpose the choosing of a variety of communication selections, which, taken together, will not only reach the audience but deliver the appeals that will catch the attention of the audience in hopes that they will then process and be influenced by the information carried in them.

Even with these considerations in mind, remember that findings into the limited power of the media and other determinations about the natural resistance of receivers to process and seek knowledge, attitudes, behaviors, and other images (note the case of how few customers read the inserts placed in utility billing statements) suggest that just reaching the audience with a message sets up no guarantees that the audience membership will process the messages. Merely getting the communication selections and built in messages to the audience does not guarantee that the audience members will pay attention to them, let alone process them and be persuaded by them. Sending out creative, appealing, or shocking messages via communication channels to resistant receivers does not ensure that the population members will be attracted to the messages. And sending out information-laden messages via accommodating channels does not mean that the audience will seek and process the messages.

I always tell my students that those of us in campaign communication or any other field within the study of communication—journalism, human resources, personnel, labor relations, technical writing, business—work in the *social sciences, not the hard sciences.* We do not work in the hard sciences where exact findings can be drawn; we are not performing chemical or physics experiments or computing mathematic equations. Our objects of analysis are people, not chemicals or scientific experiments. Trying to influence and persuade people is not an exact or a hard science that can be precisely measured. Organizations and the people who conduct communication for organizations work on the premise that people can be informed, can be persuaded to hold certain opinions, and can be influenced to enact certain behaviors. But human beings can also change their mind, hold two contrasting opinions at the same time, be reluctant to act even in situations where they want to or know they should act, and possess multiple images of one organization.

Placing Selections in the Structure of the Campaign

How the campaign places or runs the individual communication selections is another factor to be decided relative to communication selections. Following Simmons (1990), there are three patterns for placing communication selections within a campaign plan. If you run a communication selection every day of the campaign, you are following a continuous pattern. For some communication selections, for example radio or local cable television, several messages are played throughout the day, every day of the week. The continuous pattern works for selections that you can afford to run several times and for those audiences that you want to receive multiple messages consistently throughout the campaign.

The good news for campaign planners is that recent technology today provides a continuous pattern of communication selections and daily message exposure with little or no real costs. Campaign messages can be developed on a home page, on e-mail, or on electronic bulletin boards, with little cost to produce and no significant cost to receive. Faxes are also becoming very economical and cost-effective for many organizations. The minor disadvantage for computer selections and for faxes is that the organization can only send these messages to audience members who can receive messages via these technologies—not a major negative if your targeted audience members have these technologies but a problem if your intended audiences do not.

A communication selection that is started and stopped follows a flighting pattern. This pattern is very common since most selections cannot be run daily, due to cost or other considerations. For a personal communication selection of regular business meetings with the employee population, daily meetings most likely would be too time consuming and probably unnecessary. Instead, weekly meetings or biweekly or monthly meetings, following a flighting pattern, might be just as effective and practical.

The flighting pattern of placement is often used in placing media channels. Even though the campaign strategist might want to run television or newspaper paid messages or send letters or direct mailings every day, it can get very expensive, even for only a three or four month campaign. For those broadcast media that require that seconds of time be purchased or for those print media that are purchased in column inches, cost is often a prohibitive factor to daily exposure. For these media channels, the flighting pattern of one or two days of messages and then no days of messages or of placing messages only on weekends, and so on, is feasible and affordable.

The final pattern of communication placement is pulsing. This pattern is a combination of flighting and continuity, whereas messages are placed every day, and on certain days, multiple messages are added. If costs allow, certain media and personal communication selections lend themselves to this pattern of relatively intense message saturation.

And consider that some communication selections do not fit any of these patterns for placement. In the case of giving out objects engraved with the organization's or the campaign's name, or in sending routine business letters or memos, or in wearing or viewing clothing with a corporate name or logo on it, the audience might receive only one exposure to the corporation's name, albeit at no cost for the receiver. For these kinds of organization giveaways and for large communication events staged by the organization, costs can be reasonable

188   Campaign Strategies and Message Design

since expense in incurred only in the production of the communication selection and not in the placement or delivery of it to the intended audiences.

Costs for Buying Communication Selections

It is virtually impossible to estimate some kind of general costs for buying message space or message time. It can give you some ballpark figures for some of the major communication selections, but I make a big disclaimer here and caution you, the campaign professional, that these are merely general estimations. You will have to investigate the costs of each kind of selection you want to use in every single campaign situation. These costs change too rapidly to allow any kind of permanent estimation.

A full-page message in a major newspaper like *The Wall Street Journal* or *The Chicago Tribune* runs about $30,000 to $45,000 for one message, for one day. A local newspaper may run about $5,000 for an entire page. Costs will, however, be adjusted given the message's placement in the paper. Costs for radio and television are just as variable. On prime time television, network or cable, a thirty-second spot can cost around $50,000 to $100,000 for one message; however, the ratings of the show will drive the cost up or down. Probably your best bet for broadcast—television and radio—is local cable programming; it can be as reasonable as $100 per message. Radio costs are extremely variable, based on the ratings and based on market share of the station.

Personal selections can cost for setting up the place for the speech or meeting or seminar and other logistical fees. Of course, costs can be incurred for fees for the speaker. If you are contacting your audiences personally, through conversations or group meetings, you might only have to pay your own or your staff's salary for the time it takes.

My only advice when it comes to costs for buying print, broadcast, or personal communication selections is to do your research on a campaign-by-campaign basis. That is, every time you plan a campaign, do a routine check of every kind of communication selection you intend to use and get cost estimates from each one. By all means, do not assume that the media costs you incurred for your last campaign will remain the same for the next campaign.

One more tip: when you contact each station or publication, be sure to ask for any package deals. This is routine. You can get some prime slots and some off-peak slots at a more or less general figure.

STRATEGIES FOR CHOOSING COMMUNICATION SELECTIONS

Once you understand the two basic classifications of communication selections, the various typical and atypical examples of communication selections, and the patterns of placement that also define communication selections, you are ready to choose the selections that will best deliver the message components—that are already decided and formatted—to the various targeted audiences. You have before you, at the outset of this final stage of your campaign strategies decisions, the designs of the print messages, broadcast messages, and audio messages that are appropriate for each intended population.

Putting the Cart before the Horse

I am aware that finalizing the designs of the personal, print, visual, and audio messages before you have even decided the communication selections is a bit awkward at best and almost never done. For sure, almost every campaign planner chooses the communication channels in conjunction with the design of the message components or, just as common, before the decisions on message design so that the various selections can determine what message components are best accommodated by each respective selection. I appreciate that my recommendation that message designs be completed before the communication selections are chosen is, for most campaign strategists, a backward procedure.

It can be done, however, even if it seems as if you are putting the cart before the horse. The campaign planner can, based on the basic strategies conceptualized for the campaign, choose the words and visual message components and then place the print, broadcast, and personal message components into message formats for each intended audience. Communication selection decisions on what print media, broadcast media, and personal communication are best suited to each targeted population and best for delivering the message components are separate strategic considerations from what designs of message components are best for each targeted population. In other words, the decision on communication selections is a separate and distinct strategic decision from what message components should go out to each intended audience.

To suggest how these two steps can be reconciled and operationalized, assume that you have as one of your most important targeted populations your employee population. Presume, as well, that based on your basic strategies already decided for this population, that you have chosen the words and visual message components that will best facilitate and accomplish the basic strategies of goals and objectives.

Say, for example, that in this employee population you have significant numbers of employees sharing both the active status and latent status toward the organization. Also, your research findings suggest that the employees hold some inaccurate images of company policy. And, finally, the organization wants to communicate some additional, positive images of its own to the employees.

For just this one population of employees, you can, first, fashion and design several possible *print* message designs or formats. Without any thought yet for whether the print designs will end up in newspapers, or magazines, or brochures, or fact sheets, or press releases, you can create some message formats that contain copy points and visuals targeting active status positions across the population membership. These could be numerous message designs (or message formats) that contain relatively large numbers of copy points, copy points suggesting knowledge and attitudes and behaviors, copy and visuals appealing to the demographics and needs and psychographics of the employees with active images. For this same employee population, you would also be obligated to design numerous print message formats with less copy and more visuals for those employees who hold latent positions and who possess different or additional needs, demographics, or psychographics.

These print message designs appealing to both active and latent positions can also have some copy and visuals that attack the inaccurate images held by the employees and that provide those additional images the organization wants them to have. Your print messages to the employees will fulfill the three basic strategy goals revealed by the research findings: to appeal to the active and latent positions, to attack the inaccurate images, and to present new positive images desired by the organization.

Perhaps some of the message designs are almost exclusively copy points; these will most likely end up in press release selections or fact sheets or computer pages or brochures. Perhaps some of the message designs contain a lot of copy points but also dramatic visuals that appeal to the audience and reflect the desired images of the organization; these would best be accommodated by newspapers or magazines or also computer pages or brochures. Other print message designs, with a lot of visuals for the latent positions, could best be accommodated by newspapers, computer pages, magazines.

For broadcast messages, as well, you can mock up visual and audio messages that carry the appropriate copy and visuals and audio for the employees; after these are decided, they can be placed in those broadcast channels that best accommodate the message design. For personal communication, you can plan outlines for oral presentations of knowledge and attitudes and behaviors, scripts and items of discussion that appeal to the audience and reflect the concerns of the organization, visual and/or audio supplementary message components appropriate for personal communication. Then you can decide which personal communication events will best carry the information: focus groups, business meetings, speeches, interpersonal conversations, seminars, or conferences.

Thus, the campaign planner should design message formats by considering, primarily, appealing to the varying image positions across the population's membership and the varying image positions that the organization wants to deliver—not by considering what communication selections will deliver them. This is my version of putting the cart before the horse.

Conceptualizing the message components first, designing the message formats second, and choosing the communication selections last forces a more thorough conceptualization of the appropriateness of messages and communication selections than collapsing both steps into one strategic decision. Separating message design strategies from communication selection design strategies encourages the campaign strategist to examine all facets of the message composition process—from basic strategies to messages to communication selections.

For the campaign planner designing messages and choosing selections for our employee population, forcing three strategic steps encourages a more thorough communication of campaign messages. Basic strategies, message strategies, and communication selection strategies are three separate strategic decisions; they should not be collapsed into one or two steps. Do not get ahead of yourself. First, you make all your decisions on the proper basic strategies. These decisions directly inform the correct or appropriate message components and message formats. Decisions on the message formats will, in turn, dictate the best communication selection choices to deliver these messages.

Therefore, basic strategies drive decisions on message components. Message components drive decisions on message formatting. Message formats drive what the communication selections should be. The structure of message composition from the very first steps in the conceptualization process (basic strategies) to the choice of message components and design of message formats (message strategies) to the delivery of the campaign messages (communication selections) is completed in three separate strategic stages. And each stage contains its own principles that guide its completion and inform the next stage in the process.

Choosing Selections for the Audience

A major consideration in the decisions on suitable communication selections for each intended audience rests on matching the selections to the lived experiences of the audience. This consideration parallels what we did in message strategies—choosing message components and designing message formats that will appeal to the traits, characteristics, and lived experiences of the targeted populations.

In message strategies, I suggested that you use your research findings to identify the most commonly shared image positions across each of your respective audiences and, from those findings, decide on those word and visual components that are appropriate for appealing to these images in each respective audience. The same process goes for communication selection strategies. The various media and personal communication selections, just as the various word and visual message components, each contain their own inherent qualities and logistical parameters.

As such, some selections—out of both media and personal choices—are exceptional for delivering a lot of copy points and for serving as efficient and thorough channels for delivering massive amounts of information to interested, or active, positions within a population and for direct and full appeals to other demographic, psychographic, schematic, needs, or knowledge/attitude/behavior images. Other selections work better as "containers" for both visuals and words components. And at the other end of the spectrum, some selections are creative and distinctive by their very nature and are best used as selections accommodating very creative and unusual visuals and dramatic message components.

You can appreciate that communication selections, just as message components, each have certain qualities that can address the unique and multiple lived experiences within and across an audience. Let me operationalize this for you and demonstrate, again, how selections should appeal to the audience and the benefit of strategizing both messages and selections separately. If you place a content-rich, knowledge/attitude/behavior mix of copy, along with an information seeking message format *in a communication selection* that can naturally and inherently and in an unobtrusive way facilitate this kind of message format—say, for example, in a speech or a press release or a fact sheet or a computer home page or television infomercials—you have created a kind of "double whammy" for your intended audience. The message and the selection complement each other and double the persuasive power on the active and information seeking images held by a respective audience.

The same process works for other, less information-laden kinds of message formats and for the more creative, conspicuous communication selections. From the most active and interested image positions to the least interested and weak image positions, for all the possible image positions based on demographics, psychographics, needs, knowledge/opinions/actions, schema, consider that message strategies and communication selections work together to accommodate each other.

Given another example of an audience with significant uninterested, or latent and nonpublic, image positions toward the organization, perhaps images of low information processing and seeking, along with unique demographic, psychographic, and needs consistent with these images, the message and selection strategies shift in order to address these particular image positions. These image positions dictate that more creative, innovative, and attention-grabbing *messages* and *selections* be used to communicate to this audience. Messages with less copy and dynamic visuals are complemented with communication selections such as billboards, television, artifacts or giveaway products, and possibly interpersonal conversations or group discussions.

Your experience with and knowledge of message components and your awareness of the capabilities of each kind of communication selection can afford you a common sense approach to placing a message in a compatible communication selection. Before you can bring the two together, however, you must theorize and consider each separately. Decide which message components best address all the various images held by a population. Then decide on the communication selections that best address the various images held by a population, either because they are unobtrusive "containers" or because they are dynamic, attention-getting channels in their own right. *Then,* place the messages with the proper selections to deliver your "double whammy" of persuasive communication appropriate to your various audiences.

Choosing Selections to Reflect the Organization's Interests

The next consideration concerning decisions on suitable communication selections for each intended audience rests on delivering the organization's desired images to the respective audiences. In addition to your mission to deliver messages that appeal to the lived experiences of your audiences' memberships, you also need to represent to these audiences the information that the organization wants its relevant audiences to know, believe, and act on. As noted above in both basic strategies and message strategies, recall that you should have in mind a two-pronged attack in campaigning to your audiences: in messages that appeal to the audiences' interests and in messages that reflect the organization's interests.

Let us turn now to how you can use communication selections to represent the organization to your intended populations. These considerations do not change significantly from the principles that informed using communication selections to appeal directly to audience interests. Virtually the same considerations and strategies that dictated what kind of messages go with what kind of selections is at work in this situation.

Your choice of communication selections should be consistent with the nature of the messages that you intend for each audience. Designing the messages that incorporate the desired images that the organization wants the respective populations to hold is, inherently, a more creative and flexible process that trying to appeal to certain lived experiences in the respective audiences. In those messages that are exclusively the information and content desired by the organization—and separate from information specifically targeting audience traits—the organization is free to include those images that would be desirable in the audience. That is, the organization-decided message components, as discussed above in message strategies, are simply what the organization would like the audiences to know, to believe or have an opinion about, and to do or act on.

This leaves room for message components to range from a lot or a few copy points to a lot or a few visualization factors that, in turn, suggests communication selections that accommodate a lot of copy and visuals or very little copy points and visuals. The organization has a free hand to decide its desired effects and kinds of information (basic strategies), its words and visual components and finalized message formats (message strategies), and its communication selections as its own strategic decision(s) and not a strategic decision(s) based on the relevant audiences.

The campaign planner, working to inform the audiences of the intentions and desired images of the organization has the latitude to include knowledge, attitude, behavior information, or need-oriented, psychographic-oriented, schema-oriented, or demographic-oriented information, exclusively from the organization's perspective. In this process, the organization has the option to design messages that range from messages dominated by a lot of copy points and no visuals to messages with no copy points and only visuals.

Whatever the message formats or message designs finalized according to the organization's intentions, the communication selections should be chosen to adapt to the nature and amount of message components. Just as the campaign strategist adapts the communication selections to messages that appeal to the audience, so also are communication selections chosen so that they complement messages that reflect the organization's desired images. The "double whammy" is also at work for communication selections delivering organization-related messages.

Deciding the Mix of Communication Selections

Throughout this book, in every chapter on strategies—research, basic, message strategies—and now, communication selection strategies, I return to the Collapse Model for an understanding of campaign strategy and message design. I have argued throughout that if we assume that each person who relates to an organization possesses multiple and changing images, then any campaign that is going to gain the attention and persuade this person needs to attempt to appeal to these multiple images. Admittedly, this relatively "radical" position toward campaign messages dictates that *many more and varied* messages need to be communicated to each relevant population throughout the course of a campaign than is usually done.

Considerations of the Collapse Model

I appreciate that most campaign planners seek to find the few catchy or dramatic copy points and visualization factors that will deliver a common or universal appeal to all the audiences. These "common denominator" message components are then repeated throughout all the campaign messages. However, my position toward campaign messages turns this search for common ground on its head and argues, instead, that campaign planners should be identifying the different images and targeting the differences, not some kind of common ground of lived experience that probably can never exist among or across distinct, albeit relevant, populations. Further, more effective and more persuasive messages are those that contain multiple and varied components that include content that follows a two-pronged offensive on the intended audiences: messages that appeal to the audiences' multiple and everchanging lived experiences and messages that reflect the diverse and consistent desired images of the organization.

Simply put, just as you need more messages to target the various audience images and the multiple desired corporate images, you will also need to use more communication selections to deliver these messages. Estimating the number and kinds of communication selections needed to deliver the multiple and varied message designs are two strategic decisions that are intricately bound to each other. If you find that any or all of your targeted populations have significant numbers of active images or high information processing and information seeking images, your knowledge of strategies suggests to you that more message components, more message formats, and more communication selections are required. If you find significant numbers of nonpublic images and low processing and seeking scores, you know that fewer, but more visual and creative, message components, message formats, and communication selections are appropriate.

Communication Selection Mix

Your decisions on how many communication selections are appropriate for each population can be informed by referencing the definitions of communication selections explored earlier in this chapter. It is important to begin with the concept of communication selection mix.

Every communication selection—media and personal—possesses its unique advantages and limitations. Some selections operate on reach, others on frequency. Some selections possess inherent qualities to be unobtrusive containers of massive amounts of copy points and visuals. Other channels possess inherent qualities to be attention-getting, to accommodate those creative and attention-getting message components. The campaign strategist needs to look at each population with an eye toward using a combination or a mix of selections to adapt and to conform to the images respective to each population and to put together a mix of selections that can complement each other and compensate for each's inherent limitations.

Choose Personal Communication Selections First

With this need to consider a mix of communications in mind, your next item to pursue is to envision if you can use any personal communication selections to reach any of the image positions in each respective population. Given the inherent properties of personal communications to be direct links to the audiences and to be inherently persuasive, considerations of any possible way to use personal selections is a priority. Remember that personal communications include the obvious personal channels such as interpersonal conversations, group discussions, or meetings, but personal channels also include print and broadcast channels, which, even though they are media forms, act as personal channels when they go directly to the audience members. Personal letters, direct mail, direct mail videos, brochures, annual reports, or company newsletters are personal selections when they are addressed to the audience member and when communicated directly to the audience member.

If there is any way you can use any personal selections, do so. This is not an absolute, however, since many kinds of populations exist that cannot be reached through any personal channels and that can only be reached through media channels. Obviously, when you have exhausted every channel possibility that could serve as a personal selections, you will turn to your media options.

Reach and Frequency Communication Selections

Next, decide on personal and media selections that, taken together, provide a mix of reach and frequency. Again, you are strategizing according to the principle of communication mix just mentioned. You can accomplish this easily with a mix of personal and media selections, since the personal channels tend to operate on the principle of reach and media channels tend to operate on frequency.

If, however, the characteristics and images of any of your intended audiences demand only personal selections or only media selections, as best you can, try to incorporate personal selections that follow both reach and frequency or media selections that contain both reach and frequency. This might not be feasible or even possible in all cases. But, it is the ideal situation if you can manage it.

Remember that any object or piece of clothing or commodity with the organization's name or campaign on it is a communication selection. Be creative. Use the packaging of your product or service, point-of-purchase displays, giveaway toys or other free artifacts, or any of the "atypical" communication selections defined earlier for reaching your audiences.

And, finally, in your efforts to provide a communication selection to accommodate the variety of images that need to be communicated to each population, do not lose sight of the fact that you also have a means for providing variety. Remember to include a variety of placement of your messages, using continuity, pulsing, and flighting. If you need to get great numbers of copy points out to a population, consider pulsing and continuity of certain selections that can accomplish this. If cost is a problem or audience image positions are few, you can use flighting as a pattern of placement.

Do you see how everything comes together here? All the objectives, which are operationalized as copy points and visuals, are now placed in the various communication selections in order to get all the information out to the audiences. You can use communication selection mix and the various placement patterns to serve the organization in delivering all the necessary information to the targeted populations.

HOW LONG IS THE CAMPAIGN?

The length of the campaign is probably one of the easiest decisions to make. Given all your detailed conceptualizations of strategies of goals and objectives, messages, and communication selections, it is relatively easy to decide the number of months necessary for the campaign. Simply put, if you find you have great numbers of objectives—pieces of information, also copy points—to communicate to numerous intended audiences, then you will have a longer campaign. If you have fewer populations to reach and less than a thousand objectives, then you will need fewer months to communicate your images. Cost is also a crucial factor in deciding campaign length as well; organizations can often support only three or four months of messages.

The rule of thumb here in length of campaigns is that most campaigns will run from three months, four months, five months, to six months. Three months is the minimum, and six months is the maximum. If you represent a client or an organization who wants to run a campaign longer than six months, say eight or even a year, then my advice would be to run two campaigns of six or four months each.

Deciding the length is a very subjective call on your part. If you are able to use a broad communication selection mix, with channels that accommodate large numbers of copy points, you might be able to get your information and images delivered in a shorter period of months. If your selections cannot handle much copy and you still have large numbers of copy points to communicate, you will need to extend your campaign to allow your selections to relay all the copy points. It is a matter of common sense. Look at how many copy points you need to communicate and then consider how long it should take your selections to deliver these points.

There is one important principle here when it comes to deciding campaign length. *Length is determined by how long it should take to deliver the copy points to all the audiences.* Campaign length is not decided at the convenience of the organization. It would be a mistake to plan a three-month campaign because the client or the organization has only three month's worth of money to support a campaign. In other words, the ideal situation is that the amount of information decides a campaign's length, not the campaign funds of the organization nor the convenience of the organization.

In order to conduct research and conceptualize basic strategies, message strategies, and communication selection strategies on identified audiences to address a singular campaign project or crisis, you are going to do a more thorough and precise job of communicating with a discrete time period in mind. There is another important reason to keep a reasonably short period of time per campaign. You want to allow yourself the opportunity to measure or evaluate the campaign's effects on the audiences. If you plan lengthy campaigns, your resources are devoted to the current campaign's logistics of delivering messages and costs. This will not allow you ample time to measure the impact of one campaign's messages before you continue with another campaign, if needed.

Each campaign is waged on its own research findings and on its own strategies to address the campaign situation. You cannot help but do a more thorough job of communicating to your relevant audiences when you are forced, through repeated campaign assignments, to reassess and restrategize through each campaign. As your intended audiences become more and more informed about the organization and the campaign project through repeated campaigns, you can adjust your strategies in each following, separate campaign.

IN SUMMARY

The final strategic decision for the execution of a campaign is the choice of what communication selections should be used to deliver the message components. Notice that placing the choice of selections last runs contrary to the way many campaigns are planned and executed. In many campaigns waged today the choice of communication selections is one of the first decisions made, often based on what the organization afford or on what is easiest to design and use. These traditional criteria for determining communication selections must be given up today for more thorough and strategic considerations.

Choosing communication selections should be done only after message components are decided; the amount of copy points and visualization factors determine or suggest the appropriate mix of communication selections that will accommodate and deliver the chosen message components to the targeted audiences. In turn, the message components have been decided based on the decisions of basic strategies of goals and objectives that were suggested by the research findings on the organization and the targeted populations and by information on the nature of the organization, the campaign situation, the kind of campaign, and so on.

For decisions on what communication selections are appropriate for a campaign, the campaign strategist must appreciate that each selection has unique and inherent qualities which make it personal or media, operating as reach or frequency, expensive or inexpensive, capable of accommodating a little or a lot of copy, capable of accommodating a little or a lot of visualization factors, and so on. Given the unique logistical characteristics of each potential communication selection, considerations of communication mix are crucial for the campaign planner.

And finally, understanding and applying the Collapse Model to a campaign situation suggests that because more basic strategies and more message components are necessary to match the multiple and flexible images and public positions present across any population, more communication selections are also most likely necessary. Given this model for campaign structure, considerations of the three patterns of placement, the typical length of a campaign, and the costs for buying communication selections are necessarily related to the campaign manager's decisions of communication selections.

IMPORTANT THINGS TO REMEMBER

- Two broad classifications of communication selections are media channels and personal contact.

- Personal selections are any communication of messages directly to audience members by the organization.

- Media selections are mediated communication. Messages are placed by the organization in media forms, in hopes that the audience will be exposed to the messages and process them.

- Any object or text with the organization's name on it is, technically, a communication selection.

- Communication selections are varied, subtle, or attention-getting; for example, toy giveaways, clothing, corporate-sponsored charities, or sporting events.

- Every communication selection has advantages and disadvantages attached to it. Each has unique logistical qualities that mean that some are more conducive to a lot of copy points while others are more visually accommodating.

- Communication selection mix is putting together a mixture of selections so that the advantages of one outweigh the limitations of another in order to achieve eventual saturation of an audience.

- The principle of reach is when a communication selection is received by the entire audience at about the same time.

- The principle of frequency is when a communication selection must be repeated in order to, hopefully, reach the entire audience eventually.

- Three patterns of placement of communication selections are continuity, flighting, and pulsing.

- Choosing communication selections is the last strategic decision of a campaign. Basic strategies drive message strategies. Message strategies drive communication selection strategies.

- Personal communication selections tend to be more persuasive than media selections.

- The length of a single campaign should be three, four, five, or six months maximum. The length depends on the number of copy points to be delivered and the nature of the communication selections to accommodate copy and/or visuals.

References

Alvesson, M. (1990). Organization: From substance to image? *Organization Studies.* 11(3): 373–394.
Atkin, C., & Freimuth, V. (1989). Formative evaluation research in campaign design. In C. Atkin & R. Rice (Eds.). *Public communication campaigns.* 2nd edition. (pp. 131–150). Newbury Park, CA: Sage.
Baskin, O., & Aronoff, C. (1988). *Public relations: The profession and the practice.* 2nd edition. Dubuque, IA: W. C. Brown.
Berger, A.A. (1991). *Media analysis techniques.* Newbury Park, CA: Sage.
Bogart, L. (1990). *Strategy in advertising.* Lincolnwood, IL: NTC Business Books.
Boulding, K.E. (1977). *The image: Knowledge in life and society.* Ann Arbor: The University of Michigan Press.
Bradac, J.J. (1989). *Message effects in communication science.* Newbury Park, CA: Sage.
Center, A.H., & Jackson, P. (1989). Cookie tampering threatens Girl Scout survival. *Public relations practices.* 4th edition. (pp.293–295). Englewood Cliffs, NJ: Prentice-Hall.
Clark, E. (1988). *The want makers: The world of advertising: How they make you buy.* New York: Viking.
Davison, W.P., Boylan, J., & Yu, F.T.C. (1976). *Mass media systems and effects.* New York: Holt, Rinehart, & Winston.
Dowling, G.R. (1986). Measuring corporate image. *Journal of Business Research* 17: 27–34.
Eagly, A., & Shelley, C. (1993). *The psychology of attitudes.* New York: Harcourt, Brace, & Jovanovich.
Esman, M.J. (1972). The elements of institution building. In J.W. Eaton (Ed.). *Institution building and development.* (pp. 19–40). Beverly Hills: Sage.
Festinger, L. (1957). *A theory of cognitive dissonance.* Stanford: Stanford University Press.
——— (1964). *Conflict, decision, and dissonance.* Stanford: Stanford University Press.

Flay, B., & Cook, T. (1989). Three models for summative evaluation of prevention campaigns with a mass media component. In C. Atkin & R. Rice (Eds.). *Public communication campaigns.* 2nd edition. (pp. 175–197). Newbury Park, CA: Sage.

Flora, J., Maccoby, N., & Farquhar, J. (1989). Communication campaigns to prevent cardiovascular disease: The Stanford community studies. In C. Atkin & R. Rice (Eds.). *Public communication campaigns.* 2nd edition. (pp. 233–252). Newbury Park, CA: Sage.

Fombrun, C., & Shanley, M. (1990). What's in a name? Reputation building and corporate strategy. *Academy of Management Journal* 33(2): 233–258.

Fowler, F., & Mangione, T. (1990). *Standardized survey interviewing: Minimizing interview related error.* Newbury Park, CA: Sage.

Freedman, J.L. & Sears, D.O. (1965). Selective exposure. In L. Berkowitz (Ed.). *Advances in experimental social psychology.* 2nd edition. New York: Academic Press.

Frey, L., Botan, C., Friedman, P., & Krepps, G. (1991). *Investigating communication: An introduction to research methods.* Englewood Cliffs, NJ: Prentice-Hall.

Grunig, J. (1989). Symmetrical Presuppositions of a framework for public relations theory. In C. Botan and V. Hazelton (Eds.). *Public relations theory.* (pp. 17–44). Hillsdale, NJ: Lawrence Earlbaum Associates.

Grunig, J., & Hunt, T. (1984). *Managing public relations.* New York: Holt, Rinehart, & Winston.

Grunig, J.E., Ramsey, S., & Schneider, L.A. (1985). An axiomatic theory of cognition and writing. *Journal of Technical Writing and Communication* 15(2): 110–130.

Heibert, R.E. (1988). *Precision public relations.* White Plains, NY: Longman, Inc.

Hunt, T., & Grunig, J.E. (1994). *Public relations techniques.* Fort Worth: Harcourt Brace College Publishers.

Ind, N. (1993). *Great advertising campaigns: Goals and accomplishments.* Lincolnwood, IL: NTC Business Books.

Janz, N., & Becker, M. (1984). The Health Belief Model: A decade later. *Health Education Quarterly* 11: 1–47.

Kendall, R. (1992). *Public relations campaign strategies.* New York: HarperCollins.

Kerlinger, F. (1986). *Foundations of behavioral research.* 3rd edition. New York: Holt, Rinehart, & Winston.

Kidder, L., & Judd, C.M. (1986). *Research methods in social relations.* 5th edition. New York: Holt, Rinehart, & Winston.

Krueger, R.A. (1988). *Focus groups: A practical guide for applied research.* Newbury Park, CA: Sage.

Maslow, A.H. (1943). A theory of human motivation. *Psychological Review* 50: 370–396.

────── (1970). *Motivation and personality.* 2nd edition. New York: Harper and Row.

McElreath, M.P. (1993). *Managing systematic and ethical public relations.* Madison, WI: W. C. Brown.

Moffitt, M.A. (1992). Bringing critical theory and ethical considerations to definitions of a "public." *Public Relations Review* 18(1): 17–30.

────── (1994a). Collapsing and integrating concepts of "public" and "image" into a new theory. *Public Relations Review* 20(2):159–170.

────── (1994b). A cultural studies perspective toward understanding corporate image: A case study of State Farm Insurance. *Journal of Public Relations Research* 6(1): 41–66.

Nager, N.R., & Allen, T.H. (1984). *Public relations management by objectives.* New York: Longman.

Paolillo, J.G., & Lorenzi, P. (1984). Monetary incentives and mail questionnaire response rates. *Journal of Advertising* 13: 46–48.

Petty, R.E., & Cacioppo, J.T. (1979) Issue involvement can increase or decrease persuasion by enhancing message-relevant cognitive responses. *Journal of Personality and Social Psychology* 37: 1915–1926.

Pfau, M., & Parrott, R. (1993). *Persuasive communication campaigns.* Boston: Allyn and Bacon.

Prentice-Dunn, S., & Rogers, R.W. (1986). Protection Motivation Theory and preventative health: Beyond the Health Belief Model. *Health Education Research* 1: 153–161.

Rabe, B. (1994). Beyond NIMBY: Participatory approaches to hazardous waste management in Canada and the U.S. In F. Fisher and S. Sirriani (Eds.). *Critical Studies in organizational behavior.* (pp. 622–645). Philadelphia: Temple University Press.

Rayfield, R.E., Acharya, L., Pincus, J.D., & Silvis, D.E. (1991). *Public relations writing.* Dubuque, IA: W. C. Brown.

Rippetoe, P., & Rogers, R. (1987). Effects of components of Protection-Motivation Theory on adaptive and maladaptive coping with a health threat. *Journal of Personality and Social Psychology* 52: 596–604.

Russell, J.T., & Lane, R. (1990). *Kleppner's advertising procedure.* 11th edition. Englewood Cliffs, NJ: Prentice-Hall.

Salmon, C.T. (1989). *Information campaigns: Balancing social values and social change.* Newbury Park, CA: Sage.

Salomon, G. (1979). *Interaction of media, cognition, and learning.* San Francisco: Jossey-Bass.

———— (1981). *Communication and education: Social and psychological interactions.* Beverly Hills: Sage.

———— (1987). *Interaction of Media, Cognition, and Learning: An Exploration of How Symbolic Forms Cultivate Mental Skills and Affect Knowledge Acquisition.* San Francisco: Jossey-Bass.

Schultz, D.E. (1990). *Strategic Advertising Campaigns.* 3rd edition. Lincolnwood, IL: National Textbook Company.

Schultz, D.E. & Barnes, B.E. (1995). *Strategic advertising campaigns.* 4th edition. Lincolnwood, IL: NTC Business Books.

Schultz, D.E., Martin, D., & Brown, W.P. (1984). *Strategic Advertising Campaigns.* 2nd edition. Lincolnwood, IL: National Textbook Company.

Schultz, D.E., & Tannenbaum, S.I. (1989). *Essentials of advertising strategy.* 2nd edition. Lincolnwood, IL: National Textbook Company.

Simmons, J., & Stark, N. (1993). Backyard protests to emergence, expansion, and persistence of local hazardous waste controversy. *Policy Studies Journal* 21: 470–491.

Simmons, R.E. (1990). *Communication campaign management.* New York: Longman.

Trent, J.S., & Friendenberg, R.V. (1991). *Political campaign communication.* 2nd edition. New York: Praeger.

Williams, F. (1992). *Reasoning with statistics: How to read quantitative research.* 4th edition. New York: Harcourt, Brace & Jovanovich.

Williams, S.L., & Moffitt, M.A. (1997). Corporate image as an impression formation process: Prioritizing personal, organizational, and environmental audience factors. *Journal of Public Relations Research* 9(4): 237–258.

Wimmer, R.D., & Dominick, J. (1983). *Mass media research.* 2nd edition. Belmont, CA: Wadsworth Publishing.

Index

Audience, definition of, 12–13
Audience resistance, considerations of, 186

Campaign, conceptualization model, 3–5
Campaign, definition of, 3
Campaign, guiding metaphor for business, 2–3
Campaign, kind of, how to label, 18–19
Campaign, length of, 196–197
Campaign specialist, role of, 27–28
Closed-ended questions, 51–52
Collapse Model of Corporate Image, 14–18, 88–91, 107, 143, 194
Commercial campaign, advertising, 19
Commercial campaign, marketing, 19
Commercial campaign, public relations, 19–21
Communication selection, anything can be, 177–181
Communication selection mix, 181–182, 194–196
Communication selections, cost of, 188
Communication selections, inventory of, 184
Communication selections, matching audience, 191–192
Communication selections, placement of: continuous, 187; flighting, 187; pulsing, 187
Communication selections, reflecting the organization, 192–193
Communication selections, strategies for choosing, 188–194
Content analysis: conducting, 59; planning, 58; preparing to begin, 58–59; quantifying responses, 60–61; use of theory in, 60
Copy platform, 144–146, 169, 171
Copy points, 141–144, 169, 171
Crisis, investigation of, 5–6

Data analysis: choosing analyses, 69; data entry, 67–68; forming scales, 68–69; organizing, aggregating information, 68–69; preparation for, 66–69
Demographic appeals, 102–103, 125, 131, 135
Dissonance theory, 86, 88

Encroachment, 23–25. *See also* Integrated marketing
Ethical decisions, 27–28
Evaluative research, 32
Experimental research: techniques, 61–65; quasi-experimental designs, 65–66
Experimenter effects, 35

Focus group: analyzing results, 49–50; conducting, 47–49; planning, 45–47
Focus group interviewing, 45–50
Formative research, 32
Frequency, 182–183, 195–196. *See also* Reach

Goal, appeal, 101–109: demographic, 102–103; needs, 103–105; psychographic, 105–107; schema, 107–108
Goal, change, 97–101, 121, 125, 129, 133, 135
Goal, conceptualization of, 93–97
Goal, definition of, 84–85
Grunig Typology, 37, 99–100; 111–115; 127, 162–165

Image, definition of, 14–18
Integrated marketing, 23–25. *See also* Encroachment
Interim research, 32
Interviewing, 43–44

Linkage Model: diffused linkage, 11; enabling linkage, 9; functional linkage, 9–11; normative linkage, 11;

Management by Objective, 85
Maslow, Abraham, 103
Maslow's Hierarchy of Needs, 103
Media, use versus personal communication, 176–177
Media selections, 174–175, 184
Message components, strategies for choosing, 157–165
Message components, visualization factors, 146–157, 169, 171: for broadcast media, 151–155; for personal communication, 155–156; for print media, 147–151
Message components, words, 140–146

Needs appeals, 103–105, 127, 131, 135
Nonrandom sampling: convenience/accidental, 41–42; purposive, 42; snowball/network, 42
Normal curve, 72

Objective: knowledge, attitude, behavior, image, 111–112, 121, 123, 125, 129, 131, 135
Objective, audience-centered, 110–112
Objective, conceptualization of, 109–112
Objective, definition of, 84–85
Objective, organization-centered, 110–112
Open-ended questions, 51–52
Organization, investigation of, 6–8
Organization-based strategies, 91–93

Personal selections, 175–176, 184, 195
Political campaign, 21
Population, definition of, 12–13
Population, not a public, 12–18
Populations, investigation of, 8–12
Project, investigation of, 5–6
Psychographic appeals, 105–107, 125, 131, 135
Public position, 13–18, 88–91, 162–165
Publicity campaign, 22

Quasi-experimental designs, 65–66. *See also* Experimental research

Reach, 182–183, 195–196. *See also* Frequency
Receiver-based strategies, 85–88
Research, ethics of, 34
Research, need for, 33–34
Research, original, 32
Research, secondary, 32
Research validity, definition of, 34
Research validity, threats to: history, 36–37; instrumentation/measurement, 38; maturation, 37; mortality, 38; testing, 38–39; selection, 35–36

Sampling error, 40
Sampling, research, 39–42
Sampling strategies: random, 40; sampling interval, 40; stratified, 41 systematic random, 40
Schema appeals, 107–108, 127, 131–132, 137
Selective perception theory, 86–87, 115
Skewness, interpreting, 72–73

Significance: testing for, 74–78; continuous variables, correlations, 77–80; multiple regression, 80–81; T-tests, F-tests, chi-square, 75–76
Social issue campaign, 21–22
Standard Metropolitan Statistical Area (SMSA) Reports, 102, 106–107
Statistics, descriptive, 69–74: dispersion, 71; kurtosis, 73; skewness, 71–72; standard deviation, 71; variance, 71
Statistics, central tendency, types of averages, 71–72
Strategic decisions, quantifying message copy, 161–165
Strategic decisions: visuals and spokesperson traits, 158–160; words, 158–160

Stratified sampling: disproportional, 41; proportional, 41
Survey data, collecting, 54–57
Survey, rules for writing, 52–54
Systems theory, 25–27

Terrorist campaign, 23
Theory, definition of, 25–27

U.S. Bureau of Census Reports, 102, 106–107

VALS, 106. *See also* Psychographic appeals
VALS 2, 106. *See also* Psychographic appeals

About the Author

MARY ANNE MOFFITT is Associate Professor in the Department of Communication, Illinois State University. She teaches advanced courses in public relations strategy and message design, and has published articles in the field.